1 .50

CW00665265

BRISTOL
IN THE EIGHTEENTH CENTURY

BRISTOL
IN THE EIGHTEENTH
CENTURY

Edited by Patrick McGrath

Reader in History
University of Bristol

Eight studies originally published by the
Bristol Branch of the Historical Association

DAVID & CHARLES
NEWTON ABBOT

0 7153 5726 3

Printed in Great Britain
by Lewis Reprints Ltd.
member of Brown Knight & Truscott Group
London and Tonbridge
for David & Charles (Publishers) Limited
South Devon House Newton Abbot Devon

Contents

Illustrations

Introduction

The eight studies collected here were originally published as separate pamphlets by the Bristol Branch of the Historical Association in a wide-ranging series in which particular aspects of the history of Bristol are examined by specialists. This book does not, of course, claim to deal with all the major themes of Bristol's Golden Age. The architectural and the religious history of the period do not figure to any extent, and these and other important matters will be examined in later pamphlets. Nevertheless, the eight chapters focus attention on activities which were of major significance in the life and work of a great city at a time when it could justifiably be regarded as the metropolis of the West, and they contain a considerable amount of material which cannot be found elsewhere.

The first chapter, by Professor Peter Marcy, examines the impact of Bristol on the numerous travellers who visited it for business or for pleasure, and shows that the good opinion which many Bristolians had of themselves was not, for the most part, shared by their visitors. At the same time, the descriptions of the city given by the visitors present a vivid picture of the background against which eighteenth-century Bristolians lived their vigorous, if somewhat self-satisfied, lives.

Charles James Fox once referred to Bristol as 'that rascally city'. Dr Underdown examines one aspect of the sometimes unsavoury political life and explains how the electors in 1780 came to reject the great Edmund Burke. Issues of principles were involved, but the reasons why Burke lost his seat are more complicated than has often been suggested.

The city which damaged its reputation with posterity by rejecting a great statesman also had the misfortune to show lack of appreciation of one of the few poets it has produced— Thomas Chatterton, whom Dr Cottle describes as England's 'loudest herald of the Gothic Revival'. It was unfortunate that Chatterton did not find in Bristol the patronage which he thought was his due and not surprising that he was filled with hatred of

> Bristolia's dingy piles of brick,
> Lovers of mammon, worshippers of trick . . .

But it was rejection by London rather than by Bristol which led to the end of that tragic life.

If Bristol failed to re-elect Burke and provided little help for Chatterton, it made at least one lasting contribution to civilised life which counter-balanced its pre-occupation with money-making. In 1764 the Theatre Royal, Bristol, began its long and remarkably varied existence. Miss Kathleen Barker, who has recently completed her definitive history of this theatre, examines in the fourth chapter the early successes and failures of one of the oldest surviving theatres in the country. Another feature of eighteenth-century Bristol which gave it for a time a national and international reputation was the water of the Hotwell. At the height of its fame the Bristol Hotwell drew large numbers of fashionable visitors to the city in search of health and amusement, and the water was, as Defoe noted, sent in bottles not only all over England, but all over the world. The Bristol Hotwell never rivalled the waters of Bath but it had an important part to play in the life of the city in the eighteenth century, and its rise and decline are examined by Mr Waite in the fifth chapter in this collection.

There was an immense variety of activity in eighteenth-century Bristol, and the city certainly did not live by trade alone. Nevertheless, its regional and its foreign commerce gave it a vital importance in the national economy, and Professor Minchinton's essay examines not only the way in which the port worked, but also the trades which provided the main source of its wealth. His work is a valuable corrective to the commonly held view that Bristol's Golden Age depended almost entirely on the exploitation of slaves. Bristol's role in the slave trade has received attention out of proportion to its importance from the local and the national point of view. The undoubted horrors of the slave trade lend themselves to exploitation by those who come to Bristol to take a quick look before presenting a colourful story in print or on television, and even today some Bristolians regard with a curious mixture of fascination and guilt a trade in which London and Liverpool in fact played a bigger part than Bristol. An essay by the late Professor C. M. MacInnes examines this aspect of the city's history and considers the reality which lies behind the black legend. Professor Peter Marshall here looks at the other side of the picture, which has received comparatively little attention—the part played by a number of Bristolians in securing the abolition of the slave trade.

Acknowledgements

A number of the pamphlets were published originally with the help of grants from the University of Bristol's Publication Committee, the University of McGill, Claremont Graduate School Research Fund, the Bristol Docks Committee, the Bristol Education Committee, the Gane Trust and the Bristol Civic Society. The Bristol Branch of the Historical Association wishes to record its thanks to these bodies and to Messrs David & Charles for making it possible for the work to be presented in a more permanent form for the benefit of a wider public.

The Branch is also very grateful to Mr. Stephen Sefton who kindly agreed to compile the index.

As this book has been reproduced by a photographic process it has been possible to include only a limited number of alterations and additions to the original texts.

University of Bristol   PATRICK MCGRATH

BRISTOL BRANCH

OF THE HISTORICAL ASSOCIATION

LOCAL HISTORY PAMPHLETS

1   The Bristol Hotwell by Vincent Waite (out of print).
2   Bristol and Burke by P. T. Underdown. 10p.
3   The Theatre Royal; the first seventy years by Kathleen Barker. Third edition, 20p.
4   The Merchant Adventurers of Bristol in the Fifteenth Century by E. M. Carus-Wilson (out of print).
5   The Port of Bristol in the Eighteenth Century by Walter Minchinton (out of print).
6   Thomas Chatterton by Basil Cottle. 10p.
7   Bristol and the Slave Trade by C. M. MacInnes. 15p.
8   The Steamship Great Western by Grahame Farr. 15p. (out of print).
9   Mary Carpenter of Bristol by R. J. Saywell. 15p.
10 The Chartists in Bristol by John Cannon. 15p.
11 The Steamship Great Britain by Grahame Farr. 20p.
12 Ferdinando Gorges and New England by C. M. MacInnes. 15p.
13 The Port of Bristol in the Middle Ages by J. W. Sherborne. 25p.
14 The Theatre Royal; Decline and Rebirth 1834-1934 by Kathleen Barker (out of print).
15 The Bristol Madrigal Society by Herbert Byard. 15p.
16 Eighteenth Century Views of Bristol and Bristolians by Peter T. Marcy. 15p.
17 Early Bristol Quakerism, 1654-1700, by Russell Mortimer. 15p.
18 The Industrial Archaeology of Bristol by R. A. Buchanan. 15p.
19 Captain Thomas James and the North-West Passage by C. M. MacInnes. 15p.
20 The Anti-Slave Trade Movement in Bristol by P. Marshall. 18p.
21 Sebastian Cabot and Bristol Exploration by David Quinn. 25p.
22 The Romans in the Bristol Area by K. Branigan. 20p.
23 Prehistoric Bristol by L. V. Grinsell. 20p.
24 The Medieval Churches of Bristol by M. Q. Smith. 20p.
25 John Whitson and the Merchant Community of Bristol by P. McGrath. 20p.
26 Nineteenth Century Engineers in the Port of Bristol by R. A. Buchanan. 20p.
27 Bristol Shipbuilding in the Nineteenth Century by Grahame Farr. 25p.
28 Bristol in the Early Middle Ages by David Walker. 25p.
29 Bristol Corporation of the Poor 1696-1898 by E. E. Butcher. 25p.
30 The Bristol Mint by L. V. Grinsell. 30p.

EIGHTEENTH CENTURY VIEWS OF BRISTOL AND BRISTOLIANS

PETER T. MARCY

Books of travel, guide books, and descriptive accounts of the world and its various parts were enormously popular in the eighteenth century. Perhaps the influence of Pierre Bayle and the sceptics or the new scientific interests which made the world at once larger and smaller engendered this popularity. But whatever the cause, the inquiring reader could choose from a great abundance of printed materials to satisfy his curiosity about the world. Daniel Defoe whose *Tour Thro' the Whole Island of Great Britain* underwent seven revisions by different editors in the eighteenth century was among the most perceptive of the writers. His particular work, like Thomas Cox's revision of *Magna Britannia,* was further complemented by plagiarists who freely gleaned from its pages in an age during which appropriation was as common as original writing. Though much of this material was not original—even Defoe and Cox were plagiarists—and some of it quite inaccurate, this did not in any way hinder its popularity, and Bristol readers were not immune to its attractions. The early records of the Bristol Literary Society reveal that the two books most often borrowed were books of travel. And as Bristolians were interested in the rest of the world, the rest of the world was interested in Bristol and Bristolians. Most of the major accounts and descriptions of England contained at least some mention of Bristol, although many authors were convinced that the city was part of Gloucester or of Somerset.

The purpose of this account is to try to determine what impressions were held of Bristol and Bristolians by their contemporaries in the eighteenth century. Materials published in the eighteenth century are the primary source, but contemporary private correspondence and diaries which have been subsequently published add an interesting perspective. In any case, it seems best to use the words of the writers and their editors whenever possible.

In the eighteenth century Bristol was first and foremost a city of trade and commerce. In fact, Daniel Defoe, the great novelist and essayist, noted of Bristol in the 1720's that is was "the greatest, the richest, and the best Port of Trade in Great Britain, London only excepted," and he continued:

> The Merchants of the City not only have the greatest Trade, but they Trade with a more entire Independency upon London, than any other Town in Britain. And 'tis evident in this particular, (viz.) That whatsoever Exportations they make to any part of the World, they are able to bring the full returns back to their own Port, and can dispose of it there . . . .

> But the Bristol Merchants as they have a very great Trade abroad, so they have always Buyers at Home, for their Returns, and that such Buyers at Home that no Cargo is too big for them. To this Purpose, the Shopkeepers in Bristol who in general are all Wholesale Men, have so great an inland Trade among all the Western Counties, that they maintain Carriers just as London Tradesmen do, to all the Principal Counties and Towns from Southampton in the South, even to the Banks of the Trent on the North; and Tho' they have no Navigable River that way, yet they drive a very great Trade through all those Counties.

> Add to this, That as well by Sea, as by the Navigation of two great Rivers, the Wye and the Severn, They have the whole Trade of South Wales, as it were, to themselves, and the greatest Part of North Wales; and as to their Trade to Ireland, it is not only great in itself, but is prodigiosly encreas'd in these last Thirty Years, since the Revolution, notwithstanding the great Encrease and Encroachment of the Merchants at Liverpool, in the Irish Trade, and the great Devastations of the War; The Kingdom of Ireland it self being wonderfully encreas'd since this Time. (II, p. 435)

Bristol's predominance in trade was one of the factors which drew many visitors to the city. It should not be surprising, therefore, that many of them concerned themselves with this aspect of the city's life in their descriptions. Through much of the century, there was agreement among commentators concerning Bristol's position as second trading city in the kingdom as well. However, as the century wore on, there was a growing awareness that Bristol's position was being challenged.

John Aitkin, a writer about whom very little is known, described some of the changes which had taken place in the world of

industry by 1788 in a work entitled *England Dilineated,* and the
following quotation reveals Bristol's trade in more detail than did
Defoe.

> The manufacturers of this city and its vicinity furnish it with
> several important articles of exportation. The glass-making,
> in its several articles of crown, flint, and bottle glass, is very
> considerable and on the increase. Ireland and America take
> off great quantities of these goods, especially bottles, of which
> nearly half the number are sent out filled with beer, cyder,
> perry, and Bristol water. The copper and brass manufac-
> turers were of capital importance, but are now much declined
> in consequence of a monopoly. Hard white soap, of the best
> quality, is made here in large quantities, much of which is
> sent to London, as well as to the colonies abroad. Hats,
> leather, both tanned and dressed in oil, saddlery and shoes
> white lead, gunpowder, and earthenware, are all considerable
> articles of domestic and foreign traffic. The city likewise
> possesses works for smelting lead and making lead shot, iron
> foundries, rolling and slitting mills, and the tin works, all
> which furnish very valuable commodities for exportation. Its
> former woollen manufactures are at an end.
>
> Some of the principle commodities of the surrounding
> country, exported from Bristol, are, cheese, cyder, and beer,
> a few coals, herrings taken in the channel, salt from Droit-
> which, course woollens and stockings, hardware from Birming-
> ham and Wolverhampton, and earthen-ware from Stafford-
> shire. In the exportation of these last articles, however, Liver-
> pool has gained upon Bristol, chiefly on account of the super-
> iority of the canal navigations to that town, above the difficult
> and uncertain navigation of the Severn. (pp. 317-319)

This account by Aitkin is of interest for a number of reasons. It
seems surprising that he does not mention the sugar houses and
their products which supported one of the principal trades of
Bristol. Nor did he mention the greatly diminished slave trade. He,
however, did mention the glass manufacturers, and the sight of the
glass houses proved intriguing to many of the contemporary
visitors. One of the most thorough descriptions of these houses
was made by a man styled simply as the "Irish Gentleman".

> I saw many glass houses, with which this town vastly
> abounds, as the inhabitants reckon upwards of thirty. The
> generality of them are built of brick, toperwise to the top. With-
> in side is the Chaldron wherein the metal is boiled, by means of
> a large constant fire with a chimney, by which the smoke is

conveyed through the top . . . I saw several things blown, this
is performed by a long iron tube, the end of which they dip into
the metal, and after they have given it a blast or two, they form
or shape it on an anvil. (Huth, ed., *Journey*, p. 149)

Other interesting descriptions of local industries were also offered
to the reader. Arthur Young who visited Bristol in the 1770's described the copper-works in great detail while the "Irish Gentleman" explained the workings of the lead smelting factory as well.
    Another interesting point made by Aitkin was that Liverpool
was encroaching on the trade of Bristol. This point was not
generally noted even as late as 1788. But Aitkin went further than
simply offering a tantalizing hint. He categorically stated that

> Bristol, in wealth, trade, and population, has long been
> reckoned second to London within this Kingdom; and though
> the custom house receipts of Liverpool have for some time
> past exceeded those of Bristol, yet the latter may perhaps still
> maintain its place with respect to the opulence and number of
> its inhabitants. (pp. 314-315)

Aitkin was not without support in this observation, for David
Macpherson also declared

> There were entered inward this year (1765) at Bristol
> 384 British, and 47 foreign, vessels; and outward 319 British
> and 44 foreign.
>   In Liverpool there was entered inward 1738 British and 65
> foreign, vessels; and outward 795 British and 70 foreign. . .
>   From these statements it appears, that Liverpool had
> gained greatly upon Bristol, and was henceforth to be con-
> sidered as the second port in Britain, and the commercial
> captital of the West coast. (*Annals*, III, p. 432)

There was recognition, then, that Bristol had been eclipsed
in regard to her overseas trade; however, the city remained the
second largest in terms of population in the popular mind. Un-
restrained by the facts which a general census might have provided
— there was no official census until 1801 — the authors of the
eighteenth century ordinarily over-estimated the population. Daniel
Defoe wrote in the 1720's that "It is supposed they have an
Hundred Thousand inhabitants in the City, and within three Miles
of its Circumverance," (*Tour*, II, p. 437), while Benjamin Martin,
an instrument maker and compiler, computed the houses at
"13,000 and the souls at 95,000," (*History*, p. 75). Macpherson
"perambulated it for two days, and from a near examination of
the number of houses on a new foundation, and even of entire

new streets erected since the year 1751, he could not hesitate in concluding it to contain about 100,000 souls, or to be about the magnitude of that part of London which is contained within the antient walls." He continued;

> It is confessed, that London, within the limited compass, appears to be more populous, or to have more people appearing in the streets; but that we apprehend to be occasioned chiefly by its communication with its vastly-extended suburbs, its immense commerce and shipping, the greater resort of foreigners, and the near residence of the court, nobility, gentry, and lawyers; whereas, in the streets of Bristol, which are more remote from harbour and shipping, the inhabitants are mostly either families, living on their means, or else manufacturers and workmen of many various kinds, employed mostly within doors. (*Annals*, III, p. 322-323)

There were others, however, who made more reliable estimates. William Cole, the Cambridge antiquarian who provided his friends with materials for histories and antiquarian books, numbered the houses of the seventeen Bristol parishes and the out-parish of St. Philips at 5,701 in 1735 (Cole MSS., B.M. Add. MSS. 5811: 87b). This, figure he pointed out, represented an increase of 1390 houses since his initial visit in 1712. Less convincingly he estimated the houses outside the confines of Bristol at approximately 1,000. Numbers of houses are, of course, not numbers of people, but they can help at arriving at approximate populations.

James Sketchley, a Bristol publisher, made a population count in his *Bristol Directory* of 1775. He calculated the number of houses, and multiplied that number by five and one-sixteenth. This figure was not without some foundation. He examined eighteen separate streets in Bristol noting both the quantity of houses and the number of male and female inhabitants in each. He found 703 houses with a total of 1823 male and 2185 female inhabitants, and from this he calculated that there was an average of five and one-sixteenth people to a house in Bristol. His method was commendable but his arithmetic poor, for he should have arrived at 5.7 persons per house. Altogether he found 6,570 inhabited houses and 384 empty houses in Bristol, Clifton, and Bedminster. This would have given Bristol approximately 37,449 people in 1775. Multiplying Cole's estimate of houses by the same number yields a population of 32,290 in 1735. Since the latter figure does not include Bedminster and Clifton and may not take empty houses into consideration, it is difficult to make a meaning-

ful comparison. However, it does seem reasonable to maintain that
population remained somewhat constant between 1735 and 1775.

The census of 1801 revealed that Bristol had lost her position
as second only to London in population. This fact was anticipated
by a writer in the *Gentleman's Magazine* in 1799 who also listed
other important changes.

> With regard to opulence and importance, Bristol has long
> been esteemed the second city in the Kingdom; in extent
> and population, however, it must yield to Birmingham; in
> commerce and commercial liberality to Liverpool, which is
> now rapidly upon the increase. The Merchants of Bristol enjoy
> the trade of Ireland, and of nearly the whole of North and
> South Wales. In exchanging commodities with the West
> Indies, they employ no less than seventy ships, and this is
> one of the most important branches of their commerce. They
> also traffic with Spain, Portugal, Guinea, Holland, Ham-
> burgh, Norway, Russia, America, and Newfoundland. The
> refinery of sugar, and the glass and soap making, are the
> principle manufacturers of Bristol; the woollen, and the
> copper and brass, manufacturers are now at an end. (LXIX,
> p. 1039)

Some of the contemporary writers were aware that Bristol
had suffered a relative decline in a century which was marked
by an enormous acceleration of economic activity in Great Britain.
Few writers offered reasons for this relative decline since their
primary concern was description not analysis. However, Defoe
cited several encumberances retarding the growth of Bristol early
in the century.

> The greatest Inconveniences of Bristol, are, its Situation, and
> the tenacious Folly of its Inhabitants; who by the general In-
> fatuation, the Pretence of Freedoms and Privileges, that Cor-
> poration-Tyranny, which prevents the flourishing and En-
> crease of many a good Town in England, continue obstinately
> to forbid any, who are not Subjects of their City Sovereignty,
> (that is to say, Freeman) to Trade within the Chain of their
> own Liberties; were it not for this, the City of Bristol, would
> before now, have swell'd and encres'd in Buildings and In-
> habitants, perhaps to double the Magnitude it was formerly
> of.
>
> This is evident by this one particular; There is one re-
> markable part of the City where the Liberties extend not at
> all, or but very little without the City gate. Here and no where
> else, they have an Accession of the New Inhabitants; and

abundance of New Houses, nay, some Streets are built, and the like 'tis probable would have been at all the rest of the Gates, if liberty had been given. As for the City itself, there is hardly room to set another House in it; 'tis so close built, except in the Square, the Ground about which is a little too Subject to the hazard of Inundations; So that People do not so freely enlarge that way. (*Tour*, II, pp. 55-56)

The less-outspoken revisionists of the eighth edition of Defoe's *Tour* attempted to dispel this image of a closed society. "All kinds of persons are free to exercise their trades and callings here, without molestation from the corporation; and if poor, they may, if they please, purchase the freedom of the city for a very moderate sum." (II, p. 239) There is probably some truth in this, but another assertion by the same editor concerning the convenience of Bristol for trade is more questionable. What Defoe was alluding to in his statement concerning the inconveniences of "situation" was, without much doubt, the inconvenience to trade brought about by the physical separation of Bristol from the sea. John Aitkin most graphically illustrated the problem in 1788.

The tide rushing with great violence and rising to a vast height in these narrow rivers, brings vessels of considerable burthen to the quay of Bristol which extends along the inner shores of the Froom and the Avon; Here at low water they lie a-ground in the mud; which circumstances, together with various difficulties in navigating to and from the Severn, are the disadvantages under which this port labours. (*England*, p. 315)

In like manner, he outlined the further difficulties which ships encountered on entering the Severn. "The tides from St. Georges Channel, meeting with the powerful tides from the Atlantic, enter the mouths of the Severn and its tributary with a rapid influx; and, rolling on with a lofty head, received from our earliest historians the name of *Hygra*. (II, p. 162)

The Avon and the Froom—the avenues to the Severn and thence to the sea—which dominated the economic life of the city were the objects of a considerable amount of comment. One of the most celebrated observers was Alexander Pope who visited the Hotwells in 1739 to take advantage of their curative powers.

. . . then you come in sight of Bristol, the River winding at the bottom of steeper banks to the Town where you see twenty odd Pyramids smoking over the Town (which are Glasshouses) and a vast Extent of Houses red and white. You come first to the Old Walls, and over a bridge built on both

sides like London bridge, and as much crowded with a strange
mixture of Seamen, women, children, loaded Horses, Asses,
and Sledges with Goods dragging along, all together, without
posts to separate them. From thence you come to a Key
along the Old Wall with houses on both sides, and in the
middle of the street, as far as you can see, hundreds of Ships,
their Masts as thick as they can stand by one another, which
is the oddest and most surprising sight imaginable. The street
is fuller of them, than the Thames from London Bridge to
Deptford, and at certain times only, the Water rises to carry
them out; so that other times, a Long Street full of ships in
the Middle and Houses on both sides looks like a Dream.
(Sherburn ed., IV, p. 201)

The "Irish Gentleman" was more analytic and less colourful in his
approach and view.

Next morning I went to the quay, but was very much surprised to find the river so very muddy, which I concluded to
proceed from the heavy rain that fell the night before, but on
inquiry found it was continually so. I can no better give a
just idea of it than by a witty remark a young lady of my
aquaintance made on her first seeing it, "that it seems as if
Nature had taken a purge, and that was the operation".
The filth and dirt that floats on the top makes it very loath-
some. The quays here are a prodigious height, because the tide
flows so high, and commonly with so much rapidity that it
surprised me. When it is quite ebbed, the masts of the ships
reach to the level of the quay, and the landing of goods would
be very difficult, were it not for the number of cranes which
were placed all along it; and it is worth observing that one
man with the greatest ease can raise a ton burden. The
bridge is made of timber, and, when any ship is to pass, it
opens in the middle by means of an engine on either side.
(Huth ed., pp. 142-143)

Perhaps the most caustic remarks were made by Horace Walpole.
"I did go to Bristol, the dirtiest great shop I ever saw, with so
foul a river, that had I seen the least appearance of cleanliness, I
should have concluded they washed all their linen in it, as they
do at Paris." (Lewis, *Correspondence*, X, p. 232) On the other
hand, the 1769 revisionists of Defoe's *Tour* were willing to temper
their criticism.

The River is (it is true) muddy, and unseemly at low Water;
nor do fishes, of any Value, care to inhabit so filthy a stream.
But this is amply made up by the constant Viccissitudes of

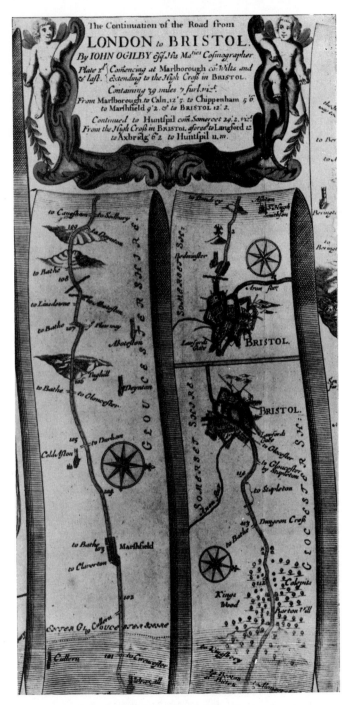

Part of John Ogilby's *Britannia* showing the road systems of England and Wales. First published in 1675 and reprinted later.

An eighteenth century view of the approach to Bristol by the Bath Road.

Photograph by Kevin Tindall

the Tides, which purify the Air. When the River is quite
full, the Tide is supposed to rise near 40 feet, the common
Tide 30; and when the ships are carried up-and-down by the
Tide, passing and repassing through the Meadows and Trees,
the Prospect is indeed enchanting; especially when the Be-
holder is so situated as to see the Rigging of the Ships, and
not the water. (II, p. 310)

The "Irish Gentleman" was so adversely impressed that he felt
it necessary to mention the river again in the rather uncomplimentary summary of his opinions of Bristol.

The Town itself is but disagreeable; the streets are generally
dirty and close built, except a few which lie from the main
body; but what contributes more to its disadvantage is the
muddy river which flows in it, and this circumstance, in my
opinion, cannot be compensated by any natural advantage
(Huth, ed., p. 151)

The Irishman, then, considered Bristol "disagreeable", and
Walpole called the city the "dirtiest great shop" that he had ever
seen.   The city did not necessarily deserve, nor did it always
receive, such harsh indictments.   One of the most succinct descriptions was made of Bristol by the famous Celia Fiennes who
visited the city in the late seventeenth century and described it in
her *Through England on a Side Saddle*.

The Buildings of ye town are pretty high, most timber work,
the streets are narrow and something darkish because the
roomes on ye upper storys are more jutting out, so Contracts
ye streete and the light.   The suburbs are better buildings and
more spacious Streetes. (Griffiths ed., p. 200)

Another early visitor, John Macky, compared Bristol to Verona
for its charm and pleasing aspect.

A River runs thro' almost the Middle of it, on which there
is a fine Stone Bridge.   The Key maybe made the finest
largest, and longest in the World, by pulling down an old
House or two. Behind the Key is a very noble Square, as
large as that of Soho in London: In which is kept the Custom-
House; and most of the eminent Merchants, who keep their
Coaches reside here. The Cathedral is on the other side of the
River, on Top of the Hill; and is the meanest I have seen in
England; But the Square or Green adjoining to it, hath
several fine Houses, and makes, by its Situation, in my
Opinion, much the pleasantest Part of the Town. There are
some Churches in the City finer than the Cathedral; and

your Merchants have their little County Seats in the adjacent
Eminencies; of which that of Mr. Southwell hath a very com-
manding Prospect both of the City, the River Severn, and
the shipping that lie below. (*Journey*, II, pp. 133-134)

As the eighteenth century wore on, Bristol rather naturally
expanded. This point was noted by Aitkin who explained that
"Bristol is closely built: but, like other opulent towns, is now
extending into suburbs by now and more airy streets," (p.
319) and by an anonymous writer in the *Gentleman's Magazine* for
1789 who went into some more detail.

The best-built parts of Bristol are the College-green, some of
the streets in the neighborhood of the green, and Queen-
Square. The suburb called King's-down abounds with good
houses; and as this part stands pleasantly in an elevated situation, removed in some degree from the smoke and noise of
the city, additions are frequently made to the number of its
inhabitants. (LIX, p. 999)

The streets in the centre of the city as in all medieval towns
were extremely narrow and inconvenient—a fact observed with
animus by the government spy and agent, R. J. Sullivan, whose
Observations were published in 1780.

When we consider Bristol as a place of trade and riches we
are greatly surprised to find the houses so meanly built, and
the streets so narrow, dirty, and ill paved. This is in some
measure owing to an ill-judged parsimony; for the houses
being mostly built in the same manner as those in London
before the fire of 1666, with the upper stories projecting in
the streets, are patched up and repaired from time to time—
But this is a very impolitic measure; for besides the expenses
attending the different repairs, and the low price of the rents,
were a fire to happen in Bristol, it would be attended with as
dreadful consequences, in proportion to the number of inhabitants, as it was in London. (pp. 91-92)

The passerby was not always safe as he walked under these
ancient buildings, for their timbers and plaster often fell into
the streets. Nor was the man who continually looked up safe, for
he risked the chance of falling into an open cellar door, or if on
horseback, of running into one of the signs which directed the
illiterate to the shops and inns. This, however, was not the least of
the hazards. As Defoe noted in the 1720's, "They draw all their
heavy Goods here on Sleds, or Sledges without Wheels, which
Kills a Multitude of Horses; and the Pavement is worn so smooth

by them, that in Wet-weather 'tis dangerous walking." (*Tour,* II, p. 437) The reasons adduced for this practice were varied. The anonymous author of *A New Present State of England* maintained that "no Carts being permited to come there, lest as some say, the Shake occasion'd by them on the Pavement, should affect their Bristol-milk, a Cant Term for their Sherry, in the Vaults, large Quantities whereof are doubtless lodg'd there, and dispos'd of both Wholesale and Retail in its utmost Purity and Perfection." (Vol. I. 1750, p. 207) R. J. Sullivan thought that the cellars ran under the streets—which is true—but the real reason for this precaution was presented by the anonymous author of a *Complete History of Somerset.* "The streets, which are very uniform and well built, are kept very neat and free from all noiseome vapours which may infect the air, by the many subterraneous vaults and channels, (called by the citizens Goutes)." This sewer system, he went on to explain, was the reason that heavy vehicles were not allowed on the streets. (p. 270) Few others, however, agreed concerning the cleanliness of the streets.

The city fathers were well aware of the many hazards and inconveniences, and they obtained parliamentary authority for various improvements. That some improvements were made is attested by the sympathetic revisionist of the eighth edition of Defoe.

The internal and trading parts of the City are partly antique, high, irregular and projecting, and built of wood and plaister, with many houses, and some entire streets, (viz. Bridge-street, Clare-street, and Union-street,) of Brick and stone; . . . The heart of the city is rather closely built, but the streets are now much widened and improved, and several are totally rebuilt . . . .

The city has of late years been newly paved, with smooth pavements on the sides for foot-passengers, executed very neatly. It has been long lighted with lamps; but of late they have been increased, and the lighting is exceeded only in London.

The city has plenty of good water from public pumps and conduits; The most remarkable of which is in Temple-street . . . . Also the river water is brought underground into every street, and may be had in every street, and may be had in every house for an annual payment. There are vaults or common sewers . . . and perhaps there is not a house which has not a communication with

the main sewers; a provision for cleanliness, not so universal
in any city in the world.   Carts and Waggons are used here
as in other places, with some sledges, or drays. (II, pp.
239-240)

Despite the improvements (which may have been exaggerated by
this edition of the *Tour*) visitors still spoke of the narrowness of
the streets. During a visit to Bristol in 1775, Thomas Hutchinson,
a prominent American and later a loyalist, echoed the old view.
"I had formed a pretty just idea from the long-continued accounts
of people who had been there, but it rather fell short: the houses
are meaner, the streets narrower and dirtier, and except the
buildings in three or four small squares (or rather some of these
buildings), and some of the Company Halls, there are no elegant
houses, scarcely fit for a first-rate tradesman To live in." (Hutchinson ed., I, p. 346) It would, indeed, appear that Hutchinson found
Bristol wholly unattractive, yet two years later this same visitor
wrote:

> Yesterday took a full view of Bristol from Brandon Hill,
> where they say Cromwell erected his battaries and beat down
> their houses. I think, take in all circumstance, and I should
> prefer living there to any place in England.   The manners
> and customs of the people are very like those of the people of
> New England, and you might pick out a set of Boston Select-
> men from any of their churches. (Hutchinson, II, p. 148)

Though the basis of the judgment differed, this does present an
interesting and strange contrast.   Others, given the same opportunity to visit Bristol a second time, might well have revised their
opinions.

Perhaps because the streets were narrow, they appeared to
many of the observers to swarm with people. Pope who had
described the bridge—which was replaced in the 1760's—as
"crowded with a strange mixture" of people and animals, also
commented that "The streets are as crowded as London, but the
best Image I can give you of it is, Tis as if Wapping and South-
wark were ten-times as big, or all their people run into London."
(Sherburn ed., IV, pp. 204-205)

To add to the confusion and crowds which were evident
throughout the city were the hawkers, peddlers, and farmers who
cried their wares through Bristol.   During the two annual fairs
and during market days ably described by one of the local historians, Barrett, the crowds were even greater.

Butter remarkable good and flesh meat, ox beef, veel and mutton, the best of every kind, together with all the produce of the kitchen-garden in great abundance, are to be had at the markets, held every Wednesday and Saturday, behind the Exchange in Union-Street; and fish at the Fish-market twice a week, Wednesday and Friday, in Union Street, besides the salmon, cod, mackeral, herring, plaice, flounders, oysters, sprats, etc. brought to the Back during the season. A market is also held on the Back every other Wednesday, where the Welch boats, arriving at spring tides, discharge the produce of their country for sale; fine salt-butter, poultry of all kinds, roasting pigs and geese ready for the spit; fruit as apples and pears, etc. The great brewhouses and malthouses, the bakers and cornfactors, are furnished with corn and flour by water carriage from the West Country and the fertile vale of Evesham, and the counties of Hereford, Monmouth, and Worcester, which is landed on St. Austin's wharf, at the head of the Quay, out of the trows; or on the Back, where convenient markethouses are built for securing it when landed from the weather, and there exposed to sale every spring tide:—here are also landed great quantities of cyder. Besides these, there was a corn-market in Wine-street, where corn was brought by the neighboring farmers for sale, now converted into a cheese-market; and a hay-market was established in Broadmead in the year 1786, every Tuesday and Friday. The great market for fat and lean cattle, sheep, (great droves of which come in from Wales) is held in St. Thomas-street every Thursday, and is much frequented also by the woollen manufacturers at the season of the year for the purchase of wool, the wool-hall being in this street. (*History*, pp. 102-103)

Another contemporary explained that "all are in a hurry, running up and down with cloudy looks, and busy faces, loading, carrying and unloading goods and merchandizes of all sorts, from place to place . . . ." (*A Complete History of Somerset*, pp. 27-28)

Even the merchants contributed to this confusion. This was the case despite the fact that a commodious exchange was completed by 1742. The "Irish Gentleman" who made his trip in 1752 left a description of the economic centre of Corn Street.

I went to the Exchange, very neat and well built, modelled from the Royal Exchange in London, but not near as to the dimensions of that pile. On the entrance is a coffee house on one side, and a tavern on the other. I was surprised to see most of the merchants assembled in the street transacting their affairs, and a very few within. As the Exchange hath been newly finished and the people never before used to it, the London merchants say, "the Bristol hogs have built a sty, but cannot find the way into it." (Huth, ed., p. 144) The merchants may not have been adjusted to their new centre, but they were used to being called hogs. Even twenty-eight years later, another visitor explained that by their meeting in the streets the merchants were "constantly exposed to the inclemency of the weather." (Sullivan, p. 92)

To add to the inconveniences suffered by the Bristolians, the glass-houses, which Pope had described as "twenty odd Pyramids smoking over the town," kept "the city, from the continual smoke arising from them, being constantly darkened and in dirt, while the inhabitants are almost suffocated with noxious effluvia." (Sullivan, p. 92) A local poet of questionable talent shed some light on this problem in a number of *Felix Farley's Bristol Journal*.

Bristol can boast of as many pleasant Walks and Rides for Airing in its Invirons, as almost any City: — And happy it is for such a populous Place to have such pleasant Hills and Downs in its Neighborhood — Here the Industrious Tradesmen after breathing the impure Air of a close Street, may sometimes retire with little Loss of Time, and Snuff the Flagrant Gales, and open his Air-pipes nigh chock'd with noisome Exhalations . . . . Here the labouring Mechanic accompanied with his Faithful Wife and little Pratlers take their Sunday's Walk, of Summer Evening Excursion . . . a perfect Terras, thrown up as it were by Art, for people to walk there and overlook the smokey Town. Kingsdown delightful spot is already begun to be dug up . . . . (Dec. 13, 1760)

The author was complaining about the loss of another green belt—a problem which is all too common today. The digging to which he alluded was elaborated on in the same paper a month later.

Each petty Tradesman here must have his Seat,
And vainly thinks the Height will make him great:
But little things look less the more they rise:
So wrens may mount until they look flies.

Haste Brewer e'er Too late, and choose thy Spot
Sell off thy Soot, and build thy Kingsdown Cot.
Come hither Pedlars, quit your dusty stalls.
Here build your Seats, on rise your gardenwalls
And when you've built it e'er call It what you will
'Twill not be Kingsdown then, but Pedlars Hill.
(January 24, 1761)

The contemporary view of Bristol, then, was not altogether flattering. It remains to discuss the opinions expressed by contemporaries of the people who lived in it. Bristol, like London, was essentially a two and not a three-class society in ordinary eighteenth-century terms. There was a middle-class and a lower-class, but the city could not boast of a noble or an aristocratic class. The organization of society was, more simply, commercial not aristocratic. Alexander Pope pointed this out in a letter to his friend Martha Blount: "The City of Bristol itself is a very unpleasant place and no civilized company in it," and he continued, "Only the Collector of the Customs would have brought me acquainted with the Merchants, of whom I hear no great Character." (Sherburn, IV, p. 204) One might assume that he was equating aristocracy and civilized man.

This make-up of society is further revealed by *Sketchley's Bristol Directory*, the first part of which was "An Alphabetical list of the Merchants, Tradesmen, Manufacturers, Captains of Ships, Custom House and Excise Officers, and every other person of note in Bristol and its environs." The leaders of this society were the merchants of whom Bristol was proud. Andrew Hooke, a local publisher, reflected a widely held opinion by noting that, "if we indulge a free Enquiry into the true Source and Origin of Honour, we shall find that Commerce is the sole foundation, and Solid Basis that supports not only secondary Dignities, but even Royality itself." (*Bristolia*, p. 111)

However, Pope was unimpressed and so were others. One of the most scathing indictments was made by the editors of the 1742 edition of Defoe's *Tour*. After discussing the narrowness of the streets, they go on to say:

> . . . we might mention also another Narrow, that is, the Minds of the Generality of its People; for, let me tell you, the Merchants of Bristol, tho' very rich, are not like the Merchants of London; The latter may be said (as of old of the Merchants of Tyre) to vie with the Princes of the Earth; whereas the former, being rais'd by good fortune, and Prizes taken in the Wars, from Masters of Ships, and blunt tars, have inbib'd the Manners of those rough Gentlemen so strongly, that they transmit it to their Descendents, only with a little more of the Sordid than is generally to be found among British Sailors; and I would advise the rich ones among them, if they would be a little more polite and generous, than they usually are, to travel, but not out of England neither, I mean only to London (that is, from the second great Trading town to the first); and

they will see Examples worth their Imitation, as well for
Princely Spirit, as upright and generous Dealings. (*Tour*, II,
pp. 269-270)

Pope and the editors of this edition of Defoe were not alone in
their vilifying appraisals. The "Irish Gentleman" noted of Bristolians that, "Their Souls are engrossed by lucre, and [they] are
very expert in affairs of merchandize; but as to politeness, it is
a thing banished from their republic as a contagious distemper."
(Huth, p. 151). Thomas Cox writing much earlier made a similar
judgment.

It is very populous; but the People give up themselves to
Trade so entirely, that nothing of the Politeness and Gaiety of
Bath is to be seen here . . . for the Trade of many Nations is
drawn hither by the Industry and the Opulency of the People.
This makes them remarkably insolent to Strangers, as well as
ungrateful to Benefactors, both naturally arising from being
bred, and become rich by Trade, as (to use their own Phrase)
to care for no Body, but whom they can gain by; but yet this
ill-bred Temper hath produced one good Effect, which our
Laws have not yet been able to do, and that is, the utter
extirpation of Beggars. (*Magna Britannia*, 1727, IV.
pp. 744-745)

Cox did find a redeeming feature, but Samuel Johnson's friend.
Richard Savage, was not so charitable.

Boast swarming vessels, whose plebeian state
Owes not to merchants but mechanics freight.
Boast nought but pedlar-fleets — in war's alarms,
Unknown to glory, as unknown to arms.
Boast thy base Tolsey, and the turn-spjit dogs,
Thy Halliers horses and thy human hogs;
Upstarts and mushrooms, proud relentless hearts;
Thou blank of sciences! thou dearth of arts!
Such foes as learning once was doom'd to see;
Huns, Goths, and Vandals were but types of thee.
    Proceed, great Bristol, in all-righteous ways,
And let one Justice heighten yet thy praise;
Still spare the catamite and swinge the whore,
and be, whate'r Gomorrha was before.
(Anon., *Savage*, II., p. 235).

These vitrolic words, it must be admitted, were written while
Savage was in Bristol's Bridewell, but even so they cannot be
ignored in light of so much corroboration.

All of these comments were made in roughly the first part
or half of the century, and much of the criticism had its origins
in the contention that Bristolians were uncultured. A Pope or a

An eighteenth century view of the High Cross, the Cathedral and the Church of St. Augustine the Less (now demolished).

From a print supplied by Messrs. Frost and Reed Ltd.

The first American consulate in England, No. 37 Queen Square. In 1797 the Polish patr
Thaddeus Kosciuszko after his release from St. Petersburg Prison and while en route
the U.S.A. was a guest here of Consul Vanderhorst and received a great ovation at this hou
Photograph by Reece Winst

Savage in particular were interested in the cultural attainments of any society, and a commercial Bristol rather naturally disappointed them. However, within the years between 1740 and 1780, there were significant improvements which might have pleased those who viewed Bristol as a cultural desert. Many of these improvements, it should be noted, were brought about jointly for the benefit of Bristolians and visitors to the Hotwell, which was brought within the confines of Bristol by 1778.

One source of enjoyment shared by both the visitors and the inhabitants was the Jacob's Well Theatre which had its origins early in the century. Located between Bristol and the Hotwells at the foot of Brandon Hill, the Theatre was inconvenient for Bristolians, and the walk to and fro was fraught with danger especially on those nights when the moon did not shine. Aware of these dangers and awakening to new cultural demands, the Bristolians constructed the King Street Theatre in 1766 amidst heated controversy. The editors of *Felix Farley's Bristol Journal* expressed their dissatisfaction over the prospect in verse, two lines of which are enough to reveal the substance of their argument.

> Newgate enlarge!. . .Yes, Quick extend its Walls; A large Play-house loudly for it calls; . . . (June 21, 1766).

And the constant visitor John Wesley, the founder of Methodism, elaborated on this view in a letter to the Mayor and Corporation of Bristol.

> The endeavors lately used to procure subscriptions for building a new play house in Bristol have given us not a little concern; and that on various accounts; not barely as most of the present stage entertainments sap the foundation of all religion, as they naturally tend to efface all traces of piety and seriousness out of the minds of men; but as they are peculiarly hurtful to a trading city, giving a wrong turn to youth especially, gay, trifling, and directly opposite to the spirit of industry and close application to business; and, as drinking and debauchery of every kind are constant attendants on these entertainments, with indolence, effeminancy, and idleness, which affect trade in an high degree. (Telford, IV, p. 279)

Unfortunately, commentators on Bristol did not write about the new theatre at any length. Only the 1778 edition of Defoe's *Tour* mentions that "It is common to see upwards of 100 carriages at the doors of the theatre or concert-room." (II, p. 240)

However, other social and cultural changes were made and some of them did draw comment. By 1778 Bristol could boast a new assembly room, a Vauxhall, and a grotto of some interest. Prior to 1756 Bristol did not have a formal assembly room, though

various company halls and a converted playhouse near St. Augus-
tinine Back were often used for that purpose. When queried
about the latter, a contemporary responded, "Twas a mighty
shabby concern I assure ye." (Smith, Biographical Memoires,
B.R.I. II, f. 290) However, it was noted in *A New Present State
of England* in 1750 that the Bristolians had "begun to improve
the city by several noble edifices, more particularly their Assem-
bly-Room, on College-Green, it is to be hop'd that their Minds
will in Time take a happier Turn, and the more considerable Part
of them will be convinc'd, that Politeness is no ways incompatible
with Trade and Commerce." (I, p. 207) It is not easy to determine
which assembly room the author is alluding to, but in 1756 the
New Musick Room on Prince Street was opened with the presentation of Handel's *Messiah*. That the New Musick Room had the
desired effect is open to question. The eighteenth century poet,
Thomas Chatterton, presented a rather uncomplimentary view in
verse.

> A mean assembly room, absurdly built,
> Boasted one gorgeous lamp of copper gilt;
> With farthing candles, chandiliers of tin,
> And services of water, rum, and gin.
> There in the dull solemnity of wigs,
> The dancing bears of commerce murder jigs;
> Here dance the dowdy belles of crocked trunk,
> And often, very often, reel home drunk;
> Here dance the bucks with infinite delight,
> And club to pay the fiddlers for the night.
> While Broderip's hum-drum symphony of flats
> Rivals the harmony of midnight cats.
> (*Kew Gardens,* Chatterton, pp. 355-356)

Of course, it must be recalled that the ill-fated Chatterton had
been rejected by Bristol.

The New Vauxhall which was opened in 1751 was visited by
the "Irish Gentleman" who was not unimpressed.

> In the evening we went to a pretty garden near the
> Hotwells, which they call Vauxhall. There are some booths
> and pleasant arbors, hung with some globe lamps, etc. an
> orchestra wherein were a good band of music. There was
> no company here this night, which rendered it very disagreable
> and several times after but very few. The Poor Man who
> owned it was at a great expense to keep it in order, but
> in a short time after was obliged to decamp. (Huth ed.,
> p. 148)

The gardens did, indeed, disappear from the Bristol scene for
some years, but a New Vauxhall was constructed in 1776, and,

if we are to believe the local journals, it was an immediate success. *Felix Farley's Bristol Journal* reported an attendance of over two thousand on the first night alone.

It is impossible to determine how popular the grotto owned by Mr. Goldney, a local merchant, was, but it was popular enough to attract Samuel Curwen, another American Loyalist, who spent some part of his exile in Bristol.

On 'change met my countryman Mr. Joseph Waldo, who procured tickets for our admission to Mr. Goldney's grotto at Clifton . . . we were soon admitted, and, attended by the gardner, were conducted through gravel-walks, kept in the nicest order, the whole bearing the appearance of care and industry; it is on a moderate scale, but well filled with orange and lemon trees, etc., and a small piece of water abounding in gold and silver fish, supplied from a natural fountain so lofty that a fire-engine is erected at one end of the terrace; the stream runs underground for a distance and discharges itself through an urn on which a neptune rests with his trident. The ground between it and the engine is made rough, scraggy, and woody, to resemble a wilderness, which I passed going through the main walk. We arrived at the door of the grotto, situated under the terrace; the object that presented itself to our view was a lion in a sitting posture, and behind, in a dark cave, a lioness, the latter so like life that I could hardly persuade myself to the contrary. The form of the grotto is octangular, its roof semi-circular, having a dome with a round window in the centre; the diameter about twenty feet on each side, from the door in front to the mouth of the cave in which the lioness is sitting; to the right and left of the entrance the roof is supported by pillars; covered as its roof and sides are with a variety of shells, stones, spars, petrifications, etc., the mountain, even the bowels of the earth and the bottom of the sea, seem to have been pillaged to furnish materials to adorn this curious subtertraneous recess. On the left hand, beyond the dome and under a rough cragged stone arch, is a small quadrangular stone basin of water supplied by small streams, issuing through almost perfect deception ever saw. On the door was a miniture of a female face with a seemingly broken glass covering it, in the same style and manner, and producing a like effect. From hence we ascended the terrace-walk four hundred feet in length, the front of the garden raised forty feet supported by a brick wall; the rear bounded by a border of flowers, and behind a shrubbery of lofty trees. On the right is an octangular structure ending in a dome eighteen feet in diameter, with seats all round, and

having as many windows as it has sides, which affords as
many prospects, except on the side of the garden, where they
are darkened, yielding three delightful perspectives. (Ward
ed. p. 154)

With all of these changes, Alexander Pope might have been more
impressed had he visited Bristol in 1780 rather than in 1739. As
the 1778 edition of Defoe's *Tour* noted.

There are many genteel houses of entertainment all about
the city, with neat walks and gardens, and very good accommodations. Convenience and elegance are now attended to at
Bristol, and it affords every gratification a reasonable person
can desire. (II, p. 241)

The same revisionists also attempted to dispel the unhappy image
of the people at Bristol which was reflected in the writing of so
many of the early visitors and writers.

Its gentry, merchants, and capital traders, are as polite, and
superb in their town and country houses, equipages, servants,
and amusements as any in the kingdom. And they cannot
well be otherwise, with Bath on the one side, and the Hotwells, a resort of nobility and gentry, under their eye. Its
shopkeepers are remarkable for their activity, industry, and
obliging upright, and punctual behaviour in their business.
Literature and genteel education are much cultivated
in Bristol; and it abounds with agreeable women,
whose mode of dress is universally approved. People
of rank and education here, as everywhere else, pronounce
with propriety; but some of the bourgeois speak a broad
dialect, much worse than the common people in the metropolis, though they are not willing to acknowledge it. (II,
p. 239)

It will be recalled that Thomas Hutchinson was also very much
impressed with the people of Bristol when he made his visit in
1777. However, these seem to have been minority opinions;
Samuel Curwen, who liked Bristol well enough to spend some
part of his exile in it, reflected the old view in his diary in 1778.

Had an hour's conversation with a stranger on 'change; a rare
event, people in England being greatly indisposed to join
with unknown persons. The Bristolians are, however, remarkable for early enquiries into the character of all
strangers, from commercial motives, and soon fasten on all
worth making a property of, if practicable; all others, of how
great estimation soever, are in general neglected. This city
is remarkable for sharp dealings; there runs a proverb, "one
Jew is equal to two Genoese, one Bristolian to two Jews."
(Ward, ed., p. 154)

R. J. Sullivan was no more generous in his appraisal in 1780, nor was G. Parker, a lecturer, soldier, and actor, who visited Bristol in the same year.

> I barely entered into London, in order to fix my route, which I determined should be to Bristol, where I got at the time of the fair, and found it almost impossible to obtain lodgings for love or money.
>
> My fears of large towns were justified in Bristol; for after repeated struggles in the course of near six months, I was unable to procure more than three Audiences, from whom the whole amount of my receipts were only seven pounds four shillings: So that had it not been for the assistance of some friends, it must have been over with me.—
>
> I often expostulated with myself on this impossibility of inducing an Audience of any consequences to visit my lecture; but what right had I to expect being attended to where Savage died neglected in a gaol, and whence Chatterton fled to perish prematurely in London . . . . (*View*, II, pp. 260-261)

These again are the bitter words of a thwarted artist, and it is apparent that George Parker was unattractive to audiences in many cities, for despite the patronage of Oliver Goldsmith and Samuel Johnson, he died in poverty. It might be mentioned here that both Dr. Johnson and Boswell visited the city in order to investigate the Chatterton papers. Unfortunately the only registered response of either man was about the inn in which they stayed. Dr. Johnson said that it was so bad that even Boswell wished he was back in Scotland, but it will be remembered that Johnson had a very poor opinion of Scotland.

The writer in the *Gentleman's Magazine* of 1799 concurred.

> Here, as I was examining one of the small brazen pillar tablets, which are placed before the entrance into the Exchange, I observed on the border this inscription.
>
> Nemo sibi nascitur
>
> [roughly translated; no man is an island unto himself.]
>
> A motto that was the more remarkable, as the general character of the people of Bristol, and particularly of the merchants, though they have this memorial so continually before their eyes, is far from being correspondent. The latter, not withstanding this elegant structure has been erected for the reception at so great an expence, always remain on tolzey, jealous of the increase of each other's affairs. But, though innumerable instances may be adduced in confirmation of this characteristic, it is not here intended to insinuate that Bristol is incapable of giving birth to men of liberal sentiment. (LXIX, pp. 1039-1040)

Even John Wesley who had been a frequent visitor for fifty-one years made a devastating judgment in a letter to a friend.

> I often wonder at the people of Bristol. They are so honest, yet so dull; 'tis scarce possible to strike any fire into them. (Telford, VIII, p. 198)

The anonymous writer of an article in the *Monthly Magazine* in 1799 offered a reason for Bristol's bad press.

> Perhaps there is no place in England where public and social amusements are so little attended to as here. From this circumstance, the inhabitants have been stigmatized with a want of taste, and described as the sordid devotees of Plutos. Another, and more plausible reason may be alleged for this singularity: no place contains, in proportion to its inhabitants so many dissenters. (June 1, 1799)

Defoe had noticed that there were "seven Meeting-Houses, two Presbyterian, one Independent, two Quakers, one Baptist: also one or two other Meetings not to be nam'd." (*Tour*, 1724, II, p. 515) There was also a great increase occasioned by the Wesleyan additions during the century, but this does not mean that the author was necessarily correct in his assumption.

The bulk of this criticism was, of course, directed towards the middle-class inhabitants of the city. The poor not only escaped criticism but also escaped notice. To be sure, there were lists of charitable projects and foundations. Bristol was justly famous for its care of the socially deprived, and John Howard, the prison reformer, described the jails in detail—crime being a peculiar province of the poor — but otherwise there was little mention of this aspect of life. Poverty and suffering were altogether too common in the eighteenth century to warrant special notice. Furthermore, the literate were writing about the literate for the literate.

If one were to judge the contemporary view of Bristol by the sheer weight of evidence, one would find the image of the city to be an uncomplimentary one throughout the century. The reader may not find this image congenial if his Bristol ancestors made up this eighteenth century population, nor will he find it all accurate. One might justly ask if many of the writers were prepared to find Bristol unpleasant. Travellers of all periods of history have had a propensity to be critical. A Pope might expect too much of a provincial city, and a Hutchinson used to wide and airy streets in the new American cities would rather naturally be adversely impressed by the narrowness of the medieval streets. Though one might indeed question the validity and recognize the prejudices of the writers, one cannot change what the world was reading about Bristol. As uncongenial as it may have been, it must stand.

BIBLIOGRAPHY

This bibliography is neither complete nor exhaustive. However, its length is justified by the hope that interested readers will want to pursue this investigation further than it goes. In most cases, the works have good indices which precludes my using page numbers. The reader might only be warned that he may find reference to Bristol under either Somerset or Gloucester.

Anonymous. *Bath and Bristol Guide.* Bath, 1760.

———— *The Beauties of England.* London, 1767.

———— *A Complete History of Somerset.* n.p., 1742.

———— *Description of the Exchange at Bristol.* Bath, 1743.

———— *A New Present State of England.* 2 Vols. London, 1750.

———— *The Pipes, Pumps, and Conduits of Bristol.* London, n.d.

———— *The Poetical Works of Thomas Chatterton.* Cam. 1842.

———— *The Tradesman's and Travellers Pocket Companion:* or *Bath and Bristol Guide.* Bath, (1750).

———— *The Works of Richard Savage.* London, 1775.

Aitkin, John. *England Delineated.* London, 1788.

Anderson, Adam. *The Origin of Commerce.* 4 vols. Lon., 1787-9.

Atkyn, Robert. *The Antient and Present State of Gloucestershire.*
                                                    n.p., 1768.

Banks, Sir Joseph. *Journal of an Excursion to Eastbury and*
                                        Bristol. n.p., n.d.

Barrett, William. *The History and Antiquities of the City of Bristol.* Bristol, 1789.

Bickham, George. *The British Monarchy.* n.p., 1743.

Campbell, John. *A Political Survey of Britain.* London, 1774.

Chambers, George. *An Historical View of the Domestic Economy of G. Britain, and Ireland.* Edinburg, 1812.

Collins, Emmanuel. Miscellanies. Bristol, 1762.

(Cox, Thomas). *Magna Britannia.* 6 Vols. 1722-31.

Curnock, Nehemiah, ed. *The Journal of the Rev. John Wesley,*
                                    A.M. 8 Vols. London, n.d.

Defoe, Daniel. *A Tour Through England and Wales.* 2 Vols.
                                            London, 1928.

———— (edited) *A Tour Thro' the Whole Island of Great*
                                Britain. 4 Vols. London, 1742.

———— (edited) *A Tour Through the Whole Island of Great*
                                Britain. 4 Vols. London, 1769.

———— (edited) *A Tour Through the Island of Great Britain.*
4 Vols. London, 1778.

Griffiths, Mrs. ed. *Through England on a Side Saddle.*
London, 1881.

Goldwin, W. *City of Bristol: A Poem.* London, 1751.

Heard, William. *A Sentimental Journey.* London, 1778.

Hooke, Andrew. *Bristolia: or Memoirs of the City of Bristol.*
London, 1748.

Howard, John. *The State of the Prisons in England and Wales.*
Warrington, 1777.

Hutchinson, P. O., ed. *Diary and Letters of Thomas Hutchinson.*
2 Vols. London, 1883-1886.

Huth, Henry, ed. *Narrative of the Journey of an Irish Gentleman
Through England in the Year* 1752. London, 1869.

Lee, Sidney, ed. *The Poems of Thomas Chatterton.* London, 1906.

Lewis, W. S., ed. *Horace Walpole's Correspondence.* 30 Vols.
London, 1937-1961.

Macky, John. *A Journey through England.* 2 Vols. 1714-1722.

Macpherson, David. *Annuals of Commerce.* 4 Vols. London, 1805.

Martin, Benjamin. *The Natural History of England.* London, 1759.

Matthews, W. *Bristol Guide.* Bristol, 1794.

Parker, G. A. *A View of the High and Low Life.* 2 Vols. Lon. 1781.

Randolf, George. *An Enquiry into the Medicinal Virtues of
Bristol-Water.* London, 1750.

Russell, P. *England Displayed.* 2 Vols. London, 1769.

Sherburn, George, ed. *Correspondence of Alexander Pope.* 5 Vols.
Oxford. 1956.

Sketchley, James, *Sketchley's Bristol Directory.* Bristol, 1775.

Smith, R. Biographical Memoires *B.R.I. MSS* 20 Vols.

Spencer, Nathaniel. *The Complete English Traveller.* London, 1773.

Sullivan, R. G. *Observations Made During a Tour Through Parts
of England, Wales, and Scotland.* London, 1780.

Telford, John, ed. *The Letters of the Rev. John Wesley,* A.M.
8 Vols., London, 1931.

(Wallace, James). *A General and Descriptive History of Liverpool.*
Liverpool, 1795.

Ward, G. A., ed. *Samuel Curwen, Journals and Letters.*
London, 1842.

Whatley, John. *England's Gazetteer.* 3 Vols. 1751.

Young, Arthur. *A Six Weeks Tour.* London, 1772.

BRISTOL AND BURKE

P. T. UNDERDOWN

I wish to be a Member of Parliament to have my share of doing good and resisting evil.

Speech at Bristol, 1780.

Burke's statue in Colston Avenue, Bristol. It is a bronze replica of the original in the Houses of Parliament and was given by Sir W. H. Wills to mark the opening of the new St. Augustine's Bridge.

Photograph by Reece Winstone

On 30 October 1894 a statute of Edmund Burke was unveiled in Bristol by the then Prime Minister, Lord Rosebery. In recognition of the occasion, G. E. Weare published **Edmund Burke's Connection with Bristol,** a study mainly concerned with the election of 1774 but giving only a short account of Burke's work as member of Parliament for the city during the ensuing six years. Since Weare's book appeared, our understanding of eighteenth century politics has been transformed as a result of the researches of Sir Lewis Namier and other modern historians. A number of collections of manuscripts have also become available to scholars, including the Fitzwilliam papers which were removed from Wentworth Woodhouse in 1948 and housed in Sheffield Public Library. These contain many previously unknown letters to and from Burke, and together with letters from smaller manuscript collections elsewhere, they have made possible a revision and amplification of Weare's book.

The six years 1774-80 during which Burke represented Bristol in Parliament constituted only a short chapter in his public career which extended over thirty years. He had previously sat at Westminster for Lord Verney's pocket borough of Wendover from 1765 to 1774; Lord Rockingham subsequently found him a seat for Malton which he represented from 1780 until his retirement in 1794. Burke was a professional politician. By 1774, he was not only the most distinguished speaker in the House of Commons, but he also acted as an unpaid agent for the Rockingham party in its negotiations with other political groups as well as in internal consultations amongst its own adherents. An Irishman by birth, easily irritated and even flustered by the attacks of his opponents, he was yet entirely loyal to his friends. If he had a real veneration for the aristocrats amongst whom he moved, he also had a great belief in himself, and this frequently enabled him to make a stand as a champion of unpopular causes. In 1774, at the age of 45, he was at the height of his powers.

Although Burke's representation of Bristol comprised only a small fraction of his parliamentary career, it presents him in an unaccustomed role. Since the political outlook of Lords Verney and Rockingham largely coincided with that of Burke, he was to a considerable extent a free agent when he sat for their pocket boroughs; but at Bristol, with its broad franchise, the number, wealth and political consciousness of his constituents introduced a new factor into Burke's position as a member of Parliament. Many of the citizens were fully alive to the chief political and economic issues of the day, especially those which affected their livelihood, the city's trade. Burke was thus in a position not simply of moulding public opinion—as was his wont—but of either truckling to it or suffering the consequences. This article tries to explain how and why he chose the latter course.

Burke as Candidate for Bristol.

In 1774 events were moving towards a crisis in British history, for the American colonies were seething with discontent. This was a matter of the deepest concern for the people of Bristol which was then the second city and port of the kingdom, for her wealth was largely derived from her colonial trade, notably with North America and the West Indies. The merchants had thus acquired great prosperity which they naturally did not want to lose.

Britain's great political and commercial rival in the eighteenth century was France, but the conquest of Canada during the Seven Years' War had largely removed any danger of French attack upon the British settlements in America. With the end of the war in 1763, the prime minister, George Grenville, decided upon a policy of retrenchment: that the colonists should help to pay off the large national debt incurred during the war and should contribute towards the upkeep of garrisons stationed in the colonies for their defence. The result was the Sugar and Stamp Acts of 1764-5.

Previously the basis of British policy had been that the colonies existed for the benefit of the Mother Country, which was therefore entitled to regulate their trade through such devices as the Navigation Laws. Grenville's Sugar Act of 1764 was a new principle in that it imposed customs duties not merely in restraint of trade but as a means of raising a revenue. It was followed in 1765 by the better-known Stamp Act which imposed further taxes upon the colonists for the same purpose. These two measures so provoked the anger of the Americans that they refused to trade with Britain, causing great losses to the British merchants and manufacturers. In 1766 Grenville's successor as prime minister, Lord Rockingham, bowed to the storm of protests and decided to repeal the Stamp Act, but at the same time Parliament passed a Declaratory Act which affirmed its basic right to tax the colonists if it so wished.

Burke had then just become Rockingham's private secretary and had entered Parliament as member for Wendover. Henceforth he remained a loyal and enthusiastic supporter of the Rockingham Whigs. The latter was only one of several groups of politicians who called themselves Whigs but whose policies were quite different from one another. It has been seen that Grenville and his supporters believed in American taxation; the Rockingham group, including Burke, believed in Britain's right of taxation but thought it might be inexpedient to use it; another more radical group led by William Pitt, Earl of Chatham, distinguished between the right of Parliament to legislate for the colonies—which they admitted —and its right to tax—which they denied. On the other side, George III and his ministerial supporters, some of whom were described by their contemporaries as ' the King's Friends ', wished to assert the undoubted and unlimited supremacy of Parliament over the colonies, and eventually, of course, this led to the outbreak of the War of Independence in 1775.

Paradoxically, it was Charles Townshend, chancellor of the exchequer in Chatham's ministry which had succeeded Rockingham's in 1766, who revived the dispute in 1767 by introducing taxes on tea and other colonial imports, at a time when Chatham lay prostrated by illness. The colonists again boycotted trade with Britain, and in 1770 Lord North's ministry repealed all the duties save that on tea. It was the Tea Act of 1773, allowing the import of East Indian tea direct to America, which finally sparked off the conflict. In retaliation for a colonial demonstration against the Act, known as the Boston Tea Party, Lord North's government passed a series of Coercion Acts, which made hostilities virtually inevitable.

There were, of course, many other issues then being discussed in the Bristol clubs, coffee houses and taverns, and on the Exchange, but it was the American question which dominated the political scene. It explains the rather unexpected dissolution in September 1774, when the Parliament elected in 1768 had yet another year to run. Lord North's government wished to avert criticism of its policy which it anticipated would follow an impending joint meeting of the colonies—the Continental Congress.

Until the Reform Act of 1832 the members of Parliament elected for each borough were chosen in many cases by a mere handful of voters. Bristol was one of the principal exceptions, having an electorate numbering about 5,000—the third largest in the kingdom. The voters comprised the forty shilling freeholders and freemen. Freedom could be acquired by birth, purchase, apprenticeship, or marriage to the daughter of a freeman.

In 1774, the retiring members of Parliament for Bristol were Lord Clare, an Irish peer who had been first elected in 1754, and

Matthew Brickdale, a Bristol merchant, elected in 1768. Although Clare is often labelled a Whig and Brickdale a Tory, their policies were almost indistinguishable. They both normally supported the government of the day and had made themselves unpopular in Bristol by supporting coercive measures against the colonists. Their candidatures had been sponsored by the two Bristol political clubs: the Union Club (Whig) meeting at the Bush tavern and the Steadfast Society (Tory) at the White Lion. In 1756 these two bodies agreed that each would support the other's candidates for the next three elections, thus avoiding the expense of a contest; a further agreement was made in 1766 to cover the election of 1768 only. If, as seems probable, the 1766 agreement superseded that of 1756, neither agreement was still operative for the 1774 election. However, for some years there had been dissatisfaction at the system whereby the city's members of Parliament were virtually elected by the committees of the two political clubs. Since the emergence of John Wilkes as the champion of popular liberty in 1763, a radical movement had developed in many parts of Britain. In Bristol it was organised as the Independent Society under the leadership of Samuel Peach, a wealthy merchant, and his son-in-law, Henry Cruger, but drawing its support largely from the artisan class. Its programme included the safeguarding of civil liberties; a vigilant scrutiny of public expenditure; the prevention of compromised elections; the repeal of the Septennial Act; a limitation of the number of placemen in Parliament, and the exclusion of pensioners and contractors from it; and the maintenance of a conciliatory policy towards the American colonies. This body had tried to 'instruct' Clare and Brickdale to vote in support of the reform of Parliament, but getting no satisfaction, it soon after adopted Cruger as its prospective candidate to oppose them at the next election.

Henry Cruger was an American merchant from New York who had come to Bristol in 1757 to take charge of a branch of his family's business. Though he had been regarded as a Tory, he was a member of a Bristol deputation sent to Parliament in 1766 to ask for the repeal of the Stamp Act. He was then elected to the Bristol Common Council[1] and became a leader of the local radical movement. The radicals at first intended putting forward as their second candidate Cruger's business partner, John Mallard, but they finally decided that as it was unlikely that they could win both seats, it would be more realistic to nominate as the second candidate a representative of one of the other Whig groups that were opposed to the government. It was customary for one of the Bristol

1. The modern City Council.

members of Parliament to be a local merchant (**e.g.,** Brickdale); the other, a politician of national reputation but with a special knowledge of economic policy (**e.g.,** Clare). The name of Edmund Burke was therefore suggested. By 1774 he had won a national reputation as " the brains and mouthpiece of the Rockingham party ", which was the more moderate and aristocratic wing of the opposition. His speeches in Parliament, his political pamphlets, especially **Thoughts on the Cause of the Present Discontents** (1769), and his appointment as British agent for the province of New York, all made him a suitable candidate—though it was perhaps surprising that the invitation should have come through Rev. Dr. Thomas Wilson, a leading radical, with whose policy Burke was wholly out of sympathy.

At this time he was already looking around for another constituency because his seat at Wendover was no longer available. The prestige to be gained by representing Bristol made him inclined to accept the offer of nomination, provided he could be assured of adequate support both in men and money to fight the election. But when the dissolution of Parliament was announced on 30 September 1774 and the adoption meetings were held, a meeting of the Bristol radicals refused to endorse Burke's nomination and resolved that Cruger should stand as the only opposition candidate. The rift between the rival opposition groups was thus revealed at this early stage.

Meanwhile Burke had been in correspondence with Richard Champion, a well-known porcelain manufacturer and merchant, who thenceforward became his most energetic and loyal supporter in Bristol. Champion was ably seconded by Joseph Harford, another prominent Bristol merchant. Champion was vehemently opposed to both the policy of the radicals and the person of Cruger, and in his efforts on Burke's behalf he even tried to do a deal with the government candidates to secure Burke's election and Cruger's rejection. Such chicanery was not uncommon in eighteenth century politics.

In those days the voting at elections was not secret and in the case of Bristol was often spread out over several weeks. The votes were recorded publicly, and the record of them can often still be consulted in the Poll Books of each election.

The poll opened on 7 October 1774 with two government candidates, Clare and Brickdale, and one opposition candidate, Cruger. But Lord Clare soon found that the number of his supporters had dwindled, and at the conclusion of the first day's voting, he withdrew. Champion and Harford at once tried to mobilise support for Burke, and joined by some of Clare's former supporters, they eventually persuaded the returning officers (the sheriffs) that it was in order to nominate Burke on the second day of the poll. Burke was then in Yorkshire, but an urgent summons was sent for him to come to Bristol, where he arrived three days later. Meanwhile, a joint committee of supporters of Cruger and Burke met and failed to reach agreement for there to be a joint election platform, although some of the expenses were shared. Both candidates maintained separate election committees, agents, and managers, and their supporters worked in almost open rivalry.

In those days it was rather unusual for there to be electioneering speeches; the candidates simply canvassed the voters and issued election leaflets, broadsides and squibs. This election was notable as being " the first instance of a great orator and statesman using the Platform for the purpose of bringing himself into frank and unreserved communication with the people."[2] On Burke's arrival in Bristol, he at once mounted the hustings and made a short speech in which he spotlighted the American problem and emphasised the necessity of solving it, but he did not refer to any of the other controversial points in the programme of his radical colleague, Cruger. That was Burke's only recorded speech in an election campaign lasting nearly a month. During that time, each candidate made strenuous efforts to produce sufficient voters to keep the poll open. Numerous squibs and broadsides were issued, many of them of a scurrilous, personal nature, but despite the imminence of the American crisis, that question proved to be only a minor issue in this pamphlet warfare. Burke was specially attacked on the ground, quite untrue, that he was a Catholic : at a time when religious prejudice waxed strong, the cry of " Jesuit ! " could be very damaging. Secondly, his disagreement with the policy of the radicals was strongly emphasised by the supporters of both his rival candidates, Brickdale and Cruger.

After twenty-three days of voting, the poll was closed with the following result :

Henry Cruger 3,565; Edmund Burke 2,707; Matthew Brickdale 2,456; Lord Clare 283.

Cruger and Burke were declared elected. As his private correspondence shows, Burke was highly elated at the result.

When the candidates made speeches of thanks to the assembled crowd, Cruger simply stated his belief " that the electors have a right to instruct their members " and that he would feel

2. H. Jephson, *The Platform. Its Rise and Progress* (1892) ii. 91.

bound to accept their directions.[3] Burke joined issue with him
on this item of radical policy, and in a long speech he sought to
refute it. He declared :

> Certainly, gentlemen, it ought to be the happiness and glory
> of a representative to live in the strictest union, the closest
> correspondence, and the most unreserved communication
> with his constituents. Their wishes ought to have great weight
> with him . . . But his unbiassed opinion, his mature judge-
> ment, his enlightened conscience, he ought not to sacrifice to
> to you, to any man or set of men living . . . Your repre-
> sentative owes you, not his industry only, but his judge-
> ment . . .

> Authoritative instructions, mandates issued, which the
> member is bound blindly and implicitly to obey, to vote and
> argue for, though contrary to the clearest conviction of his
> judgement and conscience—these are things utterly unknown
> to the laws of this land, and which arise from a fundamental
> mistake of the whole order and tenor of our constitution.
> Parliament is not a congress of ambassadors from different
> and hostile interests . . . but a deliberate assembly of one
> nation, with one interest, that of the whole . . . You choose
> a member indeed; but when you have chosen him, he is not
> member of Bristol, he is a member of Parliament.[4]

This speech epitomised the policy of the Rockingham Whigs
whose spokesman Burke was. It has been acclaimed by some of the
greatest British historians, and is quoted even today in the discussion of constitutional issues. But in view of the irreconcilable
differences which subsequently developed between the two Bristol
members, this part of Burke's address may well have sounded to
his more astute hearers like the tocsin of old, ringing out a warning
note of tumults and troubles yet to come.

Although the successful candidates joined forces for a victory
celebration, two repercussions of the election also helped to widen
the gulf between them. The defeated candidate, Brickdale,
petitioned Parliament against the result, claiming that the election
was irregular and that he ought to have been returned. Cruger
refused to join Burke in putting forward a united defence, by
briefing the same counsel and sharing the expense, and there were
frequent bickerings between their supporters before the hearing.
Nevertheless, Brickdale's petition was rejected and their election
duly confirmed. Even greater complications arose when Cruger's

3. He did not say " Ditto to Mr. Burke ! " as has sometimes been alleged.

4. *Works*, i. 447.

friends arranged that both the Bristol members should be escorted into the city in triumph after their election had been confirmed by Parliament. Although the arrangements had been advertised in the local press, Burke flatly refused to take part in "such a foolish piece of Pageantry" because he considered it his duty to attend the debates in the House of Commons. His supporters were divided on the issue, and to Burke's chagrin, several of them turned out to greet Cruger. Burke's absence did nothing to ease the tension between himself and his colleague; it probably made people feel that their new member was rather aloof—as indeed he proved to be.

Thus Bristol, almost alone of any constituency at this election, changed its representation to the advantage of America and to the discomfiture of Lord North's government. In reporting the Bristol result to George III, the prime minister described it as "the worst news," but the subsequent conduct of the two Bristol members in Parliament was to belie Lord North's greatest fears.

Burke as Member for Bristol. (i) The American War.

Although both Burke and Cruger were critical of the policies of Lord North's government, they failed to support one another either on the opposition benches in Parliament, where they advocated differing solutions to the American problem, or in their constituency, where the antagonisms of their supporters prevented the growth of strong local opposition to the government.

In the House of Commons, Lord North usually had a working majority of 100-150, and the disunity of the several opposition groups added further strength to his position. Moreover, public opinion was generally apathetic to politics but held instead an optimistic complacency. The merchants were in closer touch with overseas opinion than a ministry which derived its main strength from the landed gentry and the personal supporters of George III and Lord North. It was, therefore, in the merchants' interests to maintain friendly relations with America in order to avert the struggle, but they were not powerful enough to make an effective protest until the threatened boycott of British goods came into operation at the end of 1774.

In view of the weakness of the opposition, Burke's parliamentary reputation and abilities ensured that he should frequently be heard on nearly all the important issues that arose during the six years of his representation of Bristol in Parliament. But because, for the first time since 1754, both the Bristol members were sitting on the opposition benches, they took a less significant part in the routine business and committee work of the House. Their constituents were given neither accurate forecasts of impending legislation, nor attractive pickings of the fruits of patronage. Thus Burke and Cruger were at a considerable disadvantage both personally and in the eyes of their constituents, many of whom contrasted the new régime with the golden days of Lord Clare's representation of the city.

Burke's parliamentary activities were therefore largely confined for three principal functions : (1) formulating and mobilising support for modifications in the government's general policy; (2) presenting and advocating opposition petitions and remonstrances; and (3) ensuring that the interests of his constituents were safeguarded as far as was possible within the limits referred to above.

He was very early made aware that the last named duty was considered by the Bristol freemen to be the most important service he could render them. At the opening of the session he received an application from six of the principal American merchants of Bristol to obtain an amendment to a clause in the Corn Law of 1773 which placed a heavy duty on Indian corn. The merchants had urged the Master of the Society of Merchant Venturers to convene a Hall to discuss the matter, but the Master was Brickdale's brother-in-law, and declined to move without the approval of the Standing Committee, on which the ministerialists had a majority. The merchants accordingly wrote to Burke direct. At the instigation of Champion, Burke took immediate action and was able to get an amending Act passed, for which he received a public letter of thanks. His correspondence reveals the great importance attached by his constituents to this very minor matter. One of his Quaker supporters wrote :

> Thou are very well aware how little Minds are Affected and that it frequently happens popular Applause is gained more by trifles, than by things of much greater Consequence. The Indian Corn Bill, for instance, stands as much to thy Credit, as if thou had a great deal more trouble to effect the Business.[5]

Burke himself told Champion, however :

> I hope, if ever I merit your thanks, that you will have no occasion to distinguish my local services from my public conduct.

In other words, he continued to regard his parliamentary duties —as a sort of opposition whip—as his most urgent political duty. Accordingly, trading upon the dissatisfaction of the merchants at

5. James Harford to Burke, 2 March 1775, from the Burke MSS in the Wentworth Woodhouse collection of the Sheffield Central Public Library (quoted by kind permission of the Earl Fitzwilliam and his Trustees of the Wentworth Woodhouse Settled Estates).

the loss of their chief markets because of the American trade boycott, Burke organised a campaign of petitions to Parliament from most of the large towns complaining of the government's American policy. When, in January 1775, he forwarded the draft of a strongly-worded petition for consideration by the Bristol merchants, the delaying tactics of the Master and committee of the Society of Merchant Venturers bade fair to secure its rejection, for a second Hall (at which non-members were present to ensure a pro-Burke majority) had to be convened before the petition was adopted, and yet a third Hall to appoint the deputation to take it to London.

In contrast, Cruger's Bristol supporters, faithful to their radical creed, worked independently through a public meeting rather than through any of the existing closed organisations. Their petition was as moderate in tone as Cruger's maiden speech in Parliament had been a month previously. It provoked Champion's derision as being " more as if they were petitioning an eastern Tyrant than a British house of Commons," but he " got four or five lines of the conclusion added wch gave it a little spirit."[6]

All this activity proved nugatory. When they reached Parliament, the Bristol petitions like those from London and many other large towns were quietly shelved, despite Burke's plea that they should be given serious consideration. Nothing daunted, he wrote again to the Society of Merchant Venturers urging further action, but there was no response. The initiative then passed to the government, and despite eloquent speeches by Burke and others, Parliament continued its coercive policy with an Act to restrain the overseas trade of the New England states.

Burke did not, however, take this lying down, for in March 1775 he introduced his own conciliation proposals which in effect demanded the repeal of all coercive laws in order to remove the grounds of the American complaints. With dramatic simplification, he declared in his speech :

> The proposition is peace. Not peace through the medium of war; not peace to be hunted through the labyrinth of intricate and endless negotiations; not peace to arise out of universal discord, fomented from principle, in all parts of the empire; not peace to depend on the juridical determination of perplexing questions; or the precise marking of shadowy boundaries of a complex government. It is simple peace; sought in its natural course, and in its ordinary haunts. It is peace sought in the spirit of peace; and laid in principles purely pacific.[7]

6. Champion to Burke, 14 Jan. 1775, from the Champion Letter-book in the Manuscripts Division of New York Public Library.

7. *Works*, i. 453-4.

Burke's oratory proved fruitless, but his speech was printed and circulated in Bristol among his constituents, and it is still studied and quoted today.

Unfortunately, his relations with his colleague, Cruger, continued to deteriorate. In May 1775 in a letter to one of his relatives, Cruger described Burke as crafty, selfish and cunning, as well as neglectful of the interests of New York—for which state Burke was British agent. In August Burke seemed to prove him right by refusing to join the other colonial agents in presenting to the King a petition of the Continental Congress regarding American policy—much to Cruger's disgust.

The first year of Burke's representation of Bristol ended with one of his rare visits to his constituency in August 1775, just after the outbreak of war in America. He visited Cruger's house to try to explain his position over the American petition but the visit only produced further acrimony. He also tried to stimulate his own supporters. One outcome of this was their attempt to wreck a public meeting of government supporters which had been called by the Mayor on 28 September 1775 to adopt a loyal address directed largely against the American colonists. This episode produced a violent press campaign against the Bristol opposition leaders, and especially against Burke who had written publicly in support of the efforts of the hecklers. 'Obediah Steadfast' categorically informed him that he now had " no expectation of being chosen at a future election."[8]

The remaining war years were for Burke a depressing experience. In Parliament the duty of the opposition is to oppose, and this Burke sought to do at every opportunity, but his speeches made little impact upon the government. So exasperating did he find the situation that for several months during the 1776-7 session he, with most of the Rockingham Whigs, seceded from Parliament whenever American affairs were debated. For this policy he was so much criticised that he issued a pamphlet to explain his actions : **A Letter to the Sheriffs of Bristol.** No further petitions against the government's war policy were sent from Bristol, where loyal addresses and public subscriptions in support of the war were much more popular. Burke made only one more visit to his constituency —in 1776—but he still tried to satisfy his constituents' demands by attending to their local interests. For example, as the facsimile letter on p. 60 shows, he succeeded in getting amendments made to the Bill to Prohibit all Trade and Intercourse with the American Colonies so as to meet certain objections by the Bristol merchants.

8. *Felix Farley's Bristol Journal*, **28** Oct. 1775.

From then on, however, the Society of Merchant Venturers frequently approached the members of Parliament for other towns, besides Burke, whenever they had any important parliamentary business on hand. This greatly irritated him. For a brief period in 1779 Cruger appeared more cooperative, but the two were never cordial. Burke evidently was suspicious of Cruger's loyalty towards his fellow-countrymen in America, but it is not clear whether he had any knowledge either that Cruger was supplying the War Office with information regarding the military and economic situation in America, or that he was receiving an annual pension of £500 from the British government.

Not until a petitioning movement was begun by the Yorkshire Association in 1779-80 did the political tide turn in Burke's favour —by which time other difficulties confronted him. A substantial number of Bristol citizens who had previously opposed him came out in support of the Yorkshire movement. The Common Council, on which Burke's supporters had secured a majority, petitioned Parliament at Harford's instigation " to enquire into the Expenditure of the Public Money, and correct Abuses therein." But there the enthusiasm of the citizens stopped. Although some of them took the lead at the county meetings held for the same purpose at Gloucester and Wells, no committee of correspondence on the Yorkshire model was set up in Bristol itself, and Burke was clearly disappointed that his constituents gave no support to his attempts at Economic Reform, i.e., to reduce the number of sinecure posts in the government. The parliamentary opposition was still divided : the radicals—Cruger among them—wishing for a more thorough-going reform of Parliament than the Rockingham Whigs would countenance. So although in March 1780 Dunning's famous motion regarding the influence of the crown was duly passed, Burke's Economical Reform Bill was lost, and the ministry survived the most powerful attack to which it had yet been subjected.

(ii) Other Issues.

During 1778-80 Burke's relations with his constituents deteriorated sharply because of differences in policy on three specific questions.

In 1778 he flagrantly went counter to their wishes in supporting proposals to relax the Irish trade laws. At that time Ireland was in an unhappy plight. Her agriculture was extremely backward, while her trade, struggling against crippling restrictions, was further burdened by new duties imposed during the American War. Under the mercantilist system, she was treated commercially almost as a foreign country—a policy which the Bristol merchants wholeheartedly endorsed, for they believed that Irish participation in colonial trade would gravely prejudice their own interests.

As soon as the Society of Merchant Venturers heard about the proposals, it at once began methodical preparations to combat this threat to its interests. Not since the Stamp Act crisis had it moved with such alacrity and thoroughness : open meetings, petitions and deputations to Parliament from the Society and the Common Council, approaches to other M.Ps., circular letters to every city and borough in the kingdom, correspondence in the Bristol press—the whole apparatus of opposition was deployed. Some of Burke's closest friends such as Harford and Noble were among his critics. Although they warned him privately of the effect of his policy, Burke declined to visit Bristol to face his critics, but instead wrote numerous letters lecturing them on the moral issues involved and and the need for an unprejudiced approach to the problem. Despite the cogency of his arguments, he placed himself in a difficult position : himself an Irishman he was allying himself with Lord North's ministry whose general policy he opposed, against the whole mercantile interest to whose support he owed his seat. Popular clamour delayed any relaxation of the Irish trade laws until 1780, when the threat of revolt caused Parliament reluctantly to succumb, but Burke's part in the matter was not forgotten in Bristol.

The second question over which Burke differed from his constituents arose from a move to relax the penalties for debt. Under the existing law, debtors were liable to indefinite confinement and consequently the gaols were crowded. In 1780 Burke supported a Bill to transfer the duty of enforcing judgments for debt from the plaintiff to the judges, but even this limited reform provoked an outcry in which some of Burke's supporters joined. They considered the proposals would encourage fraud, endanger property and undermine credit. The opposition was on a smaller scale than that provoked by the Irish Bills but it used similar methods. This time, Burke did not dismiss the objections out of hand, but used every endeavour to meet them. The Bill did not pass, but Burke was most unfairly subjected to gross misrepresentation and scurrility for his part in it.

Thirdly, Burke collided with his constituents on the question of religious toleration. In view of his Catholic connections, Burke was generally cautious in voicing publicly opinions which might be misconstrued, although in his private correspondence he was a zealous advocate of religious toleration. His support for the Protestant Dissenters Relief Act of 1779 provoked no comment in Bristol, where there was a strong nonconformist element. Bills to relieve

English and Irish Catholics from the oppressive penal code also owed much of their success to Burke's unostentatious efforts behind the scenes. But when a similar measure was proposed for Scotland, Lord George Gordon incited fanatical Protestants to plunder and burn Catholic churches and houses. Burke then came out into the open with a speech strongly critical of the rioters. The trouble spread to London where Burke was a special target because of a quite untrue allegation that he had seconded the Relief Bill. Throughout the fantastic scenes of June 1780 when London was under mob rule, Burke played a courageous part. Bristol escaped any such disturbances but Burke's support for the Act was criticised by his constituents on the grounds that it had been passed too hastily and that the Catholics were "enemies of liberty and to our free constitution ".[9] Burke's thinking on this subject (as on those of Irish trade and insolvent debtors) was appreciably in advance of his time.

Burke rejected by Bristol.

Like its predecessor, the Parliament elected in 1774 lasted only for six of the seven years permitted by the Septennial Act. In the spring of 1780, in anticipation of an early dissolution, three candidates were already in the field in Bristol : Cruger, Brickdale, and another ministerial candidate, Richard Combe—a Bristol merchant, previously M.P. for Aldeburgh.

In contrast, Burke's position was most uncertain. He had not visited Bristol at all for four years and had virtually no electoral organisation to back him. So doubtful was his candidature that rumour linked Harford's name with that of Cruger as the opposition candidates, but Harford declined. Finally, a small committee of Burke's supporters was formed, and in response to urgent appeals, Burke was persuaded to visit his constituency in August 1780. Attempts were then made to buy off the opposition. Cruger was offered £2,000 to withdraw, but not surprisingly his committee rejected these proposals. However, a meeting at which Burke's withdrawal was to have been announced became so infected by enthusiasm that, ignoring financial and organisational difficulties, it became instead an adoption meeting. Apart from his adoption speech—a magnificent apologia for his stewardship during the past six years—Burke also issued a fourteen-page pamphlet, **A Review of Mr. Burke's Conduct . . .** , which sought to disprove the thesis that the Bristol freemen could not be satisfactorily represented in Parliament by a member of the opposition.

9. *Works*, ii. 163.

Two days later, at the opening of the poll, one of the ministerial candidates, Combe, died, and Burke made a further attempt to compromise with Brickdale. But his opponents, rightly confident of victory, adopted another candidate, Sir Henry Lippincott, in place of Combe and the poll proceeded. On the first day, Burke polled so poorly that with the unanimous advice of his friends, he decided to withdraw. This he did in a dignified speech which included his oft-quoted reference to Combe's death : " What shadows we are and what shadows we pursue."[10] The election then proceeded , Lippincott and Brickdale gaining an overwhelming victory over Cruger, while Burke was found a seat for Lord Rockingham's pocket borough of Malton.

Many factors contributed to Burke's defeat, but the main reason was that he made no attempt to work with Cruger at Westminster or to maintain a joint electoral organisation with him in Bristol. Fundamental differences in outlook between the two men and their supporters might have precluded an alliance on any terms, but it was never even attempted. Burke's lack of an effective election committee contrasted sharply with his three opponents who all had the advantage of being well-known local men. Two of them were also fighting on a united platform. Moreover, after the outbreak of war, opposition was deemed unpatriotic, while many of Burke's principal supporters were financially impoverished or made bankrupt by it. The other issues for which Burke had been criticised (Ireland, debtors, Catholics) merely put the issue beyond doubt.

In 1780, Burke did not entirely sever his connection with Bristol. The abstention of his supporters at that election ensured Cruger's resounding defeat—to the unconcealed satisfaction of Burke and his friends. After Burke's withdrawal, but even before the 1780 election campaign was concluded, he sought to remedy his lack of electoral organisation by supervising the resuscitation of the Union Club; but because of his antagonism towards the radicals, he made a strenuous, though unsuccessful, attempt to exclude all Cruger's supporters from membership of it. When a bye-election occurred only three months later, Burke's former supporters had come to recognise the folly of opposition disunity. His possible candidature was considered but not proceeded with, and his friends finally supported Cruger. Although Burke continued to have some tenuous links with Bristol and its citizens almost until his death in 1797, his political influence there after 1784 was slight. In his declining years he must often have re-echoed C. J. Fox's description of " that rascally city ".

10. *Ibid.*, ii. 171.

My dear Champion,

    I wrote to Paul Farr last Night to give him an account of
what I had done, & that I had shewd no remissness in any Business
that belongs to you & him or any other of our good friends. I
saw, from the moment of seeing Lord North, that a personal
application would be the best method of proceeding, especially
when the Bill was so near its final determination. If a few honest
men may save themselves from the sweeping & comprehensive
ruin of this most wicked & sacrilegious of all measures, I shall
be happy; though it cost me a Visit to the Minister. He, I believe,
is not the author of it. It is generally thought to be the manufacture
of Sandwich. They are now debating it on the second reading in
the house of Lords. I have this one day dined at home. We are
now drinking your health & that of y^r family and our friends in
Bristol which we all most sincerely wish. I am ever with great
affection

                                          My dear Champion
                                            always y^{rs}
                                          Edm Burke

Westm^r Dec. 15.   1775.

Letter of Edmund Burke to Richard Champion, 15 December 1775.

From the original in the Sheffield Public Library

SELECT BIBLIOGRAPHY

G. E. Weare, *Edmund Burke's Connection with Bristol . . .* (Bristol, 1894).

Sir E. Barker, *Burke and Bristol* (Bristol, 1931), reprinted in *Essays on Government* (Oxford, 1945).

H. C. Van Schaack, *Henry Cruger: The Colleague of Edmund Burke in the British Parliament* (New York, 1859).

The Works of the Right Honourable Edmund Burke, Bohn ed. (London, 1854).

I. R. Christie, "Henry Cruger and the End of Edmund Burke's Connection with Bristol" in *The Transactions of the Bristol and Gloucestershire Archaeological Society* (1955) lxxiv. 153-70.

P. T. Underdown, (1) "Henry Cruger and Edmund Burke: Colleagues and Rivals at the British Election of 1774" in *The William and Mary Quarterly* (1958) xv. 14-34.

    (2) "Edmund Burke, the Commissary of his Bristol Constituents" in *The English Historical Review* (1958) lxxiii. 252-69.

    (3) "Burke's Bristol Friends" in *The Transactions of the Bristol and Gloucestershire Archaeological Society* (1958) lxxvii. 127-50.

T. W. Copeland (ed.) *The Correspondence of Edmund Burke* (10 vols) Cambridge, 1961

THE THEATRE ROYAL BRISTOL
The First Seventy Years

KATHLEEN BARKER, MA

The ambiguous status of the Theatre was never better exemplified than at the period when the Theatre Royal, Bristol, came into existence. From the Elizabethan ruling that all provincial actors might be classed, and treated, as rogues and vagabonds unless they could prove themselves some Lord's " servants," grew the post-Restoration custom of obtaining Letters Patent from the King, or Licences from the Lord Chamberlain or Master of the Revels. If a Company had this backing, it was difficult for the Mayor to refuse a local licence to play.

As more and more such Companies were formed, regular provincial circuits were built up in the early part of the 18th Century. In the summer, actors from the London Theatres took engagements with them, or made up Companies of their own. From these early days, Bath and Bristol were associated. John Hippisley, the original Peachum in *The Beggar's Opera,* who was responsible for Bristol's first permanent theatre at Jacob's Well in 1729, also had plans for a Bath theatre which only his death frustrated. The site of his original Bristol theatre was carefully chosen to be outside the City boundary—for Bristol was strongly Puritanical, and several attempts at establishing theatrical performances there had been suppressed—yet it was reasonably accessible both to citizens and visitors to the Hotwells.

The Licensing Act of 1737 was intended to curb this proliferation of provincial companies, whose connection with the " Lords " they once theoretically served was no longer even nominal. It made all performances outside the London Patent Theatres illegal without special Act of Parliament. However, though the Act served as a discouragement, and in some places did provide a legal pretext for opposition, in many places it came too late : the tradition of theatrical performances was so strong that few Justices would initiate proceedings unless information were laid before them. Companies devised expedients for circumventing the letter of the law, such as advertising a Concert with " specimens of rhetoric " given free.

Certainly Jacob's Well seems never to have been seriously threatened; under Hippisley, and, after his death in 1748, under his daughter Mrs. Jane Green, the idea of a theatre became more and more accepted. Every summer a Company came to Bristol which included the leading actors and actresses of the London theatres, Woodward, Mrs. Pritchard and William Powell for

example—and the theatre continued to prosper. Powell in particu-
lar was outstandingly popular with Bristol audiences. A protégé of
Garrick's and of Hannah More's, he drew full houses, and after his
Benefit performance in 1765 he had to insert in the newspapers a
Card of Apology for the number of would-be spectators who had
been excluded for lack of room.

The expansion of the City, the prosperity of the Hotwells, and
the popularity of the leading actors all contributed to the resolution of some play-going businessmen to purchase a more central
site and erect a large building. The attitude to the theatre in the
provinces generally was becoming ever more tolerant (the first
provincial Royal Patents, to Bath and Norwich, were granted in
1768), and such an undertaking would hardly have been embarked
on if the proposers had envisaged any real risk of legal action.

The Minute Book gives vivid, if tantalisingly brief, glimpses of
the Committee of Proprietors at work. On 5th November, 1764 it
records how Messrs. Edgar and Symons " had been at Portsmᵒ
when they got the Necessary party to execute the Deed of con-
veyance [of the Theatre site] after attending his attorney, and giving
the party Two Guineas to prevail upon him to execute the Deed,
that matter being so far settled, and being only at a Distance of
72 miles from London, they set forward for Town when they
compleated the contracts wᵗʰ Messrs. Powell, Clark and Palmer,
and at Bath wᵗʰ Mr. Arthur, that they surveyed and have taken the
Measurements of both the playhouses in London, and have also
engaged a draft of Drury-lane hᵒ and consulting a very ingenious
Carpenter Mr. Saunders the carpenter of the hᵒ they have collected
such Prints as they flatter themselves will be a means of Saving
some hundreds in Building yᵉ Intended hᵒ in Bristol, that they
have also settled a plan in Order to be at a Certainty of securing
a good Sett of Players, all Subject to the Ratification of the Committee . . . Also Resolved to Have the Lott of Players now agreed
upon, and to Refuse several Others now Objected to And that Mr.
Edgar Writes to Mr. Powell accordingly."

No sooner was this settled, however, than the Committee had
the offer of another site behind the Boars Head near Limekiln Lane
(at the back of what is now Park Street) but negotiations for the
King Street site were too far forward, and the idea was dropped.
No-one could foresee that a century hence a new Theatre Royal
would rise near the very area.

The proposal published was the initial raising of £2000 in forty
shares of £50 each, every share to entitle the owner to a free sight
of every performance (the famous " Silver Tickets "). The Account
Book shows, however, that in fact fifty subscribers paid an initial
£50 and forty-seven of them an additional £30. Payment is recorded in November 1764, but it was not till the Theatre was

opened that the admittance of the further ten subscribers was regu-
larised, the original subscribers undertaking to "make up the
Whole Sum wanted to Compleat the House." Obviously the
Theatre was costing far more than anticipated; nearly £3500 had
been paid out by the Spring of 1767, and in 1769 a further call was
made on Subscribers "to make up the Sum of £5000—£1090—
Less by Sam[1] Sedgley not paid—£1040."

The Theatre in King Street was begun in the autumn of 1764.
Felix Farley's Bristol Journal of 24th November records: "The
Workmen are now employ'd in order to lay the Foundation of the
New Theatre, in King-street; which would have been done before
this Time, had not a Mistake been made in the Calculation, whereby the House would have been built 8 Feet larger in the Clear,
than the Theatre-Royal in Drury-Lane. A Model of that House has
been sent for, and the Proprietors seem determined that the Work
shall be carried on with great Spirit. The Purchases are made,
necessary for the Entrances from King-street and the Rackhay;
and another Way will be made into Baldwin-street." The foundation stone was duly laid on 30th November, 1764, and the Committee resolved that the Theatre should be built as nearly as possible
according to the Elevation Ground Plan and Section provided by
Saunders.

Thomas Paty, probably the best-known local architect of the
time, was chosen for the new theatre. Richard Smith, an ardent
theatre-goer from his boyhood in the 1780's till his death in 1843,
tells us: " the house was painted by Mr. Michael Edkins (also a
player) . . . Marmaduke Cowle an upholsterer in St. Augustine's
Parade furnished the flock paper for the boxes and crimson cur-
tains.—John French a pupil of Loutherburg[1] painted the drop
scene and many of the decorations and they were in a most mas-
terly style . . ." Edkins was a painter by profession, best known
for his work on Bristol Pottery, but he was also a fine singer and
evidently a stage-struck one; in his account book properties for the
theatre jostled with everyday orders for shop signs or carriages,
and he played minor parts and sang at the Theatre for a number
of years.

An early booking-plan of the theatre gives some idea of the
arrangement. The benched Pit was circled by nine Lower or Dress
Boxes, seating 267 people in all, each named after a British drama-
tist (Shakespeare in the centre). The sides of the present Upper
Circle were divided into six Upper Boxes taking 104, the centre
portion serving as Gallery. The present Gallery did not then exist,
and the stage came forward past the current Stage Boxes (traces
of the supports can still be seen). Proscenium doors gave the actors

1 French was actually scenic designer for Drury Lar⁻ at the time; De
  Loutherbourg joined him as collaborator in 1771.

entrance to the forepart of the stage, and above these, where our
19th Century imitations show recessed niches, two Slip Boxes were
built, seating 22 people each.

Scenery consisted largely of parallel flats run in and out
between sets of grooves. The only relics of these activities now are
one remaining set of grooves kept as a curiosity at the Theatre, and
the rapidly-mouldering " thunder-run," a slatted wooded trough in
a sloped Vee, down which iron balls, some of them now used as
counterweights on the stage trapdoors, were rolled as storm effects.

It had been hoped to open the Theatre in 1765, but it was not
completed until the Spring of 1766. On 10th April of that year,
David Garrick himself visited Bristol " and took an accurate view
of the new erected Theatre, with which he was very much pleased "
—so much so, that he wrote the doggerel Prologue and Epilogue
for the opening night on 30th May. In the first night Bill " The
Managers hope the Ladies and Gentlemen will not think the Prices
fix'd for admission exorbitant, when they will please to consider
their very great Expenses: particularly the high Charge of Rent;
that the House will be illuminated with Wax, that the Clothes,
Scenes and all Decorations are entirely new, and, That they will
spare no Pain or Expence to make the Entertainments as Elegant
and Pleasing as in the most Established Theatre." These " exorbitant " prices were 4s. for the Boxes (3s. 6d. after the first night);
2s. 6d. for the Pit; and 1s. for the Gallery (afterwards 1s. 6d.), and
they remained almost constant for seventy years.

An evening's programme consisted of an Overture, a Five Act
Play, Entertainments (dances, songs or instrumental solos) and a
Farce or other short afterpiece; the programme was changed com-
pletely every night unless a particularly popular novelty allowed
repetition. It was possible to come in at the end of Act 3 of the
Play at a reduced charge, known as the " Half Price," except where
the after-piece was the major attraction, such as a new Pantomime.
The first night's programme consisted of Steele's *The Conscious
Lovers,* Dancing and *The Citizen.* The net proceeds of Sixty
Guineas were given, as a placating gesture, to the Bristol Infirmary
Committee: a sum " which was politely received by them." The
Company was closely similar to that which had played the pre-
vious summer at Jacob's Well.

The troubles of the Committee were by no means at an end
when the Theatre eventually opened. The original negotiations
had been carried on with three London actors who had been
associated with the Jacob's Well company, William Powell and
John Palmer of Drury Lane, and Matthew Clarke of Covent Garden;
and with John Arthur (low comedian and stage director at Bath).
Arthur, however, had an unhappy knack of upsetting the Com-

panies he worked with, and though he played at Bristol in the 1766 season first Palmer and then Powell and Clark refused to share the management with him. Early in 1767 the projected lease was amended to nominate as Lessees Powell, Clark and another leading actor, Charles Holland, and the rent proposed was " Five pounds for every Hundred Pounds we shall expend or lay out in Building the said Theatre, opening the Avenues and all other Matters and Things relative thereto." This lease, too, was declined, possibly because it occurred to the lessees that it would mean their automatically paying 5 per cent interest on expenditure completely beyond their control. It was not until September 1767 that a seven-year (retrospective) lease was signed, at a fixed rent of £300 a year.

During all this time " squibs," pamphlets and sermons continued to be aimed at the new Theatre, but despite threats, the Licensing Act was never invoked against it, although as a precaution the Company initially advertised " A Concert of Music with Specimens of Rhetorick." (In 1768, when the Bath Theatre received its Patent, even this pretence was abandoned.) Each summer the theatre re-opened for three evenings a week in a well-balanced repertory. Mrs. Jane Barry, James Dodd, Ned Shuter and Mrs. Bulkley were but a few of the nationally-famous performers supporting Powell and Holland. But in 1769 the concern received heavy blows by the death of both these Managers. Powell was taken ill soon after the season started; he lodged next door to the Theatre, and performances were cancelled to preserve quiet in the street outside. On Monday, 3rd July, *Richard III* was to be acted with Holland in the lead, and Powell died at 7 o'clock, just before the play began. Holland almost broke down as he reached the words " We've all cause To mourn the dimming of our shining star," and when he came forward to announce a change of farce (Dodd had had to go to London) the audience made it clear that they would be content for the performance to end there. Holland died in London later in the year.

After these two deaths, shares in the management changed hands almost every season, with consequent restlessness among the Company. In 1772 there were a number of complaints against Dodd, a delightful player of fops and fribbles, but a less acceptable Manager. He was said to change the farces frequently at the very last moment for no good reason, and to have too many sentimental comedies in the bill, and the London correspondent of the *Bristol Gazette*, recording a poor summer in the provincial theatre generally, added: " Even Liverpool and Bristol, that used to be reckoned the best, have little to boast of this season."

No sooner was the theatre closed than Mrs. Hartley, one of the supporting actresses, wrote to *Felix Farley's Bristol Journal* to

complain of being passed over for parts to which she had a right.
She claimed that from " the 9th of July to the End of the Season,
he [Dodd, as Manager] never offered her a single Part (excepting
that of one of the Women in the Beggar's Opera by Way of insult)"
—" lest *she* should be *mistaken* for the *principal* actress," she
added with heavy sarcasm. Equally sarcastic was the rejoinder
from " The Public " the following week that " we are unanimously
of the opinion that he might very safely have ventured her playing
every Night in the Season without the least Danger of her having
been ever taken—or (as she expresses it herself) *mistaken* for the
principal Actress."

The proprietors were worried about the position.   When the
initial lease expired they restricted the new one to a term of three
years to be granted " only to Persons that are Performers " and a
special clause was to be inserted " in order to prevent the possibility of such Lease or Leases falling by Sale or otherwise into
the hands of persons who are not possessed of Theatrical Talents
for the Entertainment of the Town."

In the autumn a share in the management was offered to John
Henderson, later one of the great Falstaffs and Shylocks of the
stage, but then just a rising young provincial actor at the Bath
Theatre.   Henderson went into the question carefully, and his
decision, recorded in a letter to his biographer, John Ireland, casts
considerable light on the organisation of the Bristol Theatre at the
time :

" The most money that has been paid for any share has been
four hundred pounds. There are four partners at 400 l. each, and
one of them (the not acting manager) has forty pounds a season
allowed him for his interest of the 400 l. together with the freedom
of the Theatre for himself family and friends.   Three hundred
pounds a season is paid for the rent, and the fifty proprietors are
admitted gratis to all performances whatsoever at the Theatre,
which is thought much overloaded. It was rather a losing scheme
to Powell and Holland. It is known that Mr. King lost above
eighty pounds the season he held it; and the last season, 'tis said,
each partner lost between one and two hundred pounds.

" The whole property belonging to the partners, of clothes,
scenes, &c. is supposed to be worth under a thousand pounds, and
there are only two years to come of the lease. There are three votes
of the three acting managers in the conduct of the theatre."

Henderson must have congratulated himself later on his
decision, for a very unsettled period was to ensue. In November
1772 a touring company under Booth and Kennedy set up in the

Coopers' Hall under the old pretence of presenting "A Concert of Music" with "divers Specimens of ELOCUTION". An information was nevertheless laid and sustained by the Magistrates, the performers being fined a total of £200. The Theatre proprietors and lessees (who were suspected of being concerned in the attempted suppression) realised that their own position was no safer, and hastily embarked on an application for a Royal patent, arousing a flurry of controversy. Petitions against the Patent were sent to Members of Parliament and the Bishop of Bristol. They met with some sympathy but little action (the Bishop's reply, as quoted in the local press, is a masterpiece of evasion). The Bill for licensing the Playhouse was brought in at the beginning of March, but was blocked. This abortive attempt cost the proprietors £161, and the matter was allowed to rest until February 1778, when they obtained a Patent for Bristol with a minimum of fuss.

It is an interesting comment on the practical ineffectiveness of the 1737 Act, however, that not only did a fine penal by contemporary standards fail to deter Booth and Kennedy from completing their season at the Coopers' Hall and publicly advertising it, but they actually returned the following winter, though with much less success.

Nor was any action apparently taken against the King Street Theatre company, despite its equal "illegality." However, Dodd found himself in trouble from another quarter. He fell foul of Mrs. Green, who as Hippisley's daughter and a native of Bristol was very popular here both personally and as an actress. She declared that Dodd had "made her whole Summer disagreeable by his rude Behaviour," and that he had been heard to vow that "she should never belong to the Company *if he could help it*"; and consequently she regretfully declined playing that season. There were other accusations of public rudeness against Dodd, and at the end of the season he sold his share to Samuel Reddish, leading actor at Drury Lane.

Initially Reddish showed great zeal, engaging an excellent Company from the London theatres, improving the stock of scenery and costumes, and paying more attention to the selection of new popular plays in the repertoire. Before the 1775 season he undertook "new painting and fitting up the Theatre in a very elegant manner, and adding several new Scenes," and lighting it with spermaceti candles. Simultaneously he raised the Box price to 4s. and offered a type of "Season Ticket" admission—the first twenty-four nights of playing for Two Guineas. Henderson played for him, and, as Genest tells us,[3] "from the accidental indisposition of a

---

[3] Genest: *Some Account of the English Stage* (Bath, 1832), Vol. V. p. 535. Genest has, however, confused his dates: 17th August was not a playing day at Bristol.

performer on August the 17th he played Falstaff," a performance which was to become his most famous. Unfortunately this successful season ended on a familiar note: Quick (who made his name as the first Tony Lumpkin) accused Reddish of stopping his Benefit out of jealousy at his popularity, and Reddish, piqued by a rumour that Clarke had sold his management share to Quick, vowed he would not return to Bristol if this were true.

It was not, and both Reddish and Quick came back, but almost immediately there was trouble over the position in the Company of Reddish's wife, formerly Mrs. Canning (and by that marriage mother of the future Prime Minister). This came to a head when the Benefits took place. Mrs. Reddish was hissed during hers, and three of the leading actors, Samuel Cautherley and Mr. and Mrs. Jackson, were accused of organising the trouble. Reddish refused to act in Jackson's Benefit play because his wife had not been cast in it; accusation and counter-accusation enlivened the columns of the Bristol press, and with a month of the season to go, Reddish and his wife walked out on the Company, leaving Quick and Clarke to manage as best they might.

Robert Bensley joined as leading man for these two Managers the following season. Earnest was their quest after "Novelty," and in 1778 they reduced the Gallery price to 1s. while abolishing the "Half Price." The season ended in a blaze of glory with a visit from the tragic actress Mrs. Crawford, who had been the wife of Spranger Barry, Garrick's chief rival.

It was in 1778 that the Theatre was opened for the first time for a winter season. A Company led by Jefferson of Drury Lane opened on 30th November with *As You Like It,* and the season included the first performance in Bristol of *The School for Scandal,* which gave the Managers the excuse to raise the Gallery price to 1s. 6d. again. This evoked prompt protests, and within a fortnight the Pit prices were reduced to 2s. and the Gallery to 1s. with no Half Price. This season ended on 8th March, and two days later the Bath Theatre Company, without preliminary announcement (and in apparent contradiction of the terms of the Theatre Royal lease), took possession and began a fortnight's engagement. This Company included Mrs. Siddons, whose first recorded performance at Bristol was as the Countess of Salisbury in a play of that name on Monday, 15th March.

Supporters of the previous Managers claimed defiantly that "so far from being alarm'd at the experience of the Bath Company," they were "rather pleased by it, as it can only end with their being in future, uninterruptedly fix'd in that property—it being already pretty plain, that no receipts can possibly repay the enormous expense of bringing their company, musicians, scenes, &c. over here." Nevertheless, in April it was announced that Palmer of the Bath Theatre had been granted a 20-year lease at £200 a year plus ground rent and taxes, on his promising to "make an entire alteration to the theatre, enlarge the lobby, to build an elegant tea room and other accommodations." In consideration of this the Proprietors renounced claim to three years' rent. Palmer's Company, headed by William Wyatt Dimond and Sarah Siddons as straight leads, Mr. and Mrs. Brett as singers, and Edwin as comedian, played once a week till the end of May.

So began the formal association of the Bath and Bristol Theatres, operated in circuit from September to July. There were three performances a week in Bristol and one in Bath until mid-November; thereafter Bristol had plays on Monday nights only until the Benefits, which usually began in early June. Dimond, who became Joint Acting Manager with Keasberry early on, was a notable figure—a popular straight actor in perhaps a slightly "old-fashioned" style (though it is said Sheridan considered him the finest exponent of Joseph Surface he had seen), and an honest and much-loved Manager in days when neither adjective was commonly applied. Round him more than any other personality the Bath and Bristol Company was built, and when he retired from the stage in 1801, it was not altogether fanciful to say that something went out of the spirit of the Company which was never replaced.

It would be gratifying to local pride to claim—as in fact was often done in retrospect—that Bristol "discovered" the merits of Mrs. Siddons. It is nearer the truth to say that, successful and highly-esteemed as she was, in elegant Comedy as much as in the Tragedy we more readily associate with her name, equally laudatory notices may be read in the Bristol papers of actresses whose names have been long forgotten. When she left the Company in June 1782 after producing her famous "Three reasons for quitting this Theatre" (her three children), it was well before the end of the run of Benefits, so that while she had been able to call on all the Company to play for her, she herself was not available to lend lustre (and box-office appeal) to most of their special nights. Instead, she went off on a highly successful provincial tour of her father's old circuit. No doubt this accounts for the note of asperity detectable when one of her fellow-actresses three weeks later produced "Three Reasons for her *Continuance* on the Bristol Stage."

The leading actors from this circuit were engaged regularly, often for leading parts, at the London theatres, and the management was held in high esteem. In a period which undoubtedly represented the heyday of the provincial Stock Company, only the

York circuit could dispute its pre-eminence. Among future stars
of the British stage were Julia Betterton (later Mrs. Glover), the
singer Charles Incledon, and Robert William Elliston, the future
flamboyant manager of the Surrey Theatre, and, disastrously, of
Drury Lane. He made his first appearance in Bath on 14th April,
1791, as Tressel in *Richard III* (a part imported by Cibber into
his adaptation of Shakespeare) and repeated it in Bristol on the
25th. After a period with Tate Wilkinson at York, he returned
in October 1794 to play second leads to Dimond, gradually taking
over from him those parts requiring youthful buoyancy or comic
verve. In 1796 his Benefit realised £146.

Another popular actor was the "heavy," Charles Murray, whose
daughter married Henry Siddons, later managing the Theatre
Royal, Edinburgh (they may have met when young Siddons played
a few nights in Bristol and Bath in February 1796). So popular
was Murray that when he withdrew from playing the part of
Manly in *The Provok'd Husband,* and Dimond offered it to a comparatively minor actor, Eyre, as an encouragement, Eyre met with
hisses and catcalls when he took the stage, rumour having spread
that he had "arrogantly taken the part from Murray." The next
time a similar thing happened, Eyre took care to have it printed
in the bills that he played through the original actor's indisposition.

The even tenor of success was not, however, uninterrupted.
Bristol still had its moral censors, and when Brett, disappointed
at the failure of his wife's Benefit in 1782 (there was a 'flu epidemic, and although it was Sarah Siddons' last appearance, the
total receipts were only £24. 13s.), got drunk and created a dis-
turbance, the Managers immediately discharged him. In February
1784 illness depleted the Company's singing strength, and in
emergency Brett was invited down from London to take over.
Despite the two years' interval, and the publication of a preliminary apology in the Press and playbills, he was booed off the
stage, and promptly returned to London in understandable pique.
Eight years later, Brett's daughter caused a further sensation by
running off with the husband of another actress in the Company.

A storm broke out when Reynold's *Werter* was given its
premiere in December 1785. A long and, on balance, unfavourable
examen of the play included a complaint by the critic that "my
attention at the Theatre was much distracted by a noisy party
behind, and my sight obstructed by the immense hats of the ladies
before me" — both frequently reiterated complaints not confined
to the 18th Century.

Moreover, despite the popularity of the leading actors, there
was a good deal of criticism of the acting of minor parts, dis-
crepancies of costume (a Roman Ambassador in a powdered wig

FAMOUS BRISTOL THEATRE MANAGERS

William Powell (1735-1769) as Posthumus in *Cymbeline*, a favourite part.

Below: William M'Cready (1755-1829)

William Wyatt Dimond (c. 1740-1812) as Romeo, with Miss Wallis, later Mrs. Campbell, as Juliet.

Whale: Oh, my dear ~~Master's heart!~~ ..... you ~~cursed~~
~~Thief, bring him to life again~~ — —
Clow: Hush, you Fool, I am ~~your Master~~, the Magician
~~lives in the body of our Eleposter, but~~ I have his power
now free Colombine
& my first use of it shall be to ~~prevent his doing~~
~~further Mischief~~ Come, my good old friend, — ~~tis the~~
~~Rosycrucian now.~~ (binds ~~the Elf to Tree.~~)
Whale: Ha! ha! ha!, Egad if this is our Magician, I
find he's no Conjuror. (R) J. Bell, to raise Col.
~~Col:~~ — ~~Now Whalebone do free my Colombine~~. (touches
the Drum) Soft Music — the Drum opens, Colombine
appears, ~~She goes to Harlequin who is on the Ground~~
Col: My dearest Love! ~~no he~~
Whale: Nonsense, Child, look this, is your dearest Love
(points to Ulan.)
Col: What tho vile Magician — never!
Whale: (to Ulan.) Master you had best whip into your
own Skin again.
Ulan: By the power of this Ring, I wish to live again
my own proper form (lies down) soft Music. Har....

A page from an Ms. Prompt Book belonging to William M'Cready,
now in the City Archives; it comes from John O'Keefe's 18th C.
Pantomime, *Lord Mayor's Day, or A Flight to Lapland*. Note the
direction to ring the Trap Bell for Columbine's trick entry through
the drum.

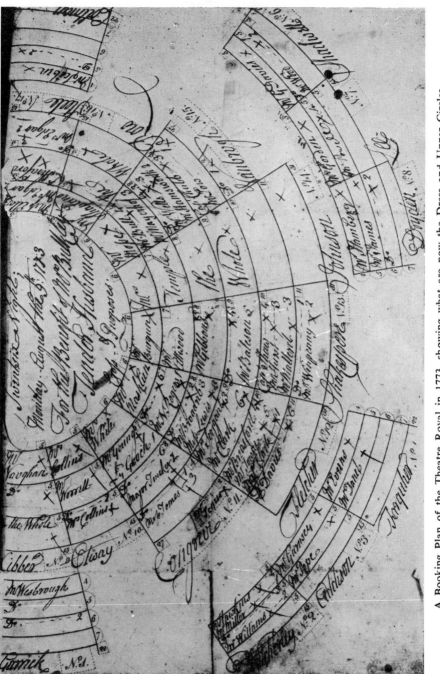

A Booking Plan of the Theatre Royal in 1773, showing what are now the Dress and Upper Circles.

To Paint[g] a Box for West Indian
repairing St Stephen Rushworts Fac 1-...

To Waxing and Varnishing the
Transparency for the Invasion
Paint[g] thereon a Castle with a
Streamer with Shakespeare wrote
Transparent ————— 2 12 6
To Paint[g] 5 Chairs both sides 1
To Paint[g] part of the Cottage in
the Invasion ————————— -3-6
To Paint[g] a Trick Table with
a fairy in Flames &c ————— 5
To Paint[g] the[e] Stump of the
Tree and Harlequins [pocket] ..... 3 ...
To Paint[g] [g] Snips Armour ——— 2 - 6
To Paint[g] Flowers Intended for
the [Palace] Wings afterwards put 10 6
on the May Pole ————————

Entries from the Account Book of Michael Edkins, singer, minor
actor and painter, showing scene- and property-painting for a
Pantomime revival, *Harlequins Invasion of the Realms of
Shakespeare*, in June 1778

and white gloves, for example), and of faults in production, such as "extras" grouped in straight lines, and actors inattentive to the play when not actually speaking. All these suggest to modern ears the amateur rather than the professional theatre, but were probably inevitable under repertory conditions.

A change gradually came over public taste: the Managers felt bound to advise Murray not to play Lear for his Benefit in 1787 because when they had last produced it three years previously they had lost heavily, and in 1790 "The Wanderer" wrote, perhaps too gloomily, in the *Bristol Journal*: "Some of our most meritorious plays are frequently represented at our Theatre, almost to empty benches; and, excepting two or three instances, the players are generally *losers* by their benefits." Melodrama, sentimental comedy and pantomime held the drawing power, and as the century neared its close, the system of having visiting "stars" from the London theatre began to grow up, to the detriment of Stock Company standards.

In 1800 Dimond and Palmer were responsible for the biggest alteration to the theatre's structure so far: the creation of a new raised ceiling so as to permit building a Gallery tier above the Upper Boxes—the form, in fact, in which we know the auditorium of the Theatre Royal to-day. The house was repainted "a stone colour, and the pannels a tender green, with gold mountings and cornices; the columns that support the two rows of boxes are cabled with stone colour and gold alternately." New lustres were fitted, and the raising of the ceiling was said greatly to improve the acoustics of the theatre. However, the "Gods" complained that the seats were not sharply enough raked to allow a clear view of the front of the stage, so in the autumn the Gallery was altered again to meet this objection. Dimond and Palmer undertook to spend not less than £1000 on this alteration and the building of a "large Commodious Scene Room."

In 1801 the Bath and Bristol Companies set up a Benevolent Fund, for which a Benefit was allowed alternate years in each city. This fund had a chequered career, and after the circuit broke up in 1817, rapidly petered out. The rather sordid story, as it affected one of the most loyal and longest-serving actresses in the Company, Miss Summers (who had supported Mrs. Siddons), can be found in Genest.[4] The same summer Dimond retired from the stage, though not from management, the Duke and Duchess of York presenting him with a "magnificent Silver Cup and Cover." This left Elliston unrivalled in the leading parts, but soon he began negotiations for London engagements which overlapped his provincial contract, and he divided his year between the two, travel-

4 Genest: *op cit.*, Vol. IX:, pp. 73 *et seq.*

ling hectically between London and Bath or Bristol until he finally left in 1804.

Charlton took over as Acting Manager—resident producer would be the nearest modern equivalent—but personally popular though he was, he had neither the principle nor the business sense of Dimond. The old favourites one by one retired, "stars" became more and more important, and after Dimond's death at the beginning of 1812 the Company began to lose its hold on the public, at least in Bristol, despite the judical closure, at the expense of £12 shared between the Proprietors and the Managers, of the "illegitimate" Regency Theatre in Prince Street.[5]

The site of the Theatre Royal, too, was beginning to prove a disadvantage. As the squares and crescents of Clifton were built in the early years of the 19th Century, there was a move out of the City area, which became very much a "trade" quarter, divorced from the social "ton." Moreover, as a newspaper correspondent complained, there was some difficulty of access, as the first permanent bridge over the Frome was well down river — roughly where Electricity House is now. Clifton began to make its own social entertainments, and the patronage of the "gentry," save for the real enthusiasts, fell gradually away.

1815, however, was a notable year: it saw Edmund Kean's first performances in Bristol, and also those of a very different actor, William Charles Macready, who was to be closely connected with the Bristol theatre personally and through his family. Macready joined the Stock Company, playing among other parts Richard II —rarely performed at that time. Bristolians, however, were beginning to resent the dominance of Bath; the action against the Regency had aroused considerable feeling; and when Palmer nevertheless sought to renew the lease in the summer of 1817, he was faced with conditions about the improvement of the property which he deemed unacceptable, and the long-standing link with Bath was broken.

Bristol was not alone in experiencing this decline: the growing dominance of London "stars," the aftermath of the Napoleonic Wars and the stirring of social unrest as the Industrial Revolution began to change the pattern of English life, all contributed to the gradual decline of provincial circuits everywhere. The break-up did not, in most cases, come till later in the century, but already in many parts of the country the once well-established Managers found themselves fighting a losing battle.

At the end of June 1817, the Committee advertised for a lessee. Elliston made a bid, offering to share " half and half in expenses

5 For a brief account of this theatre, see my article in the *Bristol Evening Post* of 5th September, 1956.

and profits" with the Proprietors, but this made no appeal. Instead,
the Theatre was let, apparently advantageously, to John Boles
Watson, already Manager of the Cheltenham and Gloucester
theatres, who promised that " under his unremitting exertions, the
Drama will assume a style of propriety, correctness and elegance
which will at once both merit and receive the approbation of those
who may honour it with their patronage." For his projected experi-
mental season of twelve nights he offered a Season Ticket system,
and promised new decorations and chandeliers "of the Grecian
make," an "Anti-Entrance Room" (sic) to the Lower Boxes for
"those who frequent the half-play," a refreshment saloon for the
Upper Boxes, and, by removing an inconvenient staircase, an
improvement to the street entrances to Pit and Gallery.

Alas for these promises! A florid redecoration of the theatre did
indeed take place, but apart from the Proprietors' action in creating separate entrances to the Upper and Lower Boxes, none of
these projected improvements was carried out. The management
soon acquired a wretched name; Richard Smith comments "The
whole House was gloomy and sombre and the stench of the tallow
intolerable—into the Bargain he could not pay his rent so that
at last the Proprietors were obliged to put an execution on his
Wardrobe and Scenes and other moveables and sold the whole—
being themselves purchasers to the amount of £250 but even then
the loss was considerable—and the Theatre in disrepute."

In these circumstances the Proprietors once more tried to treat
with the Bath Company through Dimond's son, but to no effect.
Early in 1819 the Theatre was again advertised, and four applica-
tions were received: from Henry Lee of the Taunton Theatre,
Robert Hoy, the Worcestershire manager; H. W. Grosette, one
of the Bath company, and 64 year-old William M'Cready, father
of William Charles, who had made an unsuccessful bid for the
Bristol management in 1799, and had just given up the management of the Newcastle and Whitehaven theatres. M'Cready, a
generous but quick-tempered Irishman, had spent his life in provincial theatre management, and despite more than one bankruptcy had the knack of always retaining the affection (albeit
sometimes the exasperated affection) and respect of all around
him.

No happier choice could have been made. M'Cready was a man
of unbounded energy and wide contacts, and drew largely on both.
William Charles Macready and two other stars, Daniel Terry and
Mrs. Yates, opened his "season of experiment" with Othello, and
during the summer recess M'Cready installed "that brilliant mode
of illumination, the gas-light"—an up-to-the-minute innovation
which, however, cruelly exposed the "puppet-show decorations" of

his predecessor. Between the Autumn Fair season and the winter M'Cready undertook to carry out Watson's promise of a Half-Price Saloon, but ran into trouble over Ancient Lights, and by the time the Theatre re-opened he could only offer "a 'Boudoir' . . . the best that a very limited space, shortness of time, and every other disadvantage would allow," but it was warmly received by those who previously had had to wait in a draughty, unheated courtyard.

M'Cready had engaged Charles Westmacott, who had been responsible for fitting up the Birmingham Theatre, to repaint the scenic leavings of Watson, but Westmacott, after working for some time apparently quite happily, walked out leaving the work half-done. Carroll, the Company's scene-painter, completed Westmacott's work, while Whitmore, scenic artist at Covent Garden, "in his zeal for the welfare and prosperity of Bristol theatricals under its present Director," presented the Theatre with a new drop-scene.

The house was painted a light salmon-colour; on the panels of the Boxes were the various national floral emblems in gold. The stage doors were white and gold, and the pilasters on either side of the stage were said to "appear like Sienna marble." The ceiling represented an open sky, with Cupids in different attitudes.

The first night of the season lived well up to theatrical tradition. The gas went out three times, and "for some time, a few mutton lights, collected in haste and thrust upon the stage, served to render the darkness visible, and prevented the Performers from knocking their noses against each other." The audience, in perfect good humour, sang "God Save the King" every time the lights went out, and in fact the only person who seemed at all put out was poor M'Cready, who came on to apologise profusely for the failure of supply, and was greeted with cheers and rounds of applause.

M'Cready was a shrewd man, and his programme was well-balanced. Dramatisations of Scott, 18th Century comedies (his real love, according to his son), Shakespeare and spectacle were nicely blended. A number of his prompt-books may still be examined among the City Archives. "Stars" he brought in plenty, but ensured that his Stock Company was strong enough to do without them —as for at least one season it virtually did. An elaborate production of *A Winter's Tale* and another of *Richard II* in a version specially prepared by William Charles, were mounted by the Company unassisted.

In his leading lady, Sarah Desmond, who had played for him at Newcastle, M'Cready had an impressive actress in parts ranging from Hermione to Meg Merrilees; their marriage in 1821

(M'Cready was a widower) gave her an even closer interest in the fortunes of the Theatre Royal.

M'Cready could never rest. In 1820 he had William Edkins, son of the original painter of the Theatre, redecorate it, in "warm drab," maroon and much gilt ornament on ceiling and boxes alike, and the Boudoir was at last completed. Again in 1823 Edkins went to work, and again in 1826, when M'Cready removed the Georgian proscenium doors and substituted two private boxes on the stage, continuing the line of the Dress Boxes. The "Old Fashion" of a Green Curtain was revived at the same time.

It should not be thought that M'Cready had an untroubled passage. He had to restore not only the artistic prestige but, even more important in contemporary provincial eyes, the moral standing of the theatre. He was not helped when, within months of his opening, Junius Brutus Booth, who was starring in Bristol at the same time as an acrobat known as Il Diavolo Antonio, became involved with Antonio's wife. A country expedition to Kingsdown brought matters to a head, and finally the Sunday evening peace of Queen Square was shattered by a pistol duel, in which Antonio was wounded. Booth acted as usual on Monday; on Tuesday he should have played for M'Cready's Benefit, but though he came to the theatre, he panicked and left again before the performance. Eventually the quarrel was made up, and Booth played Richard III for Antonio's Benefit (a "bumper," it is pleasing to add), but by that time the whole affair, with the inevitable trimmings of half-informed gossip, was all over the city.

There were also occasional disturbances in the theatre. Loyalty to the House of Hanover was demonstrated by the insertion of patriotic songs such as "Rule Britannia" and "God Save the King." All good Englishmen would then rise and doff their hats, but one night "a person was observed in the pit with his hat on his head . . . 'A Radical!' was immediately whispered about, and the obnoxious hat was knocked off. The whole house was thrown into confusion by this incident." At the close of the national anthem, the audience clamoured for its repetition, but the obstinate pittite still persisted in wearing his hat "until the indignation of those in the pit became so extreme, that he deemed it prudent to retire." There was, alas, rather an anti-climax to this fine demonstration of patriotism, for the naughty Radical was found instead to be a much-puzzled foreigner, "uninterested in our political afairs and almost a stranger to our language."

M'Cready's quick temper, too, led him into many disputes with the local newspapers, who, keen supporters of his enterprise as they were, would not always praise without reservation—and M'Cready took no more kindly to adverse criticism than most theatrical managers. It is clear from the often long and detailed criticisms of performances that the standard of minor actors—and sometimes of major ones—and the consistency of dress, decorations and behaviour still left much to be desired. *Macbeth*, for example, was still played with its late 17th Century spectacular witch scenes to Locke's music, and these provoked a number of cutting criticisms. "With all due humility, and strict attention to the feelings of 'families,' " wrote the critic of *The Thespian*, "we beg to record it as our opinion that the *Witches* in *Macbeth* ought to be otherwise employed than counting heads in the gallery, or waltzing to the choruses . . . As to costume, we say nothing. We have proof that the weird sisters could look into futurity, and we willingly believe that the same foresight enabled them to anticipate the fashions of modern times." A particularly heavy and unintelligent performance of Romeo drew the comment: " Friar Laurence says 'The lover may bestride the idle gossamer,' but he would have suppressed this truth if he had seen Mr. Montague."

The practical interest shown in his father's venture by William Charles Macready may no doubt be partially attributed to the fact that his money had enabled old M'Cready to assume the management in the first place. His long-standing connecton with the city, begun with the Bath and Bristol Company, was maintained by frequent visits, and his personal rectitude certainly did him no disservice in a city as strict as Bristol. The story has often been told, and can be found in full in Macready's Reminiscences, of how he interested himself in a young actress, Catherine Atkins, and introduced her to his father in 1821 for engagement with the Bristol Company. During his visits to Bristol "love approached under friendship's name," and in the summer of 1823 they became engaged, Miss Atkins leaving the stage permanently. Part of their honeymoon in 1824 was spent at Weston-super-Mare and Congresbury.

Despite the inevitable ups and downs of management, and at least one near escape from yet another bankruptcy, M'Cready and his wife evoked a strong personal feeling among Bristolians. M'Cready was a prominent Mason in the Lodge of which Richard Smith, collector of theatrical records, was Master, and their interest was always employed on his benefit night. When he died, on 11th April, 1829, the newspaper obituary spoke sober truth in saying: "His loss will be deeply felt and regretted by his family and a wide circle of friends. He was indeed universally esteemed, and the qualities both of his head and his heart, were such, as would have done honour to any profession." A tablet to his memory is in Bristol Cathedral off the passage leading to the Chapter House.

The season was completed, Fraser the Stage Manager assuming

responsibility, and William Charles coming down to play on the last night. He wrote to the Proprietors to ask if they would transfer the remainder of the existing Lease to Richard Brunton (formerly concerned with the Plymouth Theatre) and grant Brunton a further lease for three years, giving his personal guarantee for the punctual discharge of the rent. This proposal, he felt, would be "the means of material benefit to my late Father's Widow." Accordingly the Proprietors made out a lease to Brunton and Macready jointly, a lease to which is added a fascinating inventory of the fittings and scenery then stored or in use at the Theatre Royal.[6] Brunton, with the help of his father, was the active partner in running the theatre, and Macready's name was hardly mentioned although his interest can be seen from, for example, the choice of Bristol for a "try-out" of Byron's *Werner*, adapted by Macready, and with himself in the leading part, which took place on 23rd January, 1830. His stepmother, M'Cready's widow, continued in the Company as leading lady.

An absentee manager, however, is of little help in day to day affairs, and Brunton had been in financial difficulties before ever he came to Bristol. With M'Cready's death instability came again to the theatre; standards declined, houses fell off, and the biggest draw of 1830 was "the talented and stupendous ELEPHANT" for whom the Rackhay entrance was enlarged. The first season made a profit, but the second, despite some lavish operatic productions, including Rossini's *Cinderella*, and visits by Miss Smithson and Charles and Fanny Kemble, was disastrous. Brunton could not meet his obligations, and the Company was in such straits that the Kembles, though considerable sufferers themselves, offered a Benefit performance, the proceeds of which, some £150, paid off a little over a quarter of the Company's arrears of salary.

The circumstances of Brunton's bankruptcy are somewhat mysterious. Charles Mason, the leading actor, publicly averred that it was almost wholly due to the treachery of an unnamed friend of Brunton's, who had lent him money to pay off his creditors in Birmingham and enabled him to take up the Bristol lease, and at a later date had demanded additional security in the shape of the surrender of the lease itself to him. Brunton took legal advice, and told his friend this was impossible, whereupon the friend descended upon the theatre and took possession of the actual receipts at the door, including those for Charles Kemble's Benefit. The Company not unnaturally declined to continue acting "merely to put money into his pocket . . . the reply was, that the money obtained should be held in defiance of all claims," and nothing Brunton could do would, apparently, move him. The iden-

6 See *Studies in English Theatre History* (Society for Theatre Research, 1952), pp. 98-113.

tity of the treacherous friend, and the inaction of Macready, remain at present a mystery.

Brunton evaded trouble by transferring his share in the Theatre
to Macready, who promptly surrendered the lease, and eventually
the Proprietors succeeded in letting the house to General Charles
Palmer of Bath, for whom B. P. Bellamy was, as Smith puts it,
"agent and factotum," and Stage Manager. Bellamy had offered
for the theatre after M'Cready's death, without success.

Palmer and Bellamy promptly laid out a sum estimated at over
£800 in repairing and renovating the theatre thoroughly. Proscenium doors were reinstated, M'Cready's excrescent private boxes
were scrapped; the stage was re-laid; the lighting equipment was
completely overhauled, more illumination now being concentrated
on the stage and less on the auditorium. Rotten timbers were renewed. New staircases were made which would restrict the circulation of prostitutes. The lobbies of both Circles were enlarged
and heating put in, the Dress Boxes subdivided and the whole
house newly upholstered.

A successful October opening was interrupted by the Bristol
Riots, but for the re-opening at the end of November Bellamy
secured the services (such as by that time they were) of Edmund
Kean, followed by the engagement of Paganini, the virtuoso vio-
linist. On the pretext of the enormous fee demanded, the manager
raised the prices of seats to 10s., 7s. and 3s. 6d. and tried to avoid
honouring the silver tickets. His popularity was not increased when
it was revealed that the fee had been proposed by Bellamy himself. The house was filled, but at a time of national distress caused
by epidemics of cholera, comment was acid. Moreover, the
Bristol Gazette sorrowfully described Bellamy's Company as " the
worst we have ever witnessed on the Bristol boards."

A certain note of desperation creeps into the contemporary
advertisements and reviews, and after a week in which "Monsieur
Martin and his WONDERFUL TRAINED ANIMALS" starred
in a specially written piece called *The Lions of Mysore*, Bellamy
closed the theatre in July with thinly-veiled reference to his losses.

Acrimonious correspondence, related in some detail in the Minute
Books of the period, began between the Proprietors and General
Palmer over arrears of rent. Bellamy finally reopened the theatre
in February 1833 in conjunction with that at Bath, as "an almost
desperate undertaking"—the Bath Theatre being in no better case
financially. The Proprietors permitted this opening only on the
understanding that Palmer removed none of the scenery, &c., and
that the rent of £20 weekly was regularly paid. The lavish expenditure on the fabric of the theatre was no compensation, in the
eyes of the Proprietors, for a total of £595 arrears of rent from
which they might have received dividends.

The theatre closed, "rather suddenly" (as the *Bristol Gazette* put it), in June, and Bellamy claimed cautiously that his venture had been "to a certain extent, successful," but he was, with good reason, doubtful about the future. Only £240 of the arrears had been paid off, and after much bad-tempered and fruitless argument the Proprietors decided to cut their losses: once more the Theatre Royal was to let.

There had been one constant factor among the turbulence of Brunton's and Bellamy's managements: the popularity of M'Cready's widow, who continued as leading lady in every Company. With many misgivings, Sarah M'Cready offered to reopen the Theatre for three months at a rent of £100 payable by weekly instalments of £10, and was sufficiently encouraged by her success during this period to continue with the management. Even after her death in 1853, the Macready link with the Bristol theatre was maintained through their daughter Mazzerina, for her husband James Chute, who had joined the Stock Company in 1839, had for some years been helping his mother-in-law with the management, and took over the lease when she died. Thus began the Chute connection with the Bristol Theatre which lasted unbroken until the 1930's.

BIBLIOGRAPHY

A. Loewenberg: *The Theatre of the British Isles excluding London*
(Society for Theatre Research, 1950) contains a list of the
principal books and articles referring to the Bristol Theatre
Royal.

Subsequent relevant publications include:

K. M. D. Barker: The theatre proprietors' story. *Theatre Notebook*, Spring 1964.

B. G. Little: *The Theatre Royal, the Beginning of a Bicentenary.*
Bristol Building Centre, 1964.

The Story of the Theatre Royal. Trustees of the Theatre Royal,
1966.

K. M. D. Barker: The first night of the Theatre Royal Bristol.
Notes and Queries, November 1967.

Considerable information is contained also in the following:

Richard Smith Collection of playbills, &c., in the Central
Reference Library, Bristol.

Collection of Bristol playbills in the British Museum (PB 203-5).

Legal documents, Minute Books, prompt books and playbills
deposited in Bristol City Archives.

Local newspaper files in the Central Reference Library, Bristol,
and the British Museum Newspaper Library, Colindale.

ACKNOWLEDGEMENTS

I should like to thank the staff of the Central Reference and
Newspaper Libraries and of the City Archives Department for
their help and co-operation; and Miss Sybil Rosenfeld, of the
Society for Theatre Research, and Miss Barbara Mogford for
kindly reading the draft and suggesting corrections and amendments.

The extracts from the Theatre Box Book and Michael Edkins'
Account Book are reproduced by permission of the City Librarian,
and the portraits of Powell, Dimond and M'Cready by permission
of the British Museum.

THOMAS CHATTERTON

BASIL COTTLE

There is in London's Tate Gallery a melancholy but very popular painting by Henry Wallis, dated 1856 and entitled *The Death of Chatterton*: a grim garret bedroom, a heap of torn manuscripts, a misty view of St. Paul's Cathedral, a hopeful plant in flower on the sill, the gay colours of jacket and breeches, the pallor of a youth's body. The youth is Thomas Chatterton, born to poverty in Bristol in 1752, bred there in a harsh school and a dull apprenticeship, who yet against this unprivileged background began to write assured verse as a child, and went on to erect a whole medieval world of fantasy which he conveyed in his own imitation medieval English poetry, on scraps of genuine old parchment. The caprice of all this is perhaps childish; but for the performance of it there is no explanation save genius. In 1770, when he was only seventeen, his hopes crashed, and he took poison in London. Wallis painted in the very attic where the suicide occurred, and since no portrait of Chatterton was extant the figure was modelled by the poet and novelist George Meredith; even this had a gloomy ending—the artist eloped with the writer's wife two years later.

But a disservice has been done to the memory of Thomas Chatterton, English poet, by such pity and sensationalism; he has been summed up merely as 'the marvellous Boy', his faked medieval poems have been examined as a piece of linguistics and not as literature, and Wallis's painting has immortalized the pathos of the juvenile suicide in purple and puce. It is the purpose of this study to show Chatterton as England's youngest writer of sustained adult verse, but more vitally as her loudest herald of the Gothic Revival—that revival, late in the 18th century, of an interest in medieval buildings and writings.

His father was the master of the little school in Pile St., Bristol, for forty boys from Redcliffe and St. Thomas parishes, and was also a lay clerk in the Cathedral—a man proud, talented, musical, dissipated, toying with magic and owning 100 Roman coins and 150 books; the mother, half her husband's age when they married, was a nonentity from Stapleton. Three children made different kinds of gloomy entry into the world: Mary, out of wedlock; Giles Malpas, dying after four months; Thomas, posthumously, on 20 November 1752, in the north upper room of the little schoolhouse, from which the widow had not yet been ousted. The cottage still stands, in the safe hands of the City Museum, and it is fronted

by the small pedimented façade of the school, brought back into
line with the new thoroughfare slashed through the web of streets
that Chatterton knew; across this road, the spire and north porch
and bells of St. Mary Redcliffe church dominate the scene, though
in his day the spire was truncated and the church much jostled.

Mrs. Chatterton eventually moved to Redcliffe Hill, and taught
girls to sew, her dressmaker's patterns being sometimes cut from
Redcliffe muniments that her husband had filched from the
treasury' above the north porch; Mary seems to have been a
simple girl, whose mind was occasionally deranged, and a grand-
mother completed the drab and meagre household. Thomas was a
tearful and neurotic child, hiding in an attic and making no progress
with learning; yet he and his playmates had a game in which he
was their natural master, and his precocious vanity is seen in his
request to a potter of his father's kin, who had promised a figured
cup, to paint on it an angel with a trumpet ' to blow his name
about '—a request not unlike Shelley's to the West Wind. The
influence of St. Mary Redcliffe, where his uncle was sexton, was
perhaps mainly unsettling too, since, like an anachronism in an
age indifferent to Gothic buildings, he mooned inside with effigies
for company, yet never gained more than a superficial knowledge
of architecture or heraldry. He exclaims,

Thou seest this maystrie of a human hand,
The pride of Brystowe and the Westerne land;

but the poem where he says so is of vague marvel rather than of
understanding. The Pile St. School returned him to his mother
as an incurable dullard, but suddenly—through the medium of
Redcliffe parchments, his father's music folios, and a black-letter
Bible—he caught the knack of reading and thence a relish for it,
so that at seven he was ready to be nominated to Colston's School.
He had already begun scribbling, and in the ten years left of his
life he produced over 600 printed pages of poetry, as well as
pamphlets and letters in prose; works, furthermore, in the frame-
work of exacting and sustained themes and patterns.

Colston's (now superseded on its site by the Colston Hall, and
clear of the city at Stapleton) stood suggestively where the White
Friars had been; it occupied the Elizabethan Great House on St.
Augustine's Back, there were still old arches from Carmelite times,
and the boys were tonsured like little monks. But here the romance
ended. The school served the mercantile interests of the city, and
did so by the three Rs and the Church of England catechism, after
seven years of which, a boy was bound apprentice to some trade
or craft: the discipline was spartan, a boy was expelled in 1757

Poem on the Death of Thomas Phillips.
Photographed by A. R. Griffin.

for a leprosy ', and there were no humane studies whatever. Yet
Chatterton held his own, and was of course no financial burden
on his mother; one usher at least was enlightened and kindly, and
some of the boys were agreeable friends. And by voracious reading
he equipped himself more precisely for one side of his poetical
career, that of social commentator and satirist; the other came more
wonderfully.

When he was ten, he was confirmed by Bishop Newton of Bristol,
and began to use his pocket-money to borrow from a circulating
library. These happenings are reflected in his first known poem,
On the Last Epiphany, published in *Felix Farley's Journal* and
naturally contributing nothing to eschatology, yet a correct and
neat little piece; the wording is studied and Miltonic, though the
' 8-and-8 ' (with a longer line to round off) makes it sound like
a common type of hymn. There is as yet no imagery or vision,
but there is one warning of the idiom he would soon be faking
—the use of one 'olde' *-eth* inflexion amid the contemporary
grammar. The next surviving poem, from when he was perhaps
eleven, was signed ' X.Y.', the first of several pseudonyms; it is
A Hymn for Christmas Day, and the stanzas are positively clever,
since they are shaped by antithesis and they glitter with single lines
of paradox such as ' The God Eternal died '. They also show a
violation of grammatical concord by ' attraction ' (of the verb to
the number of the nearest noun) that remained a favourite trick or
error with him—' The texture of our souls were made '.

It has been as well to linger over these utter juvenilia, because
in 1763 he became his odd self, to the detriment of his innocent
scholarship, in a satire on the churchwarden who had just had the
Redcliffe churchyard cross destroyed; there are many wasted words
and derived ideas, the fun is desultory, and the gusto is forced, but
in it a child of eleven presses forward to the van of the Gothic
return, as early as Bishop Percy and Macpherson and Horace
Walpole. The scraps of Middle English, Latin, and Norman French,
that he was picking up, the curious items from antiquarians such
as Weever and Verstegan, and any of his mother's Redcliffe parchments that carried writing, were already being lumped into a strange
amalgam along with genius and mischief; and he suddenly showed
a Colston's usher the ' pastoral eclogue ' *Elinoure and Juga.* Its
parchment was ancient, its writing yellowed and strange, its rhyme-
scheme that of the Chaucerian *rime royal,* and its spelling bizarre
enough to deceive an age somewhat unmindful of pre-Miltonic
English; Chatterton passed it off as of the 15th century, and no-one
noticed the charnel-house sentiments from such poems as Gray's

Elegy, or the alexandrines from Spenser. But it would be uncharitable and uncritical to see the genesis of the poet's art in the success of a deception; a boy not yet in his teens had admittedly scored over scholars and antiquarians and fellow-pupils by an elaborate prank, but the spirit of this new work was the best and essential part of him, and it developed into his real poetic current. His double life began, and from now on his poetry has two languages, the acknowledged and the anonymous.

We may assume that he was conscious of poverty, though there was promise of material prosperity if he worked hard; he knew isolation, though he early belonged to a circle with like interests; the materialism of Bristol hurt him, though his swashbuckling descent on London would suggest that he could reckon with the hard world if it paid him enough. The dream that he erected reads like a consolation for present trials, and the troubled boy slipped back to his own inaccurate version of the 15th century and luxuriated there. It proved a temporary palliative, and in his last London days the dream faded, taking all hope with it; but while it lasted he identified himself with Thomas Rowley, priest, secretary to the enlightened magnate William Canynges, with Our Lady on the Red Cliff as his background and with the interesting duty of collecting antiquities for his patron. The name, at least, of Thomas Rowley was authentic; it is on a civilian's brass in St. John's, Bristol, where it was perilously easy for any sceptic to find it and undermine the whole elaborate story. But the rest was a charming allegory of Chatterton's own longing and his few little enjoyments; Canynges's coterie addressed verses to one another, acted in Rowley's plays, held political views, and were in various ways like any group of young Georgian scribblers, but above all there was a patron—and *that* Chatterton never found.

On 1 July 1767, not yet fifteen but with some of his Rowleiana already written, he was apprenticed to a Bristol attorney, John Lambert, possibly at his office in 37 Corn St., whither he had moved perhaps before Chatterton's arrival. The job was extraordinary in its mixture of privilege and hardship; the boy was tied to the office by himself for twelve hours a day, eating at Lambert's house with the menials in the kitchen and sleeping there with the house-boy, with two hours off in the evening and some freedom on Sunday; on the other hand, he had hardly any work to do beyond the copying of legal precedents. This life, and the quiet solitude, which could so easily have induced a morbid idleness, were put to creative purpose; and even his official leisure passed decorously—at home in the evenings, exploring the countryside on Sundays. Above all, his thwarted pride now needed the consummation of the Rowley myth, which took shape and blossomed in the dull office.

The English in which it was expressed became no more rational, and it could be argued from this alone that a deception so recklessly planned was not his main intention at all, that he was rather creating his own individual language for poetry. True, he obstinately went on disclaiming Rowley's verses, as if faithful to a childish secret; but it is clear that he eventually wrote in Rowleian almost direct, not by translating it from the idiom of his own day, and risked detection by this frankness. It must be stated at once that the language is bogus, and distressingly so to a pedant: the calligraphy has modern capitalization and no medieval contractions; in metrics it imitates writers as late as Pope; his rhymes are often not valid for the 15th century (*go*/*trow*), or made to work by mis-spelling (*note* for *night*) or bad grammar or coinings; his syllables are counted in the modern way (*inspiration* would have had five, not four), and his monotonous final *-e* is decorative, not a grammatical inflexion; constructions like ' so haveth I ' are flatly ignorant. Similarly, Rowley's diction can easily be exposed: one old glossary included the verb *houten* meaning ' halloo, hallow ', another respelt the gloss as ' hollow ', another misinterpreted this, and Rowley used it as an adjective. He copied Anglo-Saxon words from Somner's 1659 dictionary, but only as far as *ahrered*, and used ten of them (all beginning with *a*!) in a work which he dared to send to Horace Walpole. And Rowley was better read in the works of his successors than in those of his contemporaries and predecessors: *The Faerie Queene, Hamlet,* Nicholas Rowe, Gray, Pope, were pressed into service more than Chaucer, at whom, it seems, Rowley had merely glanced.

Here, it would seem, was a mouldy method of writing poetry. Yet because Chatterton could not be himself in the philistinism of a mercantile city, he became himself in this odd guise, a Romantic behind a battered casement of stained glass. His contemporary ' railing ' poems have their young genius, too, but it is as Rowley that he is a pioneer in bold expression and in metre; here he writes with splendour and great human understanding, catching at the same time the spirit of the medieval age. Bristol made many contributions to the Gothic Revival—the tower and grotto at Goldney House, the 'castle' and bath-house at Arno's Vale, the battlemented shot-tower, Blaise Castle on its hill, the ununderstood ' Gothick ' of St. Nicholas, St. Michael and St. Paul; but Chatterton's is the clearest and most authentic statement, and old Bristol is its inspiration. Rowley's set are in communication with John Lydgate, the real monk-poet of Bury St. Edmunds, but the best poems are set in Bristol. In the *Bristowe Tragedie* Syr Charles Bawdin, condemned to execution for supporting the Lancastrian cause in the Wars of the Roses, is, after a cool and defiant speech, dragged on his sled through the city streets to execution, accompanied by the non-existent *friars* of St. Augustine's in *monkish* russet, the corporation, numerous minstrels who ' tun'd the strunge bataunt ' (whatever *that* was), and other bursts of colour and sentiment. So to the High Cross (where Chatterton once fancied a St. Andrew's church on the Dutch House site); the Yorkist Edward IV sits ' Att the grete mynsterr wyndowe ' to see him go by, and suffers a fine outburst of his vituperation before the sled is out of earshot. The poem is in ballad metre; *Chevy Chase* was certainly a favourite with Rowley, and its spirit—slowed down and circumstantial now —lives on here.

The two little poems *Onn Oure Ladies Chyrche* rub their eyes with wonder, infecting us with belief in the epithet ' fetive ' and involving also the ' chapelle brighte ' built by Canynges in Westbury-on-Trym (' the Towne,/Where glassie bubblynge Trymme doth roun '). They are perhaps in deliberate contrast—one handsome in its opulent Spenserian stanzas, the other dreamy and tinkling in its short couplets.

Chatterton reached his heights in the play *Ælla: a Tragycal Enterlude*. He treats it very importantly, prefacing it with the statement that it was acted before the Duke of Norfolk in Canynges's Red House (later 97 Redcliff St., a mansion disgracefully destroyed in the 1930s); then an Epistle, then a Letter, than an Introduction. It was all commissioned by Canynges, from his Freemasons' Lodge, to mark the laying of the foundation-stone of the rebuilt St. Mary Redcliffe, and its action is set in that almost unknown city, Anglo-Saxon Bristol. We are to believe that Bristol was the core of resistance to the Danes, and Ælla, ' warde ' of the castle, is hurried from his wedding night by their irruption on to the Somerset coast. His victory near Watchet gives him a fearful wound, so that he longs only to die in the sight of his Birtha; but she meanwhile is being abducted by his disguised henchman Celmonde, who has almost accomplished his dark design when some chivalrous Danes spring out from ambush, kill him, and return her to Bristol. It is too late; Ælla, mistaking the motive of her departure, has fatally stabbed himself, and she faints on his corpse. The little plot has its oddities—the heroine does not die of grief, the hero was perhaps mortally wounded before his Tragic

Flaw upset him, the nation's enemies can behave very decently, and even the lustful villain dies bravely and repentant; but in the compass of merely 1,250 lines there is an organic development of character, an 'atmosphere' perversely sketched by 150 lines of cheerful minstrelsy, and many different narrative and metrical resources. The mournful lyric with the refrain

> Mie love ys dedde,
> Gone to hys death-bedde,
> Al under the wyllowe tree,

whatever its debt to Shakespeare, is deservedly famous, and one line is especially subtle in its alliteration, assonance, and internal rhyme: 'Come, wythe acorne-coppe and thorne'. The minstrelsy treats the joys of love and 'Whatte pleasure ytt ys to be married!'; it is here that the fifteen-year-old poet makes the statement, so extraordinary for the 18th century,

> Wommen bee made, notte for hemselves, botte manne,
> Bone of hys bone, and chyld of hys desire.

And Ælla's high speech to his troops, with its confidence that none will ever say that Bristol slept while foemen were in the land, rolls for 100 lines from its majestic opening:

> Now havynge done oure mattynes & oure vowes,
> Lette us for the intended fyghte be boune.

These astonishing poems, and the rest of the Rowley cycle, are certainly Chatterton's own work; but the motive, poetic creation, was soon coloured by the tempting chance of slight gain. He discovered that three Bristol gentlemen would welcome Rowley's effusions—Barrett, the cold surgeon and historian, who tried to make him drink, and used to argue with him for the pleasure of seeing his eyes strike fire; Catcott the pewterer, who once spat in a customer's eye because he 'had a propensity'; and Burgum, Catcott's partner, who did considerable services to music in the city. Each of these men at times performed actions that were mean and vain and foolish, yet each had the antiquities of Bristol at heart; and though Burgum's payment to Chatterton of 5/- for the 'de Bergham' pedigree was poor wages for a poor imposture, the three have perhaps been too often regarded as the evil geniuses of the boy's life. There were other bad influences, too; the male members of the 'Juvenile Society', who met in a hired tavern room to read ranting plays, and wrote squibs on one another, sound harmless enough and even promising, but so many names of authentic Bristol girls run through his correspondence and his unpublishable *curiosa* that he appears to have become recklessly promiscuous before his apprenticeship ended. We hear less, too,

of the antiquities and scenery that lie so abundantly around Bristol:
the theatre was now a greater source of inspiration—unless in this
he was following Charles Churchill. He came to write unapprec-
iatively of the grandeur outside his mutinous life, and on the
heights of Clifton there was surely no need to say

> Eager at length, I strain each aching limb
> And breathless now the mountain's summit climb.

Worst of all, Rowley had died. *Felix Farley* and the London
papers wanted up-to-the-minute lampoons and social comment,
and the acknowledged verses were soon his paramount concern.
This should not, strictly, be regretted; the Rowley game could
not last for ever, and the creature must be left behind when the
creator grew to manhood. But, in the event, the best of Chatterton
perished with Rowley, and in what remains of his life there is
almost more threat than promise; he had already recaptured
marvellously the sounds and colours of a very different age, and
made a revolutionary rediscovery of 'equivalent substitution' of
feet in his four-stress lines, a revival commonly dated from
Coleridge's *Christabel* at the end of the century. Even if the means
to these achievements were a puerile forgery, there was a poet at
work behind it; but from now on his unfailing, easy ear for rhythm
had as its main object the vignettes and pamphlets of a fickle
public, and his own testy personal outbursts.

The corpus of his acknowledged works is, however, impressive
and full of interest. It had begun, of course, with two religious
poems. He soon became religion's foe; scepticism, Wilkesism, and
philandering, became his set attitude, but a late and hymn-like
poem seems to show a return, and closes on a note of Christian
hope :

> The gloomy mantle of the night,
>   Which on my sinking spirit steals,
> Will vanish at the morning light
>   Which God, my East, my Sun, reveals.

Even the verses written on the day before his suicide beg for
Heaven's mercy and bid his mother farewell, but these sentiments
are mingled with his hatred of

> Bristolia's dingy piles of brick,
>   Lovers of mammon, worshippers of trick,

and its ' guzzling aldermanic fools '.

The elegiac verses are perhaps his feeblest. That on the Colston's
usher, Thomas Phillips, is no doubt sincerely meant, but its truths
relate most closely to Chatterton himself :

Few are the pleasures Chatterton e'er knew,
Short were the moments of his transient peace.

He laboured at this poem, and the changes in the second draft from 'cheerful' to 'frugal' and from 'friendship's potent spells' to 'necromantic spells' may cause us misgivings. Further, he so praises Phillips's forgotten Muse that we wonder how accurate is the rest of his praise. The despair is in clichés ('Farewell the laurel! Now I grasp the yew!') and fresh phrases that sound stale ('deathy tomb' and 'pitchy vapour'); the stanza is from Gray's *Elegy*, and the pathetic fallacy is everywhere: 'Wet with the dew the yellow hawthorns bow'. There are other elegies to Bristolians, with a final frigid one to Lord Mayor William Beckford of London, who had seemed likely to become the poet's patron, and the fulsome note runs through them all. Even a suicide, that may have confirmed Chatterton in his own intention, is given the shocking line 'The blood-stained tomb where Smith and comfort lie'. In addition, he parodied the elegiac mode: *February* pretends to express itself in terms of the Zodiac, but with a sudden irreverent twist of realism in 'And the spruce mercer trembles in his shop'; another poem is insincerely Gothic, with adders, meteors, levined oaks, snowy peaks, a 'shrieking lay', and the final bathos 'lady Betty's tabby cat is dead'. But the humourless elegies are careful, schoolboy stuff; *Clifton*, though it takes up a little the challenge of suggestive scenery, and mentions the Hotwell, the Gorge, Brandon Hill, and the theatre at Jacob's Well, is reminded of the death of Powell the actor, and so of death generally, thence of the Cathedral, dirges, and 'my lone abode'.

The amatory poems and letters will please us little more. He cannot be blamed for the cacophonous names of the girls in Redcliffe (Maria Rumsey, Sally Clarke, Sukey Webb, Polly Lutley, Eleanor Hoyland, the Misses Grimes and Porter), and some of the verses were written for other boys, but the sentiments are artificial and eventually sinister. Small wonder that the juvenile who began a poem of advice 'Marriage, dear Mason, is a serious thing' will give us little satisfaction on the subject of love; he made his task harder by using acrostics and by calling on the whole Pantheon of the gods; and Sally Clarke's harpsichording would have soothed King Saul. But Rowley's creator was now using a porch of St. Mary Redcliffe for his amours with the girls to whom some of the uglier trifles were addressed.

The three *African Eclogues* contain some of his best contemporary verse, and nobly uphold the cause of the slaves; he shares here the rising interest of his time in foreign parts, especially the tropics, and the landscapes are hectic and exciting. There are still conventional phrases—a tiger skin is ' the furry spoil '; but the situations are clearly conceived. The hero ' gained a mountain glaring with the dawn ', and, deprived of his beloved by the white men, cries ' O could I throw my javelin from my eyes! '. Chatterton may well be writing with feeling and vision here, and it is suggestive of his adaptable genius to turn to his one financial success, the burletta *The Revenge,* for which he got five guineas. This idle, naughty piece goes with a swing and treats the amours of Jupiter, but its pretty songs are rather of Merrie England than of the Classics; ' Away to the woodlands, away! ', and the wanton catalogue of swains called *The Virgin's Choice,* sound detached enough, but they were the work of a youth who would kill himself within three months in a Holborn garret.

All these miscellaneous modern poems yield in bulk, and usually in merit, to what he now considered his calling, satire. We have seen that he had struck the vein early, when the Redcliffe cross was felled; not long after this, he satirized *Apostate Will* for becoming a Methodist and then recanting. Eventually, with the pardonable cross-grained perkiness of youth, he was prepared to flay any individual and any cause. Had he reflected, his pride might have been diminished at the thought that he was throwing himself away as a hack for a number of indifferent periodicals, especially when London engulfed him; and now and then the poet in him repented, and a few flowers grew in the mud. For instance, *The Exhibition,* written in London on 1-3 May 1770, is just filthy in its onslaught on certain Bristol notables, but is there not nostalgia in this little picture?—

> Flying on silken wings of dusty Grey,
> The cooling evening clos'd a sultry day.
> The Cit walk'd out to Arno's dusty Vale
> To take a smack of Politicks and Ale,
> Whilst rock'd in clumsy Coach about the Town
> The prudent Mayor jogg'd his Dinner down.

The long and ornate *Kew Gardens,* so full of names in asterisks that it is quite unintelligible, is the showpiece of his satirical skill, with its pretended wrath, its ephemeral politics, its wasted oratory, and its poor jokes. Yet here, and throughout the satires, there are flashes of phrase, and consolidations of idea, that impress and even delight: a fat man called ' an animated hill of oil ', an outraged dowager who ' dined upon her nails ', ' the drilling rain ', the ' swimming elegance ' of a preacher, sermons as ' flimsy wires from reason's ingot drawn '; a frontal attack on Bute, North, and

the other boobies who alienated America; his belief in a God
working ceaselessly through natural laws; his self-knowledge (which
was considerable), and its witty link with Macpherson's faked
poems of Ossian—' Alas! I was not born beyond the Tweed! ';
good influences from Dryden, over-riding influences from Churchill,
and even echoes from Pope:

> Here conversation takes a nobler flight,
> For Nature leads the theme, and all is right.

However breathless is the more presumptuous satire, the moments
of gravity rise far beyond the poet's seventeen years and the political
climate of 1770:

> Alas! America, thy ruined cause
> Displays the ministry's contempt of laws.
> Unrepresented thou art taxed, excised,
> By creatures much too vile to be despised;
> The outcast of an outed gang are sent
> To bless thy commerce with a government.
> Whilst pity rises to behold thy fate,
> We saw thee in this worst of troubles great.

The last, hurtling days of his life do not belong to Bristol. His
eagerness for a career, and his impatience with his drudgery, had
forced on him some desperate and foolish measures. Dodsley the
publisher was sent the bait of some Rowley, but did not rise to it;
Horace Walpole was blandly pleased—indeed, his courtesy warms
us—but his investigations into his correspondent, and the flat
judgment of Gray and Mason against the poems as genuine,
excusably hardened him. Chatterton drew up some savage lines
to send him, ' but my Sister persuaded me out of it '; the poem
exploits the contrast of luxurious wordling and penniless boy,
and brightly accuses Walpole of writing ' Prosy Chapters ' and
' twaddling Letters to some Fair ', but it is cleverest in its defence
of Rowley. ' Who wrote Otranto ? ' it asks with vicious pertinence;
and the last lines are almost a confession of authorship—

> But I shall live & Stand
> By Rowley's side—when *Thou* art dead & damned.

Posterity may feel that he should have sent it.

But the irksome constriction that he felt in Bristol, his dowdy
family whom he promised to enrich, the free thought and the
slackening morals, were all preparing him for flight. The first
necessity was to slip out of his indentures. A suicide threat, left on
his desk at Lambert's, alarmed his master and drew a kindly
sermon from Barrett, whereat he wept and afterwards wrote Barrett

a letter blaming ' my PRIDE, my damn'd, native, unconquerable Pride '. Soon after, however, on 14 April 1770, an enormous *Last Will and Testament* turned up in the same place, written ' in the utmost Distress of Mind ' but certainly imitated from a mock will in *Town and Country;* the next day was Easter Sunday, and he proposed to take his own life on ' the feast of the resurrection '. There are verses for Burgum, Catcott, and Barrett—only the last being let off lightly; he hopes the Coroner will ' bring it in Lunacy ', and then he wants to be buried ' in the Tomb of my Fathers', with a monument 4' 5" high and six tablets: one in French to Gualeroine Chatterton (†1260), and one in Latin to Alanus Chatterton (†1415) and Alicia his wife—these two slabs to be ' engraven in old English Characters '; one to his father, and one to himself, both in Roman lettering; and two non-existent coats of arms. The testament itself is all an impudent and malicious bestowal of qualities on Bristolians in need of them, save that his two womenfolk are left ' to the protection of my Friends if I have any '. A codicil requests that the will be printed in *Felix Farley;* but it did not have to reach so far to be effective, and Lambert released him at once.

Thus in April 1770 he sold his masterpiece, *Ælla,* to Catcott, was given a collection by his friends, distributed some gingerbread on St. Mary Redcliffe steps, and hastened off to London from ' Bristol's narrow streets / Where pride and luxury with meanness meets '. His letters home are buoyant from the start, and *Kew Gardens,* which tilts at Dr. Johnson's play *Irene,* is equally emphatic about Bristol:

> Lost to all learning, elegance, and sense.
> Long had the famous city told her pence;
> Avarice sat brooding in her white-washed cell.
> And pleasure had a hut at Jacob's Well . . .
> A mean assembly-room, absurdly built,
> Boasted one gorgeous lamp of copper gilt:
> With farthing candles, chandeliers of tin,
> And services of water, rum, and gin.
> There, in the dull solemnity of wigs,
> The dancing bears of commerce murder jigs.
> Here dance the dowdy belles of crooked trunk,
> And often, very often, reel home drunk.

His mother is told of the superiority of London, the guineas promised by various magazines, the patronage of Wilkes, the influential people who show him favour, the Chapter Coffee House and its ' geniuses ', his Shoreditch lodgings ' in one of Mr.

Walmsley's best rooms ', and the ' trifling presents ' he has bought
for his family. Only the last of these triumphs is strictly accurate,
and the room was shared with another boy; but the brave pretence
continued, flowering into fantasies like his being suggested as
companion to the young Duke of Northumberland on the Grand
Tour. ' Bravo, hey boys, up we go! '—and nothing is wrong at all.
But in June 1770 he moved from the Shoreditch house, where he
had a relative to keep an eye on him, to the house of Mrs. Angel,
who made ' sacques ' (women's loose coats and gowns) in Brooke
St., Holborn; the area was a slum, and his room an attic. The
unfortunate poet, Richard Savage, born in Holborn, had died in
Bristol Newgate; and Chatterton was aware of this example-in-
reverse. He went on writing with all the old fury—lampoons, personal letters on architecture and music, burlettas, even another
African Eclogue—but his notebook, and other evidence and conjecture, suggest that he was receiving almost nothing for his
productions, except for the decent fee that he earned with *The
Revenge.*

Only one old Bristol friend came to comfort him in his adversity
—Rowley, bringing with him that most moving of all his poems,
An Excelente Balade of Charitie; here Chatterton, with a frank
dependence on the Parable of the Good Samaritan, surely sees
himself in the character of the stricken man :

> Look in his glommed face, his sprighte there scanne;
> Howe woe-be-gone, how withered, forwynd, deade!

The music is as rich as ever, and what material is derived is made
his own; but *Town and Country* would not print it. Off to his
family went his box of promised presents—china, dress-patterns,
snuff-box, fans, tobacco; a picaresque story, *The Memoirs of a
Sad Dog,* was formed hastily and competently; a last letter to his
sister, on 20 July, is a brief jotting about an intended oratorio, a
promise to visit them during the year, the next *Town and Country*
filled by him, his company ' courted everywhere ', and of course
' the ladies '. But the death of Lord Mayor Beckford was a real
blow to his hopes, however callously he may have reckoned that
he was ' glad he is dead by ' £3 13s. 6d. gained on elegies and
essays; and the discrediting of his chosen political party involved
him in its toils. That he was suffering also from venereal disease,
an assertion made by several after his death, is not proven and, in
view of his other misfortunes and the horrors of his combined
adolescence and genius, is certainly not needed to explain the final
catastrophe.

After some days apparently without food, though Mrs. Angel offered him a dinner, he took arsenic in water, possibly after opium to deaden the pain, and died on the night of 24-25 August 1770. His body was buried in a common pit in the burial ground of Shoe Lane workhouse; there is an impossible legend of its secret reinterment at St. Mary Redcliffe. He was aged only 17 years and 277 days.

The amazing monument of his fame was erected in two stages. First came the protracted and learned controversy over the authorship of the Rowley poems, when scholarship was divided into two camps, with Dean Milles of Exeter leading the utterly mistaken Rowleians. The campaign at least led to editions of the antiquated poems, especially Tyrwhitt's sensible volume of 1777. In 1803, Longman published both sides of the poetry, as complete as it could be made, edited by Robert Southey and Joseph Cottle; this was done entirely for the benefit of Chatterton's sister, now widowed and left with one of her four children. A note in Cottle's writing mentions a profit of £504 to come to her, and she certainly left £300; her spinster daughter, Marianne, died at the house of Mr. Bampfylde, a cooper, in West St., on 7 September 1807, and was the last of the melancholy family.

But far more important was his sudden renown among poets. The feeling that he had died for poetry inspired a number of famous writers in their youth. Coleridge, when only sixteen, wrote a *Monody* on him; Wordsworth in *Resolution and Independence* called him ' the marvellous Boy, / The sleepless Soul that perished in his pride '; Shelley devoted a harrowing stanza to him in *Adonais;* Keats ' with a bowed mind ' dedicated *Endymion* to him as ' the most English of Poets except Shakespeare ', and was much influenced by him. And, though Hazlitt and Carlyle were censorious, poets as various as Crabbe, Scott, Byron, and Rossetti, were loud in his praise, along with a host of poetasters that included Ann Yearsley the Bristol milkwoman. In France, the rising Romantics acknowledged his example : Alfred de Vigny's *Chatterton* is a prose play by a poet, with the bald thesis of a spiritual man stifled by a materialist society, and with an absurd plot. Vigny invents a family called Bell, with whom the pure-souled youth lives in London (Mrs. Kitty Bell falling in love with him), a Quaker to advise him, a set of English lords full of *rosbif,* and a complete meet coming into his digs. It was this play that Ruggiero Leoncavallo used for his opera *Chatterton;* but, unlike his *Pagliacci,* it was a failure.

13.

have had from me assuring them that they need be under no Apprehensions from the Appearance of my Ghost for I aye for none of them —

Item I leave all my Debts in the whole not five Pounds to the Payment of the Charitable and generous Chamber of Bristol On Penalty if refused to hinder every Member from over eating a good Dinner by appearing in the form of a Bailiff — If in Defiance of this terrible Spectre they obstinately persist in refusing to discharge my Debts Let my two Creditors apply to the Supporters of the Bill of Rights

Item I leave my Mother & Sister to the protection of my Friends if I have any

Executed in the presence of Omniscience this 14th Day of April 1770

T. Chatterton

Chatterton's Mock Will, 14 April 1770.
Photographed by A. R. Griffin.

The Chatterton Memorial which formerly stood in St. Mary Redcliffe Churchyard; to its left, the façade of the Pile Street School, re-set against Chatterton's birthplace.
Photographed by Reece Winstone.

The poet's name survives in Redcliffe as the name of a square and of a block of council flats. The plan for a monument was started in 1792, met protests from Rowleians and moralists, and was crowned in 1840 by a tall stone Gothic pentagon with a puppet-statue of a bluecoat boy holding *'Ella'* on a scroll; even this left Redcliffe churchyard for the crypt in 1846, but stood on unconsecrated ground, facing the birthplace, from 1857 to 1967. It was then demolished as being decayed past restoration. In the same year a collateral descendant of Joseph Cottle, his 1803 publisher, gave the modest oval stone plaque in the south transept, set in the wall just by Canynges' tomb, and lettered by the sculptor, Richard Reid of York: 'THOMAS CHATTERTON/of this parish/ 1752–1770/Poet'. In the bicentenary year, 1970, *Ella* received its first performance; fittingly, at Colston's School, Stapleton, and with great success.

Bibliography

The Complete Works of Thomas Chatterton: a Bicentenary Edition, ed. D. S. Taylor and B. B. Hoover, 2 vols (Oxford 1971); it runs to 687 pages.

E. H. W. Meyerstein, *A Life of Thomas Chatterton* (1930) is essential for any study of the poet.

F. A. Hyett and W. Bazeley, *Chattertoniana* (1914), was for its time a very good bibliography.

THE BRISTOL HOTWELL

VINCENT WAITE

From a coloured sketch of the old Hotwell House by J. M. W. Turner
(By permission of Bristol City Art Gallery)

The second Hotwell House ' in the Tuscan style '

The Hotwell Pump in the Grotto, c. 1900

One of the outstanding features of the Bristol Hotwell spa is the rapidity of its rise to fame and its equally swift decline and decay. At the height of its popularity it was a crowded fashionable spa which was a rendezvous for elegant society figures like the Duchess of Marlborough, the Duchess of Kent, and other visitors described with a curious mixture of sycophancy and scurrility in *Characters at the Hotwell*, a slim folio published in 1723. At this period London newspapers were displaying advertisements like the following :

" Famous Bristol Hotwell water, fresh from the Well, will be sold and delivered to any part of the town at six shillings per dozen bottles. These bottles are of the largest size, and by the extraordinary favour of the winds arrived but last week, in eight days from Bristol, the common passage being a month or six weeks."

Addison, Cowper, Gay, Pope, Sheridan, and Mrs. Thrale were among the many famous literary figures who visited the spa. Smollett set the opening chapters of *Humphrey Clinker* here, and Fanny Burney followed fashion by sending the eponymous heroine of *Evelina* to the Hotwell which she described as " a most delightful spot; the prospect is beautiful, the air pure, and the weather very favourable to invalids." The Poet Laureate, William Whitehead, remarkable for his insignificance in a whole series of indifferent 18th century Poets Laureate, published an extravagantly laudatory and excessively lengthy *Hymn to the Nymph of the Bristol Spring*. And yet by the end of the 18th century the gay elegant throng of the Hotwell season had dwindled to a handful of doomed patients. Finally the Pump Room itself disappeared and all that was left was a legacy of bankrupt lodging-house keepers, a few faded carriages with shabby drivers and still shabbier horses, and rows of decaying houses.

Bristolians habitually use the plural form " Hotwells," and there were in fact several spa springs in Bristol at various periods. Here we shall deal exclusively with the original Hotwell spring which gushed out of an opening at the foot of St. Vincent's rock, almost under the span of the modern Suspension Bridge, but to avoid confusion it might be well to mention the more important of the other springs.

1. The " New " Hotwell, first mentioned about 1702, flowed into the Avon further along the river bank, about two hundred yards beyond Blackrock quarry. A few intrepid travellers clambered over the stony pathway by the river or rode down the precipitous horsetrack leading to it from Durdham Downs. In 1754 John Wesley attributed his sudden recovery from a " greedy consumption " to the virtues of this spring. This gave it a short-lived celebrity; a small Pump Room and lodging-house were built, but the place was unbearably lonely. " The nearest dwelling is a mile distant, and the only human objects ordinarily visible are the gibbeted remains of two murderers," one visitor wrote. It is hardly surprising that the New Hotwell could not compete with its older rival, and by 1792 the buildings were occupied by quarrymen. In 1894 the Corporation was persuaded to build a drinking-fountain for the spring, now styled " St. Vincent's Spring," and this still remains on the Portway.

2. About 1786 a spring was discovered near the Mardyke ferry in Hotwells Road behind " The Tennis-Court House." The proprietor built a small Pump Room round the spring, but by 1810 the site was converted into Poole's Mineral Spa Coal Wharf.

3. Sion Spring was discovered in 1793 when a local attorney living on Sion Hill made a boring through the limestone rock to obtain water for his house. He, too, built a small Pump Room and set up in competition with the old Hotwell below the cliff, but in five years the building was up for sale as " suitable for any genteel business." The building which was put up in 1850 in a short-lived attempt to revive the Sion Hill Spa is now transformed into a hotel bar.

4. The spa of the Grand Spa Hotel was built in 1893 when George Newnes planned the hydraulic cliff railway from Hotwells Road to Sion Hill. He was given permission to construct the railway on condition that he revived the old Clifton Spa by building a Pump Room at the end of Prince's Buildings. From the very beginning the enterprise seemed doomed to failure, and the building finally became an ordinary hotel. The ornate building which once housed the spring water and mineral baths can still be seen with the initials G.N. woven in the masonry.

The original Hotwell spring, the subject of this account, was at high tide some twenty-six feet below the river level, but when the tide had ebbed it poured out ten feet above the level

of the water at a rate of some sixty gallons a minute. The term
" hot " well was a misnomer : its temperature was 76 degrees.

It has been traditionally supposed that the spring was known
in the earliest times to sailors who used the water to treat scurvy,
that former scourge of seafaring men, but the first known written
record was made by that indefatigable measurer of walls and pacer
of distances, the 15th century Bristol topographical scholar, William
Worcester. "Fons ibidem in parte de Gyhston Cliff in fundo
aquae, et est ita callidus sicut lac, vel aqua Badonis," is his
description of it. (In the same place is a fountain on the side of
Ghyston Cliff, towards the bottom of the river, and it is as warm
as milk or like the water of Bath.)

At the beginning of the 17th century the Hotwell water
began to be more generally known. In 1634 a young officer visited
the spring and described it as " gushing and pouring out of a mighty
stony Rocke into the Streame, so nigh thereto that every Tyde it
overflows it. To it we descended by a rocky and steep-winding
and craggy way—neere 200 slippery steps."* One of the earliest
writers to describe the theraputic value of the water was Dr.
Thomas Johnson in *Mercurius Botanicus*. He visited the Hotwell in
the same year and wrote : " Here from the clefts of the rocks issues
forth a spring of warm water pleasant to the taste. It is a water of
some repute, and much commended for . . . affections of the
kidneys, taken inwardly, and for old sores, applied outwardly. It is
in pretty frequent use, and not without success as I am informed by
those who have experienced it."

The virtues of the spring were known well enough to be
described in several books later in the century. Thomas Fuller
mentions it in his *Book of Worthies* (1662) as being " sovereign
for sores and sickness, to be washed in, or drank of, to be either
outwardly or inwardly applied . . . Dr. Samuel Ward, living in
Sidney College, Cambridge, was prescribed the constant drinking
thereof, though it was costly to bring it through the Severn and
narrow seas, and thence by river to Cambridge." In 1650 a Dr.
Venner laid special stress on the virtues of the Hotwell water for
those " who have hot livers, feeble brains, and red pimply faces "
—a combination of symptoms recalling the literature of later
patent medicines. After 1680 the spring became well-known as a
remedy for yet another disease. The circumstances of the discovery
of this cure are related by Dr. Randolph in his *Bristol Hotwell:*

Relation of a Short Survey of 26 Counties.

"It happened about the year 1680 that two or three persons
of note in Bristol died of the diabetes, the physicians acknowledging
and bewailing the inefficiency of their art in such manner as it was
looked upon by everybody to be incurable. One Mr. Gagg, a baker
who lived in Castle Street, being seized with it, was accordingly
despaired of by all that knew him. But dreaming one night that he
drank plentifully of the Hotwell water, and was wonderfully
refreshed by it, he was much inclined the next morning to quench
his thirst with it, and found it to answer to his wish so effectually
that by continuing the use of it, in a few days he came abroad,
gathered flesh and strength daily, and recovered to the great surprise
of everybody that knew him. This one remarkable instance was
sufficient to recommend this water to others labouring under the
same disorder, and accordingly it was found to answer expectation,
and was soon brought into reputation for it."

Royal patronage of the Hotwell dates back to the visit of
that unhappy neglected queen, Catherine of Braganza, who visited
it in 1677. She drove along the rough track to the spring attended
by the Earl of Ossory and other members of her entourage, but the
city records do not say if she went down the "neere 200 slippery
steps." At the beginning of the 17th century a small brick
reservoir had been built round the spring, but when the tide rose
the spring water was contaminated in the reservoir, and it continued
polluted for some time after the river level had fallen. In an effort
to prevent this the Mayor of Bristol in 1691 built a high stone
enclosure around the spring. This had an unexpected result : the
pressure of the greatly increased volume of water began to divert
the course of the spring, and it was feared for a time that it would
be driven underground and entirely lost.

A more successful attempt to solve this problem was made
four years later when the Society of Merchant Venturers, lords of
the manor of Clifton, granted a lease of the Well to a group of
Bristol citizens. Under their auspices the Hotwell House was built
in 1696 on a small rocky ledge jutting out into the river. Contemporary prints show it as a somewhat gaunt, austere building,
but from its rooms facing the Avon there was a fine view of the
river, and the gorge was still almost unspoilt by quarrying. But
even the view had its disadvantages according to Smollett's
H mphrey Clinker in which Jerry Melford says :

"I was the other day much diverted with a conversation that passed in the Pump Room betwixt my uncle and
the famous Doctor Linden who is come to ply at the Well

for Patients. My uncle was complaining of the stink occasioned by the vast quantity of mud and slime which the river leaves at low ebb under the windows of the Pump Room."

On the other hand we find that Lydia exclaims in the same novel :

"This is a charming romantic place. The air is so pure, the Downs so agreeable, the furze in full blossom, the ground enamelled with daisies, primroses and cowslips . . . For variety we go down to the Bristol spring where the company is assembled before dinner; so good-natured, so free, so easy; and there we drink the water . . . The ships and boats going up and down the river, close under the windows of the Pump Room, afford such an enchanting variety of moving pictures."

Probably the truth lay somewhere between these two pictures. Neither the old man nor the young girl was a reliable witness—he was suffering from gout and a disordered liver; and she was violently in love.

A special foundation had been built for this Pump Room to enable the pumps to raise the water thirty feet. Valves in the pipes allowed the waste well-water to flow back into the river, but shut against the river-water at high tide. This at least is what in their theory should have happened, and what the Guide Books claimed did happen, but one Hotwell doctor confessed : " It is found by experience that the high tides will mix with the spring and foul it (which they can do no other way than by some unknown clefts in the rock) and the water continues foul for some time after the tide is sunk."

Towards the beginning of the 18th century the Hotwell added tuberculosis of the lungs to the list of diseases which were treated at the spa, and in 1745 Dr. Randolph wrote :

"Of all the disorders which seek relief from Bristol water there is none more common than *phthisis pulmonaria;* none in which more is expected of it; none in which the hopes of our patients are oftener deceived. Some come not till 'tis too late to help them; others with symptoms the water will not reach; all expecting miracles, not considering the great variety of cases comprehended under this one name, or that what might have been of service in the beginning becomes of little or no efficacy in the later stages."

These are frank words written by a physician who was himself in practice at the Hotwell and who showed more professional acumen and honesty than many of his contemporaries by stressing that the Hotwell water could not work miracles. The disease must be taken in time, and it was the rest, fresh air and exercise of the spa's regimen which effected a cure rather than any magical properties of the water itself. A Hotwell guide published towards the end of the century was even more emphatic on the subject— " We do not wish to cast any reflection on the gentlemen of the faculty whose advice is consulted, but we are afraid it is too often a practice with them not to part with a patient whilst they have the least probability of success. When they find their art ineffectual, and the case desperate, then and not till then the physician consigns his patient to the Bristol Hotwell to try the effect of the water, by which he avoids the imputation of their dying under his hands." Patients of this kind were so common in one set of lodging-houses that they were known by the grim nickname of " Death Row."

Nevertheless many contemporary medical works continued to be filled with reports of cases cured which are scarcely credible to a more sceptical generation, although they were always " carefully attested, either by the persons themselves or by other trustworthy eyewitnesses so as to obviate all suspicion of falsehood." The following is a fair sample of these " carefully attested " cures :

" The Rev. Dr. Hammond, of Christ Church, Oxford, about four years since, spared neither care nor cost for the recovery of Christopher Pyman, his then servitor, and now of the same college. After the doctor had left him past hope of recovery, with his funeral directions, a dismal spectacle, wasted to the last degree, at the prime of life, forsaken by his physicians, and left to the merciless hand of death by his friends, was perfectly cured by drinking the Hotwell water, and now remains a living, healthful testimony of this truth."

" By easy journeys, Miss Lee, of Birmingham, was conveyed to the Well. To the dregs of the measles she owed her consumption, and she was reduced to skin and bone. She was so weak that she could not walk to the pump. She drank the water from her chair for the first six weeks without the least visible amendment. After this it began to have a sensible effect. It threw out large boils on her back. At the end of three months her blood vessels seemed to be filled with fresh juices. She ate heartily, walked firmly, and rode on the Downs. After five years she now continues well."

"Mr. Ralph Millard, Innkeeper at the Swan, Coleman Street, London, aged 50, in the spring of 1700, after a great medick expense, and given over by his physicians in a diabetes, was directed to the Hotwell, to which place he got with great difficulty, not being able to scramble to his bed without help. By drinking the water three weeks he was so invigorated that Mr. Eaglestone, of College Green, saw him lift a barrel of ale up several steps, which three other men failed to perform. In three weeks more he returned to London, riding the hundred miles in two days."

The bottling of the Hotwell water was a considerable industry in the 18th century. Defoe noted in 1724 that there were no fewer than fifteen glass-houses in Bristol, "which are more than in London . . . and vast numbers of bottles are used for sending the water of the Hotwell not only over England but all over the world." Later another visitor recorded that the water " was not only drunk on the spot at the Pump Room, but every morning cried in the streets, like milk." Those who bought water in bottles were given detailed instructions on the best method of reviving some of its original characteristics, but the poet Pope, who has left an interesting account of his visit to the Hotwell in 1739, confirmed the general opinion—" I am satisfied that the water at the Well is different from what it is anywhere else." The water fresh from the spring was officially described as " uniformly 76 degrees on issuing from the pump, and it cannot offend the most irritable stomach. It is sparkling and abounding with air-bubbles of a whitish colour which gradually goes off as it grows cool, and therefore in perfection only at the spring. Thus taken, it is brisk and soft to the palate, grateful to the stomach, wholly free from odour, and cooling to the system. It leaves a slightly styptic impression on the palate by no means unpleasant; and though hard for the purpose of the laundress, has the remarkable quality of making excellent tea."

One interesting event occurred at the spring in 1755 which was later accepted as proof that the spa water was "influenced to an unusual degree by the subterranean fire of the earth, and has an evident sympathy with volcanic agencies." On the first of November the Hotwell suddenly became as red as blood, and so turbid that it could not be drunk. Many conjectures were made as to the cause of this phenomenon, but news was later received that the disastrous earthquake at Lisbon had taken place on that very day.

Rooms on the upper floor of the Pump House were limited in number and at the beginning of the Hotwell's popularity most of the visitors were accommodated in lodgings around College Green. During the first half of the 18th century the houses of Dowry Square and Dowry Parade were built to provide additional accommodation. The Hotwell season began in late April and lasted until the end of September. The fashionable procedure for " taking the waters " was to ride in a carriage to the Pump Room in the morning, drink the prescribed number of glasses, and then sit with the company, talking scandal, playing cards, and listening to the small orchestra which exacted a season's subscription of five shillings from each visitor. For the benefit of those who preferred fresh air and exercise there was a tree-lined promenade along the river bank, and for wet weather a small colonnade was built about 1786, part of which still remains. This colonnade replaced a small piazza which can be seen in some earlier drawings of the Hotwells. At five o'clock the company gathered again to take the water in the Pump Room, and after the first two or three days the amount was often increased to as much as twelve glasses daily. A somewhat different, sterner regimen was described by one physician under the title " The Invalid's Day." " At six in the morning take asses' milk. Rest about an hour after it in bed. Should perspiration ensue, which is frequently the case, rest rather upon the bed, lightly clad. Rise at seven, or earlier. Be at the Well by half past seven. There take the first glass of the water; and having walked in the open air, if the weather permits, otherwise under the colonnade, for twenty or thirty minutes, take the second glass. Ride on horseback, or in a carriage, from eight to nine. Breakfast and the private avocations of the morning will engage till twelve, when a customary medicine is to be taken. At one o'clock go to the waters and drink two glasses in the same way as in the morning. From half past one ride on the Downs, or elsewhere, till four. Dinner. Remain quiet after it, or perhaps repose on a couch till six. Half hour after six, Tea, or such habitual beverage. At seven, walk; or if debility forbids, ride. At eight or soon after, be returned home. At nine, or soon after, Supper. At eleven, take the night medicine, and retire to rest."

Various organised amusements were provided for visitors who were well enough to be amused, and these were a fair proportion, especially when the Hotwell cure was part of the yearly round for fashionable society folk, or was regarded as a temporary rest cure for the typical toper and glutton of the period. Riding or driving on the Downs was a favourite pastime and there was such a

120 The Bristol Hotwell

demand for horses that in 1754 it was stated that " the best lady attending the Hotwell will not refuse riding behind a man, for such is the custom here, and numbers of what they call ' double horses ' are kept for that purpose." Another favourite amusement was sailing down the river, often accompanied by another boat with musicians on board " whose music, when echoed and re-echoed by the rocks, has a most delightful effect, not only on those on the water but also to the auditors on land. Companies of visitors often sail down as far as Portishead, and if they take a cold collation with them, go ashore and dine in the woods. And many ladies and gentlemen cross the river at Rownham ferry and walk to the sweet and wholesome village of Ashton to eat strawberries or raspberries with cream." Sometimes a visit to the spa coincided with the races on Durdham Downs which lasted for several days and always proved a popular attraction.

In 1729 a small theatre was built at Jacob's Well " lying convenient for coaches as well as for the Rope-Walk leading to the Hotwell." It was a cramped little building but it had the advantage of sharing a party wall with an alehouse, and through a hole in this wall liquid refreshment was handed to the actors and to the privileged spectators who sat on the stage. Evening balls and private parties were held in the public rooms owned by the Pump Room—the Old, or Upper Long Room, and later the Lower, or New Long Room, part of which still survives as a school. One Hotwell physician regretted " that the female invalids, who are for the most part at that period of life when public entertainments have their peculiar relish, err in no one instance so much as in the indulgence of dancing, an exercise most salutary to lungs that are sound, but as injurious to those that are unsound." It appears to have been the height of fashion to give public breakfasts "with cotillions and country dances," an outstanding example of the vigour of our ancestors that even companies of invalids could take hearty exercise of this kind during what in a softer generation has degenerated into the silent meal of the day.

The Bristol Hotwell was, of course, much smaller than the neighbouring spa of Bath, and it was in no sense a rival but rather a supplementary cure, for many people combined visits to the two resorts. After 1785 the Hotwell imitated Bath by appointing a Master of Ceremonies, " William Pennington Esquire," who wore a gold medallion strung on a blue ribbon to emphasise the dignity of his office. In order to preserve decorum in the public entertainments he issued the following regulations :

1. That a certain row of seats be set apart at the upper end of the room for ladies of precedence and foreigners of fashion.

2. That every lady who has a right of precedence deliver her card to the Master of Ceremonies on her entering the room.

3. That no gentleman appear with a sword or with spurs in these rooms, or on a ball night, in boots.

4. That on ball nights when minuets are danced, ladies who intend dancing there will sit in a front row for the convenience of being taken out and returning to their places.

5. That on all occasions ladies are admitted to these rooms in hats, not excepting the balls given to the Master of the Ceremonies.

6. That the subscription balls will begin as soon as possible after 7 o'clock and conclude at 11, on account of the health of the company.

7. It is earnestly requested that when a lady has gone down the dance she will be so polite as not to retire till it is concluded.

During the 18th century the popularity of the spa was maintained by its reasonable charges. The fee for drinking the water was merely nominal. Lodgings were only ten shillings a week for a room in summer, and five shillings in winter, with half price for servants. The public breakfasts cost one shilling and sixpence. The season's subscription to the balls (giving two tickets) was one guinea, and five shillings was charged for the use of the Rooms and Gardens.

The gay, fashionable character of the spa lasted until the last decade of the 18th century, and then at the height of its prosperity there came a dramatic decline and decay. In 1784 the Society of Merchant Venturers had advertised for a new tenant of the Hotwell. As the lessee was required to spend at least £1,000 on building a quay wall along the river bank in front of the Pump Room, £500 in protecting the spring from the tide, and a considerable sum on repairs to the Pump Room itself, it is not surprising that the lease was not taken up. The Society had to appoint a salaried caretaker of the spa and undertake the necessary repairs and improvements. In 1790 Samuel Powell became the new tenant. The rent had been considerably increased, and understandably Powell increased his charges. But the increase was so much and so sudden that the throng of visitors dwindled to a mere handful in a few seasons. In 1816 Dr. Carrick, a Clifton physician, described the spa as he had known it some thirty years before :

"It was then during the summer one of the best frequented and most crowded watering-places in the kingdom. Scores of the nobility were to be found there every season, and such a crowd of invalids of all ranks resorted to the waters that it was often difficult for them to provide themselves with any sort of lodgings. About that period a considerable number of lodging-house keepers had in the course of a few years realised very handsome fortunes without any complaints of extortionate exactions. Three extensive taverns were constantly full and two spacious ballrooms were profitably kept open. There was a well-attended ball, a public breakfast, and a promenade every week, and often twice a week. The Pump Room was all day long the resort of invalids who left with the keeper of the Well many hundreds a year in voluntary donations, and from 12 to 2 o'clock it was generally so crowded that there was often some difficulty in getting up to drink the water. The adjoining walk was filled with fashionable company; the sublime scenery of the cliffs was enlivened by the sounds of music. The Downs and all the avenues to the Hotwell were filled with strings of carriages and with parties on horseback and on foot."

Then he went on to describe how the place had changed by 1816 :

"It has the silence of the grave, to which it seems the inlet. Not a carriage to be seen once an hour, and scarcely more frequently does a solitary invalid approach the neglected spring. One of the ballrooms and taverns has been long ago shut up, and the other with great difficulty kept open. The lodging-houses, or such of them as still remain open, are almost entirely empty in summer, and not very profitably filled even in winter."

It is not difficult to trace the chief causes of this decline in popularity of a once flourishing spa. Firstly, there were the increased charges : for example, instead of the former ten shillings fee per season for a whole family to drink the water, each individual was now charged twenty-six shillings. As a result of this, families which once went to the spa for pleasure as well as for health were now attracted elsewhere. Hotwell visitors thus became mostly incurable consumptives nursing a last despairing hope of a miraculous cure. This in turn resulted in a mortality rate among the patients, which was bound to give a sinister reputation to a so-called "curative" spa. Dr. Carrick remarked on yet another deterrent for the nervous or delicate visitors—the dangerous, precipitous way leading down from Clifton to the Well. "To many the hire of a carriage twice or thrice a day at the increased charge, and the fatigue and terror of riding up and down Granby Hill is an insuperable obstacle." Finally, as Latimer very pertinently points out, the conclusion of the long war with France had made it possible for the more wealthy English families to patronise foreign spas once again.

In 1822 the old Hotwell House was demolished so that the road, later called Bridge Valley Road, could be built. At the same time an energetic attempt to revive the spa was made by a Mr. James Bolton. A new Pump Room "in Tuscan style" was built, and a suite of baths added to the building; visitors had always complained of the lack of proper facilities for mineral baths in the old Pump Room. Charges seem to have been rather high—three-pence a glass for the water, which meant up to three shillings a day if you were taking the cure. Only paupers were allowed to draw from the free tap set up in a back yard to conform with the prescriptive right of Bristolians and Cliftonians to have free access to the Well. This free tap was in fact removed in 1831, but another was set up in 1837 as a result of threatened legal action by a section of the Bristol public.

Mr. Bolton was obviously a shrewd business man. He combined with his spa water and mineral baths the sale of stationery, guide books, local views, "Indian soap as prepared at Delhi (' Nature gives much!—But Art's assisting power will aid her efforts, and her blooms secure '); fancy articles in lava; oiled silk caps and respirators; portable seats and stools; flesh rubbers and brushes; foreign cigars; umbrellas; lozenges; marine and fresh-water animals; fossils of the neighbourhood, both in their natural state and in the form of inkstands, shawl-pins, etc.; Kent's patent knife-cleaning machines; White's family flour-mill; Hotwell toothpowder; and boomerangs."

This spirited, all-embracing commercial activity won the admiration of his patrons. Some were even moved to poetical effusions such as

> " I drink thy limpid wave and feel
> Its balm in every vein—
> Endow'd by Heaven with powers to heal,
> And lull despotic pain.
> I bathe, and from thy waters win
> What gave old Jordan fame—
> An infant's smoothness on my skin,
> A glow through all my frame."

But it was of no avail; his attempt to revive the Hotwell spa failed, and in 1867 the new Pump Room was in turn demolished so that Hotwell Point could be removed and river navigation made safer. Thus the spring was lost after a long and eventful history. After much public agitation and complaining in the local press the spring was enclosed and piped to a small grotto hollowed out in the rock. Here a pump was set up in 1877 and an attendant provided by the Bristol Docks committee. In 1880 Dr. Griffin wrote a warning letter to the newspapers claiming that his analysis of this pump water proved that it was not from the original spring which in any case was too far away to retain its correct temperature. Yet up to 1913 the pump was still in use, and sometimes supplied as many as 350 persons a day. Then the long-threatened pollution of the water by the river became too obvious to be ignored and the pump was closed. The entrance, blocked up by a small wooden door, can still be seen in Hotwells Road near the Suspension Bridge. Attempts have been made to find the unpolluted original spring again. Borings were made after 1913 down to a depth of over one hundred and forty feet with no success, and another trial in 1925 was equally abortive.

Only one reminder of the old Hotwell is now left to Bristolians—part of the colonnade which still stands in Hotwells Road. In the daytime it is just a quaint little crescent of shabby houses with a busy clatter of traffic roaring past, but at night when the street lamps glitter across the river the old houses seem to glimmer like the ghosts of a vanished glory which indeed they are. This interesting relic of the past is already falling into sad decay. If neglected for much longer it must inevitably disappear like so much of the inheritance history has bequeathed to Bristol.

CHEMICAL ANALYSIS OF THE HOTWELL WATER
BY THE CHEMIST WILLIAM HERAPATH

One imperial gallon contains :

	CUBIC INCHES
Carbonic acid gas	8·75
Nitrogen	6·56

SOLID MATTERS	GRAINS
Chloride of magnesium	2·18
Nitrate of magnesia	2·909
Chloride of sodium	5·891
Sulphate of soda	3·017
Sulphate of magnesia	1·267
Carbonate of lime	17·7
Carbonate of magnesia	·66
Carbonate of iron	·103
Bitumen	·15
Sulphate of lime	9·868
Silicia	·270

Grains 44·015

ACKNOWLEDGMENTS

Mr. Waite wishes to express his thanks to the City Art Gallery for help in choosing the illustrations; to the Bristol Central Library for generously putting works of reference at his disposal; and to J. Knee, Esq., for preparing the illustrations for the printer.

The Bristol Branch of the Historical Association would like to thank the Gane Educational Trust, the Bristol Education Committee and the Bristol Civic Society for their generous donations.

The proposal that the Branch should issue a series of pamphlets on local history was first put forward by Mr. Peter Harris, who has played the major part in overcoming the many difficulties in the way of publication.

Patrick McGrath.

SOME BOOKS RELATING TO THE HOTWELL

Matthew's New History of Bristol and Directory for 1793-4.
Evans : **History of Bristol** (1824).
W. Herapath : **Handbook for Visitors to the Bristol & Clifton Hotwells** (c. 1855).
Bolton's Guide to Clifton, Bristol, & Hotwells (c. 1860).
Chilcott's Descriptive History of Bath (various dates).
Latimer : **Annals of Bristol.** 17th, 18th & 19th centuries (1887-1902).
Hutton : **Bristol and its famous Associations** (1907).

* * *

John Underhill : **Account of the Bristol Hotwell Water** (1703).
Dr. Wynter : **The Medicinal Waters of Bath and Bristol** (1725).
Dr. Keir : **The Medicinal Waters of Bristol** (1739).
John Shebbeare : **Analysis of the Bristol Waters** (1740).
Dr. Randolph : **Enquiry into the Medicinal Virtues of Bath and Bristol Waters** (1750).
Dr. Rutty : **Synopsis of Mineral Waters** (1757).
Dr. Sutherland : **Nature and Qualities of Bristol Water** (1758).
Dr. Nott : **Of the Hotwell Waters** (1793).
Dr. Carrick : **Bristol Hotwell Water** (1796).
Bristol Medico-Chirurgical Journal March, June, Sept. 1902.

References in :—

Dr. Jorden : **Discourse of Natural Baths & Mineral Waters** (1632).
Thos. Johnson : **Mercurius Botanicus** (1634).
Dr. Venner : **Via Recta ad Vitam Longam** (1638).
Dr. Malpet : **Letter to Dr. Bate** (1655).
Thos. Fuller : **Book of Worthies** (1662).
Clemontius : **De Aere, Aquis, et Locis Terrae Angliae** (1672).
Thos. Guidot : **De Thermis Britannicis Tractatus** (1691).
Sir Robert Atkyns : **State of Gloucestershire** (1712).
Dr. Granville : **The Spas of England** (1841).

THE PORT OF BRISTOL
IN THE EIGHTEENTH CENTURY

WALTER MINCHINTON

The eighteenth century was Bristol's golden age. For most of this period, except for London, Bristol was the leading English port. It occupied a key role in overseas commerce and at the same time it was the focus of the economic, social and cultural life of much of South Wales and the south west of England. Already in the seventeenth century the second largest port in the country, Bristol had, by growing faster than Norwich, become the second largest town in England in 1700. It continued to grow in the eighteenth century and its population rose from about 20,000 in 1700 to 64,000 in 1801. This expansion of the city is still clearly visible on the face of Bristol. Queen's Square was laid out, the Corn Exchange was erected and St. Thomas Church was built. Across the Froom there was new building around the Lord Mayor's Chapel, of which Orchard Street is the best surviving example; while to the north of the city St. James Square was formed. Later in the century, buildings began to push further out, Park Street was built and the Pinneys moved into residence in Great George Street. In the speculative building boom at the end of the century, Royal York Crescent was begun and Clifton gradually assumed the appearance of cultured elegance which is still to be seen. As the evidence of the successive maps of Bristol shows, it was in the eighteenth century that Bristol really broke out of the bondage of the mediaeval city and began to colonise the surrounding countryside. And not only in Bristol and Clifton but further afield at Stapleton. Frenchay and Mangotsfield, merchants' houses were built.

The dynamic for this expansion was provided by the growth of trade and by the increase in industrial activity in the city which was the concomitant of the commercial boom. For long Bristol had been an important seaport, most of its trade being carried on with markets near to hand in Ireland, France and the Iberian peninsular. During the eighteenth century Bristol merchants continued to engage in these trades but her pre-eminence in that century was based on new trades, on the growth of transatlantic commerce. From about the mid-seventeenth century, trade with Virginia, the Carolinas and the West Indies had begun to grow. The tonnage of shipping entering the port from the West Indies rose from 1,900 in 1670 to 5,200 in 1700: in 1659/60 14 ships came from Virginia, in 1699/1700 the number had increased to 29. And to the sugar and tobacco trades, as a result of the Act which permitted anyone to trade with Africa on payment of a ten per cent tax on imports and exports, was added in 1698 that most contentious of trades, the slave trade. The pattern was set for the following century. Rum, slaves, tobacco, and sugar were the main ingredients of Bristol's prosperity in the eighteenth century, with sugar the most important.

The best index of the growth of Bristol's trade in the course of this hundred years is provided by the figures of shipping using the port. In 1687 240 ships cleared from Bristol, thirty years later in 1717 the number had increased to 375 and in 1787 448 vessels left Bristol in a year. And the figures of shipping entering the port tell the same story of expansion: in 1700, 240 vessels arrived from ports outside Great Britain, whereas the total in 1787 amounted to 485. But these totals understate the growth of trade since the size of vessels rose during the century. In 1701 the average tonnage of ships owned by Bristol merchants was 105 tons, by the end of the century it was 144 tons. The tonnage of shipping using the port of Bristol therefore shows a greater increase than the number of ships. In 1700 the total tonnage of shipping entering the port was 19,878 tons, in 1791 it was 76,000 tons. Commerce was the mainspring of Bristol's activity. Here where "the very clergy talk of nothing but trade and how to turn the penny,"[1] commented a contemporary observer, "all are in a hurry, running up and down with cloudy looks and busy faces, loading, carrying and unloading goods and merchandizes of all sorts from place to place; for the trade of many nations is drawn hither by the industry and opulency of the people."[2]

Throughout the century, the most constant overseas trade was with Ireland. Vessels traded with all the Irish ports, the greatest number being concerned in the trade with Dublin and the ports of southern Ireland—Cork, Limerick, Waterford and Youghall. At the beginning of the century about 70 vessels, at the end between 100 and 120 were employed in the carriage of dairy produce, salted beef and pork, linen and yarn, leather, hides and timber to the city and in supplying Ireland with manufactured goods and colonial products. The ports of southern Ireland also served as victualling stations for Bristol ships in the oceanic trades. A number of the vessels which left Bristol for Africa, the West Indies or the mainland American colonies called at an Irish port for provisions, water and sometimes linen and yarn before they set out on their long transatlantic voyages. Although neither risky nor spectacular, the Irish trade provided a solid basis for Bristol's eighteenth-century commerce.

If the Irish entries were the most numerous, the West Indian were the most important. While some ships engaged in roundabout trades via Africa or North America, many vessels sailed directly between Bristol and the West Indies. In *A West-India Fortune*, Richard Pares gave an excellent picture of the Nevis trade (as well as of the Bristol sugar market). Though almost all the West Indian islands fell within Bristol's orbit, the trade with Jamaica dominated Bristol's West India trade. The outward cargo consisted of articles for the clothing and maintenance of white and negro, for the furnishing of their houses, the construction of their mills and distilleries and the cultivation of their lands and the manufacture of its produce. Molasses, rum, cotton, dyewoods and other goods found their place in the return cargoes but the most important item was sugar which was refined in the twenty or so sugar houses in Bristol. Bristol imported 12,330 hogsheads of sugar in 1770, 16,416 hogsheads in 1780, 18,700 hogsheads in 1790 and 19,381 hogsheads in 1801. In 1788 the goods sent to the West Indies were valued at between £250,000 and £300,000 and the return cargoes at about £800,000. At this date the trade employed between 70 and 80 ships of from 200 to 350 tons burthen and about 1,500 seamen.

Of the trade with the mainland of North America, the plantation trade was the most important. From Virginia, Bristol imported tobacco and iron, and from South Carolina, rice, skins and naval stores were obtained. The trade with the temperate colonies was smaller and of a more miscellaneous character. Bristol ships were also to be found in the Newfoundland fisheries. A few brought their cargoes of fish and train oil directly back to Bristol but most of them carried their cargoes to Spain, Portugal or other destinations in the Mediterranean. They returned to Bristol with oil, fruit and wine. In addition there was some direct trade from Bristol to the Mediterranean. Of chief importance was the cargoes of wool from Spain for the west of England cloth industry.

Bristol also carried on trade with more traditional markets in north-western Europe and the Baltic. Paper, steel, wine and brandy, linen and other fabrics came from Rotterdam, Dunkirk or Hamburg, while timber, naval stores and iron were the chief imports from Stockholm, Riga, St. Petersburg and Danzig. The exports to these places were very small and ships trading with these areas either went in ballast or carried a cargo of plantation goods.

Finally there was the part played by Bristol in the Atlantic migration of the eighteenth century. Both the plantation colonies and the West Indies had an acute shortage of labour at this time which was relieved through the agency of English merchants who transported slaves from the coast of Africa and free immigrants, indentured servants and convicts from England—the former a flood, the latter a trickle by comparison. For a brief period in the middle of the century when the Africa trade was regarded as "the principal and most considerable branch belonging to the city," Bristol dominated the trade. But as Bristol had wrested the leadership from London, so in its turn it had to yield to Liverpool. The number of Bristol ships in the trade declined from a peak of 52 in 1739 to between 22 and 33 a year in the third quarter of the century. In the last decade, Bristol's interest fell right away and only a total of 29 vessels sailed for Africa from the port in the decade between 1795 and 1804.

In the course of the century, there were no major changes in the direction of Bristol's trade but there was a shift in emphasis. The Virginia and Africa trades waxed and waned and fewer ships came to be employed in the Newfoundland fishery. Other trades, among them the Spanish trade, grew in size and all the time, the Irish trade continued to play a significant role in the life of the port. But though widely extended, as the following table shows, the dominant feature in Bristol's eighteenth century trade was its participation in West Indian commerce. The vessels engaging in that trade were larger and their cargoes more valuable than in any other trade.

DISTRIBUTION OF BRISTOL'S OVERSEAS TRADE, 1700-1801[3]

(a) Ships IN

	1700	1787	1801	
Africa	—	15	2	
Europe	79	179	93	
Ireland	68	161	116	
West Indies	55	71	70	
North America	38	44	85	
Others	—	30	22	(17 Channel Isles)
TOTAL	240	485	386	

(b) Ships OUT

	1717	1787	1801	
Africa	8	30	6	
Europe	86	120	38	
Ireland	118	139	109	
West Indies	76	73	73	
North America	73	68	63	
Others	14	18	25	(20 Channel Isles)
TOTAL	375	448	314	

During war, trade proved for some merchants less attractive than privateering, to which they turned in the hope of windfall gains

Early in the century at least, privateering was surrounded with an aura of glamour, as this song of the *Blandford* Privateer suggests:

Ye seaman who've a mind to go in pursuit of new adventure,
Repair on board the Blandford with Captain Stonehouse enter,
Who cruizing goes to meet his foes, such pastimes sure must please us,
We'll prizes make of all we take; this will to fortune raise us.

Most famous of the Bristol privateering voyages was that of Woodes Rogers who, with his two ships the *Duke* and *Duchess,* circumnavigated the world between 1708 and 1711. These were but two of the 123 Bristol vessels which sailed as privateers between 1702 and 1713. During the War of Austrian Succession 92 privateers put out from Bristol; during the Seven Years' War, 162; and during the War of American Independence 157 Bristol vessels carried letters of marque. But thereafter Bristol merchants seem to have lost their ardour for this hazardous undertaking and during the whole of the French Revolutionary and Napoleonic Wars only 63 Bristol ships sailed as privateers.

Apart from the vessels engaged in overseas trade, the Avon was thronged with market boats and coasting craft which, in the days before the railways and the improved roads, provided the main transport for goods from one part of Great Britain to another. In 1788, a contemporary estimated that "upon the coasting trade from the various ports of England Scotland and Wales, exclusive of the navigation of the Severn, about one thousand three hundred vessels of various burthen arrive annually." Towards the end of the century, the Bristol directories provided a timetable of the sailings of these vessels. The Severn trows for Bewdley, Bridgnorth, Frampton, Gloucester, Newnham, Stroud, Tewkesbury, Upton and Worcester left from the head of the Quay on every spring tide; the market boats to Caerleon, Chepstow and Newport arrived each Wednesday and departed each Thursday; the "constant coasters" sailed at given times for ports as far distant as London and Greenock as well as to all the ports within the Bristol Channel. Each had its special part of the quay, of which the Welsh Back is perhaps the most vivid reminder.

Supplementing the water-borne commerce was that carried by road. Although the improvements of the eighteenth century increased the ease of road communication, there was a considerable volume of road traffic before these changes took place. Bristol stood at the meeting point of five main roads. Neither the clay lands of the vale of Berkeley to the north nor the flats of Somerset to the south had roads which were passable in all weathers, but the three roads to the east, to Tetbury and Oxford, to Chippenham and London and to Bath and Warminster were in better condition. By these roads, Bristol merchants, Defoe tells us, maintain carriers just as the London tradesmen do, to all the principal countries and towns from Southampton in the south, even to the banks of the Trent north; and tho' they have no navigable river that way, yet they drive a very great trade through all these countries.[4]

Though dearer than water transport, road carriage was both safer and more regular. By 1750 there were ninety-four carriers plying to and from the city to Leeds, Nottingham and other distant towns and an even more extensive service was in existence by the end of the century. Standing at the centre of this web of land and water communications, Bristol was the commercial capital of the west. "If we consider domestic trade or inland Navigation," Campbell stated in 1774, "Bristol is without rival."[5] Her geographical position considered widely in this manner as a regional centre was the second source of Bristol's importance.

By land and river and sea, the produce of its hinterland was brought to Bristol which served several functions. First of all, it was the main market for agricultural produce. Of the grain crops, wheat came chiefly from the Midlands, barley from west Wales and Gloucestershire and oats from Cardigan and Carmarthen. Dairy produce and meat came chiefly from South Wales while regular supplies of vegetables were brought from the Vale of Evesham and the vale of Glamorgan. Bristol was also a market for industrial raw materials. Timber came from the Forest of Dean for shipbuilding, teazles from Somerset for the textile trades, wool from Milford or Cardiff for the Cotswold woollen industry, and tin from Cornwall for the tinplate works in South Wales or the Midlands. For these commodities, Bristol served as a distribution point. Other cargoes of raw materials were brought to Bristol to supply the needs of local industries, which also used materials brought from overseas. Even at the end of the eighteenth century, Bristol was "not more a commercial than a manufacturing town."[6]

Among its industries, sugar refining, based on an imported raw material, kept fifteen or sixteen sugar houses generally at work and a distilling industry had grown up alongside them, which produced spirits both for export and for sale at home. There were eleven glassworks in the city by the end of the century. They made glass bottles in which beer, cider, perry, wine and Hotwell water were sold and they also produced large quantities of window glass which they supplied to the west of England, to south Wales and to America and Ireland. Hard white soap, made in Bristol, was held by contemporaries to be superior to any made in England. The copper and brass works at Baptist Mills made wire and ornaments for the Guinea trade, copper sheets for sheathing ships and copper pans for sugar making. Bricks and tiles, made locally, were, it is said, the chief ballast of all the West India ships. In St. Phillip's there were iron foundries for casting all kinds of iron utensils and cannon as well as a leadworks which produced sheets and pipes.

Along the banks of the Avon there were some yards and slips used for shipbuilding and the repair of vessels. James Martin Hilhouse (founder of the firm now known as Charles Hill & Son) had his yard towards Hotwells; Sydenham Teast and William Blannin built ships at Wapping (Bristol); and Richard Tombs had his yard on Dean's Marsh. In addition there were a number of other boat builders. No returns of shipbuilding in the port exist until the end of the century but from one which survives we know that between 1787 and 1800, 176 vessels with a total tonnage of 22,644 tons were built. Most of them were small but some large vessels were also launched, including one of 458 tons in 1790; of 403 tons in 1794; of 402 tons in 1799; and of 464 tons in 1800. In addition fourteen vessels were built for the Royal Navy in these years. By 1804 there were 123 shipwrights employed in the trade there. Clearly Bristol was a shipbuilding centre of some importance at this time.

Amongst the other industries which were carried on in the city were woollen cloth, silk, lace, sailcloth, earthenware and tobacco. Many of these manufactures benefited from the cheapness of coal and other fuels which were available locally. Some of these industries used imported raw materials but all contributed to Bristol's outward trade, whether overseas, coastwise or by land through the west of England and the south-west Midlands.

It was the combination of participation in a lucrative import trade in tobacco, sugar, rum and other plantation products and in an export trade based on local industries and the products of her hinterland which made Bristol in the early eighteenth century, as Defoe described her, "the greatest, the richest, and the best port of trade in Great Britain, London only excepted." And he went on to add:

The merchants of this city not only have the greatest trade, but they trade with a more entire independency upon London than any other town in Britain. And 'tis evident in this particular, (viz.) That whatsoever exportations they make to any part of the world, they are able to bring the full returns back to their own port, and can dispose of it there.

This is not the case in any other port in England.

Thus Bristol's prosperity depended not only on her oceanic commerce, it also derived from her position as "the metropolis of the west."

But Bristol's prosperity depended rather on her imports than her exports, on the tobacco, sugar and rum brought from beyond the seas. With the growth of Britain's extra-European trade, her commerce had flourished. By the end of the eighteenth century, however, although her merchants carried on transactions widely across the seas, her trade had become dangerously concentrated on the West Indies. As her commerce grew less rapidly than that of her rivals, by 1800 she had already lost her position as the leading outport. Consequently Bristol entered the nineteenth century with less confidence than she had entered the eighteenth.

II—THE OPERATION OF THE PORT

From this discussion of the nature and direction of Bristol's trade in the eighteenth century, we can now turn to consider how the port operated. Let us follow the passage of a ship coming from overseas to the port of Bristol. Sailing up the Bristol Channel, she would probably pick up a pilot off Lundy or Ilfracombe, though occasionally some of these pilots went into the English Channel to Penzance, or into St. George's Channel and over to Ireland. There was keen rivalry to board vessels and sometimes the pilots demanded exorbitant sums as fees. Occasionally vessels ran aground while under the charge of the pilot. To deal with such matters, the Society of Merchant Venturers ordained that pilots should board vessels only when invited to do so by the master. Further, the Society laid down a scale of charges and decreed that complaints of misconduct should be examined by the haven master, one of the port officials appointed by the Society. In 1782 he reduced the charges claimed by William Capper for the pilotage of the brig *Two Friends,* from £11 1s. 5½d. to £8 19s. 6½d. since William Capper was "an idle man and frequently in liquor." The following year the Society considered a complaint against John Dickens, pilot, "for running on shore below Minehead a Spanish vessel, *San Joseph y Animas,* which became a loss occasioned by his conduct as pilot." Found guilty, Dickens was suspended from his office as pilot. Not till seven years later was he reinstated.

Most of the pilots lived, as they still do, at Pill, then known as Crockerne Pill, a village on the Somerset bank of the Avon about a mile from its mouth. Candidates for the office were examined by the haven master who reported to the Society of Merchant Venturers. In turn, the Society made its recommendations to the Common Council of the city, which made the appointment. Like other official posts, the appointments came up for formal renewal each year. When the pilots were too old for work they were given a superannuation allowance by the Council. In the course of the eighteenth century, the number of pilots increased. This provides a rather crude index of the expansion of the trade of the port. In 1748 there were 14 pilots, in 1757 24, in 1770 34, and in 1784 45.

A landmark on a vessel's passage up the Bristol Channel was Flat Holme, where a lighthouse was built in 1737. Seventy feet high and visible for 7 leagues, the lighthouse remained in private

View from Durdham Down, 1787, by Nicholas Pocock. This shows a vessel being towed up the Avon.

Plate 2

City Art Gallery, Bristol

St. Vincent's Rock and the Hotwells, c.1756, by Thomas Smith.

hands until it was taken over by Trinity House in 1823. Passing
the island brought the vessel within the limits of the port of Bristol
which in 1724 were defined as extending from

the westernmost parts of the Channell eastwards to Aust in the
county of Gloucester and from the said Holmes southwarde
athwart the Channell to a place called Uphill which is included
and from thence along the coast of shoar eastwards in the
county to Gloucester hath been for many years past a creek
place called Holes Mouth in King Road up the river Avon to the
said city of Bristoll, together with the severall pills lying upon
the said river. And we doe further certifye that a place called
Bechesley scituate on the north side of the river Severne in the
country of Gloucester hath been for many years past a creek
and belonging to the said port of Bristoll and we doe conceive
the same fitt to be continued.

These limits remained in force until they were more clearly
defined by the Bristol Channel Pilotage Act (47 George III c. 33)
of 1807.

On the way up the Channel the vessel may have sighted the
revenue cutter on patrol but she came under direct customs control
if she dropped anchor in the sheltered waters of Kingroad to await
a favourable tide to carry her up the Avon. There she would be
boarded by one of the 45 tidewaiters of the customs service who
would remain on board till she came to the quay. His job was to
prevent goods being smuggled ashore and to check the goods which
were unloaded by some of the larger ships into lighters which
carried them up the Avon to Bristol. Kingroad, the roadstead off
Portishead, was one of the two roadsteads used by shipping to and
from the port of Bristol. Here there was room for about 30 vessels
to anchor in safety, "the ground being so good that it very rarely
happens in the severest gales, that a ship drags her anchor." As
well as incoming ships, vessels outward bound waited here for
a wind or for the purpose of taking their crews and passengers on
board.

The other anchorage was Hungroad about three miles from
Kingroad which a vessel would reach after entering the Avon and
passing Crockerne Pill. Here almost all the timber ships from the
Baltic discharged, sending their cargoes to Bristol in rafts or in
lighters. Here, too, some vessels careened and here vessels waited
for favourable tides. For the security of vessels lying there, mooring
rings were provided. In 1728, for example, £600 was spent on
moorings for 14 ships. Periodically, too, work had to be carried
out to prevent the road-stead silting up. In 1745 when "an engine"
was employed, almost £300 was spent in removing shoals.

Not till a licence was obtained from the haven master were ships
permitted to move up the serpentine course of the Avon and then

only when the tide was high enough. Indication of this was given by a post set in the river at Hungroad. When this post was covered, vessels could begin their passage up the Avon. On its way a vessel passed the dock at Sea Mills. Encouraged by similar attempts in the Thames at Rotherhithe in 1696 and at Liverpool in 1709, Joshua Franklyn and a group of Bristol merchants had constructed the third wet dock in the kingdom at a cost of approximately £9,600 between 1712 and 1717. Although the dock provided a safe anchorage, it never found favour with the majority of Bristol merchants who considered it to be too far from the city. It was therefore little used save as a base for privateers during the War of Austrian Succession (1739-48) and the Seven Years' War (1759-63) and by a short-lived whaling enterprise organised by some Bristol merchants in the 1750s. Ships were sent out each year from 1749 to 1758 when the trade appears to have ceased. No further use was found for the dock which in 1779 was reported as being "utterly abandoned".

Because of the swiftness of the current, the crookedness of the river and the fitfulness of the wind through the Avon Gorge, sails were rarely of any use, so most ocean-going vessels were assisted in their passage by towboats (see Plate 2). Small vessels often needed only one boat, but larger ones required eight or ten boats each, with from one hundred to one hundred and fifty men. Some idea of the scale of charges is given by the following account, in this case of a vessel passing down the Avon.

Ship *Blaze Castle.*

	To Robert Parkhouse, pilot	Dr.		
1773		£	s.	d.
March 11th	From Bristol to Pill 9 boats and 29 men	5	2	6
	From Pill to Kingroad 6 boats and 14 men	4	3	0
	To my pilotage from Bristol to Kingroad		15	0
	To an assisting pilot		5	0
	To 1 boat and 10 men new berthing the do		11	6
	To the pilot staying on board 2 days		6	0
	To 1 boat and 4 men rowing the captain on board	5		6
	Total	11	8	6

In the course of the eighteenth century the cost of pilotage rose; in 1714 the fee for a vessel of 200 tons was 12s.; in 1800 it was 20s.

Soon after passing Sea Mills, a vessel entered the narrow gorge at St. Vincent's Rock which extends for two miles to Hotwells. Here vessels sometimes became stranded. After Hotwells, the valley widens considerably at Rownham, where on the eastern bank William Champion in 1765 built a wet dock, able to accommodate "thirty-six sail of the largest ships which frequent the port." Alongside were two graving docks suitable for shipbuilding. The cost of construction outstripped Champion's resources and he was forced to offer the docks for sale in 1770 when they were purchased by the Society of Merchant Venturers and became known as the Merchants Docks. Though much nearer to the centre of the city than the Sea Mill Docks, merchants were still reluctant to use them. To secure some business for their dock, the Society in 1776 sponsored an Act of Parliament "to remove the danger of fire amongst the ships in the port of Bristol". This prohibited the landing of timber, tar, etc. except at the Merchants Dock where the Society was empowered to erect warehouses for the purpose. The dock was declared a "lawful key for the landing of all sorts and kinds of timber including mahogany, planks and boards, deals and stones, tar, pitch, rosin and turpentine in whatever quantities the same shall from time to time be imported". The incendiary activities of Jack the Painter who set fire to ships and warehouses in Bristol in 1777 "frightened the people out of their senses" and underlined the need for fire precautions. But the Act proved difficult to enforce and attempts were made to evade it. In 1779 Paul Farr drew the attention of the Society to the fact that a ship belonging to Deidrich Meyerhoff laden with timber had moored at the Quay. Farr added "unless such ships as these are compelled to land their cargoes at the Dock we might as well have been without the Act at all". When approached, Meyerhoff agreed to move his ship to the dock. But the timber merchants continued to be dissatisfied with the position and in 1787/8 brought the case of the *Roehampton*, a vessel which had unloaded at the dock, before the Society. They alleged that timber fetched a lower price at the Dock—staves 10s. per 1,000 less and timber 2d. per foot—and that in consequence the vessel made a loss of £77 because it landed its cargo there instead of a profit of £22 10s. if the timber and staves had been landed at the Quay, "a mortifying experience for the proprietors".

The Society of Merchant Venturers found the dock a no more profitable possession than did Champion. Extensions carried out under the 1776 Act were expensive and revenue fell short of expectations. In consequence, too little was done to keep the dock in good order. In 1789 Robert Claxton wrote to the Master of the Society complaining of "the shameful state of the floating dock . . . The Society," he said, "cannot expect to be paid for vessels lying afloat if they are really lying in mud". The Merchants Dock proved of less value to the port of Bristol than its sponsor hoped.

A vessel carrying neither naval stores nor timber, continued past the Merchants Dock to what Shiercliff writing in 1793, with perhaps excessive local patriotism, called "one of the finest mercantile havens in Europe". Then as now, ships came right into the heart of the city. This sight invariably aroused comment from visitors to Bristol. Thus Alexander Pope wrote in 1739:

> . . . in the middle of the street, as far as you can see, hundreds of ships, their masts as thick as they can stand by one another, which is the oddest and most surprising sight imaginable. This street is fuller of them than the Thames from London Bridge to Deptford, and at certain times only, the water rises to carry them out; so that at other times, a long street, full of ships in the middle, and houses on both sides, looks like a dream.[10]

A ship was directed where to berth by the haven master, the chief port official, who was responsible for the "superintendence of the port". His duties included the control of the pilots, the enforcement of fire regulations, the issuing of licences to ships over 60 tons to permit them to come up to the quays and, as ballast master, the control of ballast. Each year he accompanied the committee of the Society of Merchant Venturers to inspect the port and the river. Sunken vessels, the attempts of merchants to extend their private wharfs, and the detritus of industrial enterprises (lime kilns, brickyards, glass houses, quarries and lead-works) all gave rise to complaints about the safety of navigation. In 1797, for example, the Merchants sent a petition to the city Council complaining that:

> There are considerable breaches in the banks of the river Avon on the south-east side, the lowest breach being nearly opposite the floating dock, the next breach nearly opposite the Limekiln Dock and the third breach considerably below the Glasshouse.

They added "That the navigation of the river Avon is materially affected by such breaches". The haven master, together with the inspector of nuisances and the quay scavenger, had a constant battle to maintain the port facilities.

To assist the haven master, there were two other officials: the water bailiff, responsible for the regulation and management of shipping on Bristol Back, Redcliff Back and the banks of the Avon, and the quay warden who carried out the same functions on the Quay, St. Augustine's Back and, towards the end of the century, the new quay at Clifton. They levied a toll of 5s. on ships over 100 tons and 2s. 6d. on ships under 100 tons, and this formed part of the income of the Society of Merchants.

The ships which unloaded at the quays were afloat when the tide was high but they rested on the mud bed of the rivers when the tide ebbed. Large ships were not completely water-borne except at high water for about six days every fortnight. The great tidal range of 45 feet at Bristol severely restricted the periods during which ships could come up to the quays. As a contemporary report stated: "In every alternate week no ship of burthen can

PLAN OF PROPOSED PC

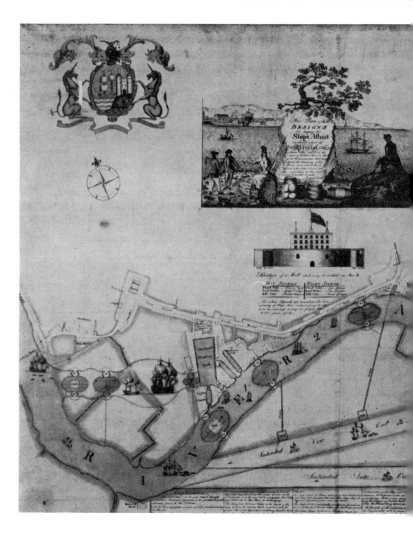

The plan of two designs for keeping the ships afloat in the harbour of Bristol
(without being subject to the danger of freshes, frost and other great inconveniences that might attend the damning of the rivers Avon and Froom) is offered
to his'fellow citizens for their consideration by their most obedient and humble
servant
Richard Tombs Cannons Marsh Dock Yard April, 1792

Plate 4   143

IPROVEMENT SCHEME 1792

Apart from showing how Mr. Tombs proposed to improve the harbour of Bristol, this plan also shows in detail many features of the eighteenth-century port. In particular, the position of the various docks, the rope walks and the position of the cranes can be seen. The drawing of the vessels show them being towed by towboats.

Bristol Harbour, showing the Cathedral, 1786, by Nicholas Pocock.

Plate 5   145

Broad Quay, Bristol, early eighteenth century, attributed to Peter Monamy.

come up to, or go from Bristol, but those inward bound are obliged
to remain either in Kingroad or Hungroad from the time of their
arrival till the period of the spring tides and the outward bound
at the Quay till the like opportunity. The floodtide in Kingroad runs
about five hours, at Hungroad about four and a half, and at Bristol
only three and three quarter hours". Despite these limitations,
"ships of the greatest burthen, fully laden" were able to come up to
Bristol. And certainly merchants preferred ships to come right into
the port because they claimed goods were liable to be pilfered
from lighters and that they got a poorer price if they unloaded
cargo elsewhere.

Once the ship had come to the wharf, unloading could begin.
By the mid-eighteenth century, most of the wharfs were equipped
with cranes for this purpose. In 1774, it was reported that there
were 14 cranes available, including "a building, erected on fourteen
pillars of cast iron, called the Great Crane . . . a curious piece of
mechanism, constructed by the ingenious Mr. Padmore". (Plate 7)
Most of the cranes were erected by the Society of Merchants or by
their lessees but a few were owned by the city. The craneowners
paid the Society or the Common Council for their leases and
collected the cranage dues which they paid over to the Society after
deducting their commission. From 1773 to 1805, the new receipts
of the cranage averaged £1,123 a year, a valuable source of revenue
for the Society.

The unloading of the vessels was checked by the "hungry and
nimble-handed harpies at the Custom House" to use a contemporary description. The principal offices of Customer, Controller
and Collector provided useful sinecures for supporters of the
Government. The Royal Librarian, for instance, became Controller for Bristol in 1782. These offices were carried out by
deputies. In addition there was a large staff at the Custom House,
newly built in Queen's Square in 1711. Of these the weigher was
responsible for weighing all goods on which duty was levied
by weight while the gauger assessed the contents of irregularly-
shaped containers taxed by volume. Loading and unloading was
checked by the landwaiters, who had huts by the cranes The
details of inward and outward cargoes were entered by clerks in
large parchment volumes, known as the port books, which still
survive in an incomplete series to 1784. Each quarter a summary
of the customs receipts of the port was made and each year the
port books for foreign and coastwise trade were sent to London to
the Receiver of the Customs.

The main business of the customs officials was the administration
of the customs system—the recording of imports and exports, the
collection of duties and the payment of drawbacks. These last
were payments which were made on imported goods which had paid

a duty when they were re-exported—to-day the use of bonded warehouses has reduced the importance of drawbacks. The revenue
system was extremely complicated. It was based on the book of
rates of 1660 but these rates were considerably amended and altered
by later enactments. The high rates of duty encouraged evasion
by fraudulent statements or by smuggling and the complexity of
the system gave rise to disputes between merchants and customs
officials. Many of these were about the classification of goods.
In 1739, for example, some merchants protested that soap which
had been brought from Leghorn had been taxed as French soap
and not as Italian soap. It must have required considerable
expertise to distinguish Italian from French soap, and in this
particular case, the situation was complicated because the vessel
did not come straight from Leghorn to Bristol but called in at a
French port on the way. Perhaps the customs officials were right
after all—or perhaps the merchants had carelessly omitted to make
the right financial arrangement with the customs officials. Another
frequent cause of disagreement was about particular provisions
which were in force for a fixed period. On each occasion there
were complaints from merchants that because of some eventuality or
other they had not been able to load or unload their cargoes within
the stated time.

With the coasting trade the object was not the direct collection
of customs dues—for ordinarily no such dues were collected—but
the prevention of fraud and evasion in the payment of customs for
goods exported to or imported from foreign countries. The government wanted to ensure that goods in coastal craft were in fact
carried coastwise: the shipper that imported goods, on which he had
already paid duty, should not be chargeable a second time when
he carried coastwise. The main device was the issue of cocquets
in return for a bond given by the shipper which was cancelled
when a certificate that the goods had been landed at an English
port was produced. In 1729 it was decided that cargoes from
Cardiff and Newport to Bristol did not require cocquets and bonds
because the vessels did not have to go into the open sea but trade
to other ports remained under this control for most of the eighteenth
century. Coastwise cargoes, like imports and exports, were
entered in the port books.

In addition to their primary function of collecting revenue, the
customs officials had to carry out various other duties. In particular they were responsible for administering the provisions of the
Navigation Laws. The regulations that the "enumerated commodities," which included sugar, tobacco and dyewoods, should not
be shipped directly from the colonies to a foreign port were
required to be enforced. The customs officers had also to check
that ships in the colonial trade were either British or plantation-

built and that three-fourths of their crews were British. They had also to see that vessels in the Newfoundland trade carried a proportion of "green" seamen since this fishery was expected to serve as a nursery for seamen. Details relating to the tonnage, place of construction and ownership of British and colonial shipping had to be recorded by the customs. Further, these officials were responsible for the enforcement of regulations relating to quarantine (vessels from the Mediterranean were particularly involved) and for seeing that embargoes on the movement of ships—usually imposed to secure men for the navy—were obeyed.

Inevitably the custom officers were criticised, particularly because the system of deputies did not make for efficient administration and effective control. In 1718 it was alleged by former officers who had been dismissed that the "customs revenues (at Bristol) had been prejudiced and diminished by corruption, avarice and unskilfulness". But on examination it was reported that "though Bristol is the greatest port of business next to London, yet by their diligence, care and example, a strict discipline is preserved in that port, the books and accounts regularly kept and returned, the King's money remitted and the merchants' bonds paid from time to time as they fall due". There were several more general complaints levelled at the Customs: that ships were allowed to unload at private wharves instead of at the legal quays, that the official hours of daily business were too short, and that the customs fees should be ·abolished. But only the complaint about hours eventually received favourable consideration.

When the goods were unloaded from the ships or lighters, they were usually taken to the merchants' own stores, or to one of the city warehouses, though sometimes they were left on the quayside to become an obstruction and a cause of complaint. The principal warehouse was the Back Hall, owned by the Corporation. Its management proved troublesome early in the century when a manager ran the hall for the Corporation and it was then decided to farm out the lease. Rates were laid down for storing goods in the cellars and lofts of the building. In addition, in the course of the century, sheds were erected on the quays for the storage of goods,. At the end of the century ten warehouses, financed by a tontine,[11] were erected at the head of the Quay.

The loading and unloading of ships and the carriage of goods about the city was done by the porters who had become incorporated as a city company in 1671. As with the pilots, while the Common Council was ultimately responsible for the control of the porters, it referred many of the matters concerning them to the Society of Merchants who were more immediately concerned. They helped to draw up the disciplinary code and the schedule of wages and they dealt with various other problems which arose. In 1740—a war year—the porters petitioned against "the putting up of more cranes on the key of this city" because of the poverty of the company and "the great decay of commerce and navigation". They alleged that "by putting up of cranes above 60 poor families would be fatally ruined".

In addition to the cranage and pilotage dues already discussed, which were payments for particular services, every vessel using the port had to pay dues. On the ship itself anchorage and moorage charges were paid to the Society of Merchants, and mayor's dues were paid to the city. These fell particularly heavily on ships which made frequent short voyages. On the merchandise carried in the ships, the Society of Merchant Venturers levied wharfage dues and the Common Council town dues. The system was complicated and its origins obscure, but its incidence can be illustrated from the account book of the snow *Africa*, a vessel of 100 tons. The total charges paid by that vessel in 1775 were:

	£	s.	d.
Reporting at the Custom House		2	6
Milford light, 1d. per ton; Holmes light 1½d. per ton; Bridge tax, 2½d. per ton.	2	1	8
Anchorage and moorage etc.		18	4
Mayor's dues and key warden's dues	2	5	0
Cranage		4	4
Pilotage	6	13	1
Total	£12	6	11

Thus shipping paid a contribution towards the provision of lighthouses and the construction of the new Bristol Bridge, erected between 1764 and 1768, as well as toward the operation of the port.

Inevitably with this complicated system of dues, there were attempts at evasion. One such is recorded in the accounts of the mayor's dues for 1792. The entry reads:

Daniel Beeby of Dumfries for voyage 1 May 1791 when Beeby imposed on Isaac Matthews, the water bailiff, by producing a false register for 59 tons though the register at our Custom House stated 63 tons. Made pay 40s. this 19 April 1792.

Apart from attempts to avoid payment, there were more straightforward attempts to question the legality of the various levies. At one time or another in the course of the eighteenth century, wharfage, cranage, the mayor's dues and the town dues were all challenged. Unfortunately we know too little of the reasons which

View of Welsh Back and St. Mary Redcliff, 1787, by Nicholas Pocock.

Plate 7   151

The Great Crane.

prompted the particular actions. In 1735 a number of the leading merchants refused to pay the mayor's dues, claiming these dues were not an ancient and laudable custom but a recent imposition. Thereupon the mayor, Lionel Lyde, sued one of the defaulters, William Hart & Co. and secured a judgment which upheld the legality of the dues. But this did not settle the issue and the right to levy these dues was challenged, again unsuccessfully, in 1788 in the case of Edgar v. Lewis. Despite these two defeats, a third attempt to test the right to levy these dues was made in the early nineteenth century. And, on this occasion a reduction was achieved.

The challenge to the other three dues was made in the 1770s. Henry Cruger, John Mallard and William Miles contested the town dues, Henry Cruger and William Miles the wharfage dues and William Miles endeavoured to get the cranage rates lowered. Only the first action was taken to court. Cruger alleged that "the town dues had within fifty years advanced more than treble and that if continued at the present level must put a stop to the trade of the town". It may be that he was speaking not of the town dues alone but of all the dues levied in the port. The case was a protracted piece of litigation in the course of which John Mallard became bankrupt while Henry Cruger, now M.P. and alderman, entered no defence. Eventually in 1787 judgment was given in favour of the city which then began slowly to collect the arrears of dues. On this broad issue of the incidence of the dues, the city was divided, the opposition stating that "the dues are trifling in comparison with the profits of the trade and never prevented any ship coming to the port".

There is nothing unusual in a port financing its government in this way. Before the existence of the modern rating system, it was the obvious solution. But Bristol in the eighteenth century seems to have evolved a more burdensome system than other ports. There has been no adequate discussion of the problem of port charges in terms of income and expenditure, so it is difficult to assess fairly contemporary allegations about them. The available evidence seems to suggest that the port charges at Bristol were higher than in some other ports. And it therefore seems fair to conclude that to the other factors making for the relative decline of the port must be added the heaviness of the port charges. Certainly the apparent arbitrariness of the dues aroused criticism.

Therefore be it enacted, to end all dispute
About Town or Mayor's Dues, that whene'er it shall suit
Our sage corporation in Council to sit,
They may manage the Town dues as they shall think fit.

III—PORT IMPROVEMENT

The growth of Bristol's trade led to congestion in the port and from the end of the seventeenth century there was pressure for port improvement. From 1661 this was the responsibility of the Society of Merchant Venturers who leased the quays from the City.. In 1690 the lease had been renewed for a period of eighty years on condition that the Society extended the quay wall along the Frome and erected more cranes. Some of this work had been carried out by 1712 when the Society of Merchants were granted a renewal of the lease until 1791 in return for surrendering, to facilitate street improvements, the Rope Walk which they owned. Further alterations were then carried out. .The Great Tower, which had originally been erected for the defence of the city and which had for a long time been a considerable obstruction on Broad Quay was purchased and demolished in 1720 and separate accommodation was provided for particular trades by 1725. A wharf was built on Welsh Back for "the landing of corn and other goods out of market boats and other vessels" and a separate quay was built on St. Augustine's Back for timber and naval stores. On his visit to the city in 1739, Alexander Pope noted that further construction had been carried out and that "the quay went half way round Queen Square".

Noteworthy as such development was, it lagged behind the demand for accommodation. In periods of rapidly growing trade, there was usually a shortage of space at the quays. In December 1755, a committee of the Common Council reported that "no human prudence could prevent the growing danger to ships without provision were made for further room, the want whereof doth greatly endanger the safety of the ships, and by which they daily sustain considerable damage". The fall in trade during the Seven Years' War temporarily removed the pressure and the Society of Merchants were reluctant to carry out further improvements with such a relatively short period of their lease to run. Their lease was accordingly renewed in 1764 on condition that the Society extended the quay on the east bank of the Froom and on the north bank of the Avon to Welsh Back and built a new quay at the Grove and on St. Augustine's Back on the west bank of the Froom. In the following years these works were built, so that Shiercliff could report in 1793 that accommodation at the quays

> is upwards of a mile in extent, reaching from St. Gile's Bridge to Bristol Bridge and is all the way embanked by a firm wall coped with large hewn stone, from which to the front buildings is such a considerable breadth, without interruption, as to make it one continued wharf. It goes under several distinct names, the part of it from Bristol Bridge to the turn of the river opposite Redcliff Parade is called The Back; and

The Port of Bristol

from hence following the course of the river downward is
called the Grove . . . from hence to the mouth of the river
Froom is called the Gibb."[12]
Finally along the bank of the Froom itself was the Broad Quay.

But even this extensive building programme did not completely
solve the problem of accommodation because of the long period
which some ships required for loading and unloading. Periodically
the Court of Quarter Sessions attempted to deal with this problem
and in 1770 laid down that "all ships laden with tobacco should
discharge their cargoes in forty working days: all vessels from
other foreign parts in 21 working days and all vessels bound
for foreign parts should take in their loading in eighty working
days". Thus anything from seventeen to twenty weeks was allowed
between arrival and departure. Nearly twenty years later there
were complaints that the quays were occupied by ships awaiting
sale, thus preventing their use for legitimate trade.

It may be that a quicker turn-round of ships would have helped
reduce the congestion in the port but this was only part of the
problem which faced shipping using the port of Bristol. As the
size of vessels in overseas trade rose it came to be recognised that
the great tidal range of the Avon was a constant threat to the safety
of large heavily laden vessels and that the harbour formed an
inadequate anchorage. In the preamble to the Dock Act of 1803
the situation was well-described:

Ships and vessels lying at the quays are by the reflux of the
tide left dry twice in every twenty-four hours, which prevents
many foreign vessels and others of a sharp construction from
frequenting the port.

From about the middle of the eighteenth century some interest
was shown in remedying this situation. In February 1758 the city
Council advertised "for persons to survey the rivers Avon and
Froom, and consider of proper measures for making some convenient part thereof into a wet dock". But no action followed. Six
years later, in the post-war boom, a meeting of merchants at the
Guildhall on 25 July 1764 resolved to raise £34,000 to carry out
a scheme for keeping the ships in the harbour afloat. But many
merchants were not enthusiastic and only about £10,000 was
obtained. This initiative was not without effect, however, for the
Society of Merchants and the city Council thereupon agreed to
commission a report on the practicability of making "the quays
and part of the Avon a wet dock". John Smeaton was then
engaged to produce a plan. His proposal was the comparatively
simple one of building a dam across the Froom and making that
part of the harbour a dry dock. Meantime William Champion
had been building his dock. As a result of this experience he put
forward a more far-reaching proposal, published in 1767, of

constructing lock gates across the Avon below its confluence with
the Froom thus making the whole of the port a "floating harbour".
But the estimated cost of these schemes appeared so great—
Smeaton's was to cost £25,000 and Champion's between £30,000
and £37,000—that the expense was sufficient to quash the enter-
prizes. Moreover, those opposing port improvement employed
an engineer, W. C. Mylne, to discredit Champion's scheme. Mylne
reported that £60,000 "would scarcely suffice to carry out the
design". Other alternatives were discussed in a brief flurry of
controversy in the local paper, *Felix Farley's Bristol Journal*, but
the division of opinion amongst the merchants and other interested
parties was sufficient to secure inaction.

No further proposals were made for twenty years. The Society
of Merchant Venturers found its attentions—and its finances—
absorbed by the problems which followed the purchase of Champion's Dock on the right bank of the Avon near Rownham in
1770 for £1,420 and the securing of the Act in 1776 "to remove the
danger of fire amongst the ships in the port of Bristol" in an attempt
to force merchants to use the dock more. Then the outbreak of the
War of American Independence led to a reduction of trade and to
a preoccupation with other matters. The upsurge of English foreign
trade after 1785 led to a general interest in the extension of dock
accommodation in which Bristol shared. At a meeting of the
Society of Merchants in 1787, William Miles, a leading merchant,
revived the question of port improvement. Accordingly fresh
plans were invited and between 1787 and 1790 reports were made
by three engineers, Joseph Nickalls, William Jessop and John
Smeaton again. These were considered by the Society of Merchants
in 1791. By that date the Merchants had recognised:

> That the harbour is by nature inferior to that of many
> British ports, and that local shipowners are not on an equal
> footing with those of other ports, either as regards security of
> ships whilst in port, or as to ease and expedition in discharging
> and loading. That from the same cause the ships of strangers
> and the charters of such ships are under similar inconveniences.
> That the losses sustained by these causes amount to a very
> large sum annually.

Their resolution went on to suggest that the continued prosperity
of the port was linked with the question of improvement, and at
the same time they endeavoured to meet the criticisms of the
opponents of such schemes. They stated:

> That the existing great inconveniences may be remedied
> without impediment to trade, or injury to health or property by
> erecting a dam across the Avon at the Red Cliff, and by
> cutting a canal, with locks and sluices, in Rownham Meads,
> agreeably to the plans of Mr. Smeaton and Mr. Jessop, and by

adopting such of Mr. Nickall's provisions as shall be deemed expedient.

They also tried to allay fears about the cost of the scheme, stating:

There is every reason to believe that the whole expense of executing this improvement, and of indemnifying those whose property may be injured, will not be greater than the advantages acquired by it will much more than counterbalance . . . and that such adequate revenue will be produced by the proposed bridge over the dam, and by a tax on shipping not exceeding the dock rates paid at Liverpool, calculating only on the present trade of the port which the improvement will doubtless considerably increase .

This resolution of the Society of Merchants was referred by the Common Council to a committee which endorsed the proposals in December 1791. In the following years, between 1791 and 1793, other plans were put forward, including those of Richard Tombs, the Bristol shipwright (see Plate 4) and William Milton, Vicar of Temple Church, Bristol, but the "spirit of unambitious caution" continued to animate discussions of port improvement in Bristol. With trade booming, the opposition became more vocal but although more vessels suffered damage in the harbour nothing was done. Eventually in September 1793 the Society of Merchants proposed that an Act for the improvement of the port should be promoted in the next session of Parliament. The Society agreed to "contribute to so desirable an object to the utmost of its ability should the corporation be inclined to co-operate" and it proposed that work should be carried out by commissioners or trustees for the general good and not for private profit. Jessop then made another report but the necessary legislation was not secured and again war intervened. Politics, parsimony, lethargy and conservatism defeated all attempts to improve the port of Bristol in the later eighteenth century.

With the French Revolutionary War came a decline in trade which underlined the need for improvement. Bristol merchants had virtually withdrawn from the African trade, and now her West Indian commerce showed signs of decline. At the beginning of the new century, *Felix Farley's Bristol Journal* recorded on 29 March 1800 that "several cargoes of West Indian and American produce have recently been imported into this city from Liverpool." The need for action was urgent. In 1800, William Miles again persuaded the Society of Merchant Venturers to confer with the Common Council. Concurrently between July and November 1800 three improvement schemes were put forward by James Palmer, J.T., and J. A. Wright. But still the city Council procrastinated and only a further enquiry from the Society of Merchant Venturers

about "the scheme of damming the river" in July 1801 stirred it
into activity. William Jessop, who had made an earlier proposal
in 1788, was asked to report on the various schemes for the improvement of the harbour. He found all the plans so far put
forward unsatisfactory and submitted a new proposal of his own for
a basin at Canon's Marsh. But as the quays at the Grove and the
Back were not included in this plan, it was rejected. Jessop was
thereupon asked to submit a further scheme which should include
all the quays within the harbour. This new plan, based substantially on a plan drawn up by William Milton in 1791, which
Jessop put forward in 1802, provided for the creation of a Floating
Harbour and the digging of a new course or "New Cut" for the
Avon. This was substantially on the lines which were subsequently
followed and its appearance is familiar to Bristolians today.
Jessop's plan was quickly accepted by the Merchant Venturers on
25 August 1802 when they resolved to support the application to
parliament for a bill to authorise the improvement of the harbour.
Both the nature of the proposals and the cost of the scheme,
estimated at £300,000, aroused determined opposition throughout
the city. But the declining trade of the port lent a feeling of
urgency to the proceedings which had been absent when previous
proposals had been considered. A Dock Company was founded
in 1802 and a Dock Act (43 Geo. III c. 140) authorising the im-
plementation of Jessop's scheme was secured in the following
year. But still opposition continued. A number of leading merchants, including Bailey, Bright, Gibbs, King, Protheroe and
Pinney, attacked the Dock Bill when it was considered in Parliament, and John Pinney continued his opposition after the passage
of the Act. In 1807 he fiercely condemned the proposal of the
Dock Company in face of rising costs to charge a duty on all commodities brought to Bristol coastwise and to raise it on all other
articles. "The poor planter," he wrote, "does not escape. He is
to pay 2s. instead of 1s. per hogshead on his sugar and other
produce."[14] But Parliament disregarded his protest. Meantime the
work of construction had begun in 1804 and the Floating Harbour
was completed in 1809 at a cost of £600,000, twice the original
figure. Harbour improvement had at last been achieved. The
Floating Harbour and the New Cut transformed the port of Bristol.

IV

Towards the end of the eighteenth century the position of Bristol
as a port began to decline, a decline which continued into the
nineteenth century. For this there were a number of reasons.
First, its importance as a metropolis of the west had been founded
on a network of predominantly river and sea communications. The
construction of canals in the north Midlands in the later eighteenth

century shifted the outlet of trade away from Bristol, and goods
which formerly came south for export now went to Liverpool. Then,
while Lancashire, the hinterland of Liverpool, was the theatre of the
classical period of the industrial revolution, there was no comparable industrialisation of the south-west of England and the
development of Swansea and later Cardiff and Newport took away
the trade of south Wales from Bristol. Overseas, Bristol lost
ground in the West Indian trade while the American trade did not
recover after the War of Independence. In addition, part of the
explanation is to be found in the attitude of leading Bristol
merchants. In the later eighteenth century, they seem to have been
less aggressively competitive than their rivals in other ports. As
Richard Pares has written:

> It would not have been very genteel for fellow members of a
> small dining club, connected together by the marriages of their
> children, to wage war to the knife by cutting freight rates or
> instructing their captains to snatch consignments from each
> other's ships or to utilise some of the other weapons in the
> armoury of competitive enterprise.[15]

Though considerable attention has sometimes been given to the
question of port improvement, this factor seems to rank less highly
than the others already mentioned. The shift in the economic centre
of gravity of Great Britain was the main cause of the relative decline
of Bristol as a port, the other factors merely contributed to it. The
trade of Bristol did not recover when port improvement took place,
it recovered when new staples were found. And whatever the
relative weight to be assigned to each, all such factors were
cumulative in effect. By the end of the eighteenth century, Bristol
had, as a result, surrendered her position as the second largest city
in England and the second most important port. Though her
population and trade had increased in the course of the century,
both had expanded less rapidly than those of her rivals in a
period of rapid economic growth. By 1800, her golden age was
at an end.

A Note on Nicholas Pocock, 1740-1821

Pocock is exactly the right person to illustrate an account on the port of
Bristol in the 18th century. Born in Bristol, the son of a merchant, he became
the master of vessels, owned by Richard Champion, Bristol merchant and friend
of Burke, sailing from this port to the West Indies and South Carolina. Some of
his logbooks of these voyages illustrated by Pocock with drawings of sailing
vessels, still survive in the National Maritime Museum. Later he abandoned the
sea for art. He exhibited at the Royal Academy 1782-1815, mostly pictures of
naval battles. A founder member of the Old Watercolour Society, he died at
Maidenhead.

NOTES

1 See E. H. Meyerstein, *Chatterton,* p. 20.

2 Thomas Cox, *Magna Britannia et Hibernia: Somersetshire* (1720-31), p. 745.

3 As the figures in this table are drawn from different sources they are not strictly comparable but they do indicate the general trend. The figures for 1700 are from British Museum, Add Mss 9764 fos. 115-6; for 1717 from Public Record Office CO 390/8C; for 1787 from W. Barratt, *The History and Antiquities of the City of Bristol* (1789), p. 190; and for 1801, derived from Bristol Reference Library, Bristol Presentments (in C. N. Parkinson, *Trade Winds,* p. 67).

4 *A Tour Through England and Wales* (Everyman edn.) II. 36.

5 J. Campbell, *Political Survey of Britain* (1774), p. 147.

6 F. M. Eden, *The State of the Poor* (1797), II, 183.

7 *A Tour . . .,* II, 36.

8 The two islands, Steep and Flat Holm. in the Bristol Channel.

9 Or creeks.

10 *Letters to Martha Blount,* ed. Elwin and Courthope, p. 326.

11 A form of loan by which the shares of the participants increase as subscribers die until the last surviving subscriber gets all.

12 *Bristol and Hotwell Guide,* pp. 59-60.

13 Reprinted in C. Wells. *A Short History of the Port of Bristol,* pp. 28-9.

14 Letter to James Tobin of Nevis, 13 April 1807 cited by C. M. MacInnes, ' The port of Bristol ' in *Essays in British and Irish History,* ed. H. A. Cronne. T. W. Moody and D. B. Quinn, p. 208.

15 *A West-India Fortune,* p. 212.

SELECT BIBLIOGRÁPHY

(a) TRADE

John Latimer, *Annals of Bristol in the eighteenth century* (Bristol, 1893).

Charles M. MacInnes, *Gateway of empire* (Bristol: Arrowsmith, 1939; Newton Abbot: David & Charles, 1968).

Walter E. Minchinton, 'The voyage of the snow *Africa*', *Mariner's Mirror*, XXXVII (1951) 187–96.

—————, 'Bristol—metropolis of the west in the eighteenth century', *Trans. R. Hist. Soc.* 5th series, IV (1954) 69–89.

—————, *The trade of Bristol in the eighteenth century* (Bristol Record Society, XX, 1957).

—————, 'The Virginia letters of Isaac Hobhouse, merchant of Bristol', *Virginia Magazine of History and Biography*, LXVI (1958) 278–301.

—————, 'Shipbuilding in colonial Rhode Island' *Rhode Island History*, XX (1961) 119–24.

—————, 'Richard Champion, Nicholas Pocock and the Carolina trade', *South Carolina Historical Magazine*, LXV (1964) 87–97 and a note, LXX (1969) 97–103.

Richard Pares, *A West-India fortune* (Longmans, 1950)

(b) THE PORT

Grahame Farr, 'Bristol Channel pilotage: historical notes on its administration and craft', *Mariner's Mirror*, XXXIX (1953) 27–44.

Stanley J. Jones, 'The growth of Bristol', *Trans. Inst. Brit. Geographers*, II (1946) 57–83.

Charles M. MacInnes, 'Bristol' in Cyril Northcote Parkinson, ed. *The trade winds: a study of British overseas trade during the French Wars, 1793–1815* (Allen & Unwin, 1948) pp. 64–71.

—————, 'The port of Bristol' in Henry A. Cronne, Theodore T. Moody and David B. Quinn, ed. *Essays in British and Irish history in honour of James Eadie Todd* (Muller, 1949) pp. 200–17.

Charles Wells, *A short history of the port of Bristol* (Bristol: Arrowsmith, 1909).

Alan F. Williams, 'Bristol port plans and improvement schemes of the eighteenth century', *Trans. Bristol & Glos. Archaeol. Soc.* LXXXI (1962) 138–88.

(c) POLITICS AND THE PORT

Walter E. Minchinton, *Politics and the port of Bristol in the eighteenth century: the petitions of the Society of Merchant Venturers, 1698–1803* (Bristol Record Society, XXIII, 1963).

—————, 'The Stamp Act crisis: Bristol and Virginia', *Virginia Magazine of History and Biography*, LXXIII (1965) 145–55.

—————, 'The political activities of Bristol merchants with respect to the southern colonies before the revolution', *Virginia Magazine of History and Biography*, LXXIX (1971).

BRISTOL
AND THE SLAVE TRADE

C. M. MacINNES

About the beginning of May 1552 Captain Thomas Wyndham of Marshfield Park in Somerset began a voyage to Barbary. On this occasion he sailed from Kingroad, near Bristol, in command of three ships whose cargoes consisted of a " good quantity of linen and woollen cloth, coral, amber, jet and divers other things well accepted by the Moors ". So began the long association of the port of Bristol with the African trade, though it is possible that some previous Bristol ships had touched on the Barbary coast. During the later years of the sixteenth century, however, Bristol appears to have taken little interest in the African trade and successive African companies of the late sixteenth and seventeenth centuries were London concerns. There is some evidence, however, that by the 1630s there was a growing spirit of resentment in Bristol against the privileges enjoyed by the metropolis. By that time, indeed, if not earlier, it seems probable, though there is nothing more than conjecture to proceed upon, that Bristol ships occasionally sailed for the Guinea coast to trade in gold, ivory and forest products.

It was the proud boast of Englishmen in the opening decades of the seventeenth century that, whatever other nations might think or do, they abhorred the trade in human flesh. Yet within a few years of the foundation of English colonies in the New World slaves were imported and by the time of the Restoration of Charles II in 1660 a revolution in public opinion on this subject had already taken place. The large plantations in Virginia and the West Indian colonies that were by then replacing the small farms of the first settlers required an abundant supply of cheap labour. The great numbers of political, sectarian and other offenders that were transported to the plantations, however, could not meet this need. Men, women and children were therefore kidnapped in the seaport towns and spirited away into bondage. This was a trade in which Bristol had a particularly sinister reputation. Thus when Judge Jeffreys visited Bristol in 1685

" . . . . he found all the aldermen and justices concerned in this kidnapping trade, more or less, and the mayor himself as bad as any. He thereupon turns to the mayor, accoutred with his scarlet and furs, and gave him all the ill names that scolding eloquence could supply; and so with rating and staring, as his way was, never left till he made him quit the bench and go down to the criminall's post at the bar; there he pleaded for himself, as a common rogue or thief must have done; and when the mayor hesitated a little or slackened *his pace, he bawled at him and stamping called for his guards . . .* "[1]

In addition there were large numbers of voluntary emigrants who went as indentured servants. They were given a free passage to the plantations and an undertaking that they would be given land at the end of their term of service[2]. Nevertheless, supply still lagged far behind demand. Moreover, even if there had been enough of these voluntary and involuntary emigrants to meet the need, it was coming to be realised that such people were not suited to heavy plantation labour. The mortality among them was appalling. The planters, therefore, turned their attention to Africa, and England threw herself with zest into the trade in negroes.

Though well aware of the King's wish that the chartered Company should monopolise this traffic, Bristol was determined to have her share and so, while she petitioned Parliament to throw the trade open, it seems fairly evident from indirect references that increasing numbers of her ships resorted to the African coast. That this trade was important to the outports would appear to be shown as early as 1667. In that year, Sir Paul.Painter, Ferdinando Gorges and other gentlemen and merchants in a petition to the House of Commons on behalf of themselves and of others concerned in the plantation trade declared that, thanks to the labour of negroes, the trade with the colonies had become one of the most important branches of the nation's commerce. They asserted that it had always been free—which was not strictly true. It was further implied that the importation of slaves from Africa had been open, and certainly during the period of the Civil Wars and the Commonwealth the Dutch had landed cargoes of slaves in the English plantations. In consequence of this freedom, the petitioners argued, the English plantations had been plentifully supplied with slaves at low rates. The recently erected company trading into Africa had obstructed English ships and as it had undertaken to supply large numbers of Africans to the Spanish colonies the English planters were now neglected. Unless some remedy was speedily found they would be destroyed through lack of labour.

The arguments used by the petitioners against the continuance of the Company's monopoly would appear to suggest that by then Bristol, the leading outport, laid great store by the African trade, in the conduct of which apparently her merchants were already well-versed. Indeed, it can be surmised that from 1660 to 1750 and later an intermittent struggle for the African trade went on between

1. Jessop, A. (ed. by), *The Lives of the Norths*, vol. 1. p. 285.

2. See A. E. Smith, *Colonists in Bondage*, University of North Carolina, 1947. The names of some 10,000 emigrants who sailed from Bristol are recorded in two large volumes in the Bristol Archives Office.

London and the outports. The former stood for controlled commerce which it wished to monopolise while the latter demanded that the trade should be open. Each side adduced masses of alleged facts in support of its case but, while this wordy struggle continued and the London Company's monopoly still stood, it seems that Bristol, in defiance of both Company and King, went on expanding her illegal traffic. Certainly great store was laid by it before the end of the seventeenth century. During the reign of William and Mary the Royal African Company, like the East India Company, became very unpopular outside of London. It had enjoyed the special patronage of Charles II and James II, and the lucrative possibilities of the slave trade were now well understood.

John Cary, a citizen of Bristol and a noted economic writer of the time, in 1695 testified to the value of the African trade which he declared is:

" a Trade of the most Advantage to this kingdom of any we drive, and as it were all Profit."

the traffic in negroes

" being indeed the best Traffick the Kingdom hath, as it doth occasionally give so vast an Imployment to our People both by Sea and Land."[1]

In 1696 Bristol joined in the fray with a petition to the House of Commons against the continuance of the Company's monopoly. This was supported shortly afterwards by another petition from the clothiers and weavers of the city to the same effect. At length, in 1698,[2] the position of the private traders was legalised by a modification of the Company's monopoly. The African trade was thrown open to all who paid 10% on all goods imported into and exported from Africa, except redwood which paid 5%, gold, silver and negroes which were free. This Act also required the Company to continue to bear the cost of the maintenance of the forts on the West Coast.

In spite of the concessions which it made to them, this measure was as much detested by Bristol and other outports as by London, which during the next half century repeatedly attempted to have it repealed. In 1707/8, for example, the Merchant Venturers of Bristol heard with dismay that the Company was seeking to have its former monopoly restored. A petition from the merchants of the city " trading to Africa, the West Indies and all other Her Majesty's plantations in America " was therefore forwarded to Parliament against a design which if carried into effect would cripple

1. Cary, J. An Essay on the State of England, in relation to its Trade, its Poor and its Taxes, for carrying on the present war against France, pp. 74-75.

2. 9 & 10 William III, c. 26.

the trade of the city. In the following year (February 2nd, 1708/9) another petition from the Merchant Venturers of the City of Bristol was presented to Parliament. Since the trade was thrown open, this document states, it had much increased and the plantations were better supplied with negroes than when the Company had it only, though, the petitioners went on to say, the present Act was far from satisfactory. The 10% export and import duties were unjust as the Company denied its protection to the private traders, and its agents on the coast discouraged the local inhabitants from trading with them. The petitioners therefore prayed that the trade of Africa would be put under such regulations that all the subjects of Her Majesty might be equal sharers therein.

As in the following year Bristol paid £1,577 5s. 0½d. in duties to the Company, its declared trade to Africa would appear to be still considerable and there is, of course, no record of the value of cargoes carried to the African coast by Bristol ships unknown to the Company. So the battle raged. In one broadsheet the Company's champions proved by statistics, carefully selected of course, that it alone had preserved and developed this important trade and that the free traders would ruin it if permitted to encroach upon it as they then did. They were guilty of grossly erroneous computations about the volume of their exports and the numbers of negroes carried by them to the plantations. To this the free traders retorted that since it was thrown open the trade had more than doubled. This was proved, they asserted, by the official returns made by the colonial governments to the Lords Commissioners of Trade and Plantations. The Company, however, believed in carrying the war into the enemy's country. So in February 1712/13 a letter was sent by it to the Mayor, Aldermen and Common Council of Bristol asking them to support its attempt to have the trade regulated and its former monopoly restored. No record remains of the manner in which this astonishing letter was received, but unless the character of Bristolians has altered radically since then the scene must have been a lively one.

Undaunted by its failures during the reign of Queen Anne, the Company returned to the attack on various occasions after that, but Bristol was always ready for these assaults. Thus, during the twenties, it spent considerable sums in defeating the Company's schemes. Again, in the forties, the fight was on once more. In 1744 the Board of Trade and Plantations was in communication with the Bristol Society of Merchant Venturers on this subject. In March of the following year, in a letter to one of the city's representatives in Parliament, the Society declared that the proposed engraftment of Bristol and other outport traders into the Company would be

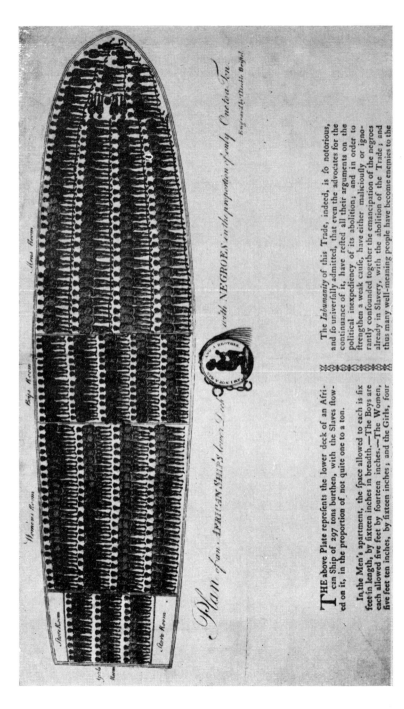

" Am I not a man and a brother ? " Broadside attacking abuses in the slave trade, engraved for the Plymouth Committee by T. Deeble, Bristol.

Bristol City Library   Photographed by A. R. Griffin.

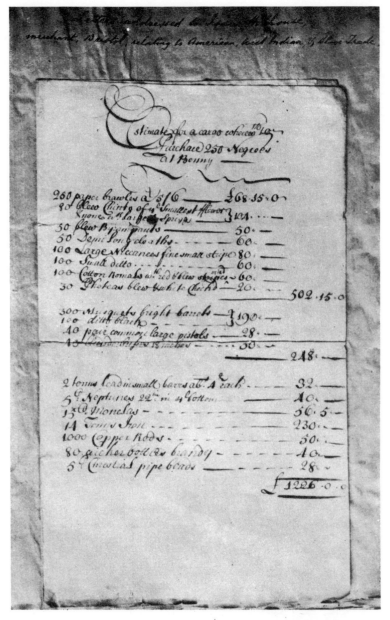

Cloth, guns, beads and other goods purchased by a Bristol merchant ni preparation for a slave voyage.

Bristol City Library: Jefferies MSS. XIII, p. 9.   Photographed by A. R. Griffin.

injurious. It went on to say that it had no advice to offer the Government about what should be done if the Company declined to maintain the African forts, which it regarded as of little use. In 1747/8, however, the African Committee of the Society conceded that James Fort and Cape Coast Castle were of some value. It recommended that if the Royal African Company was to be replaced by some other body then the admission fee for new members should not exceed 40 shillings.

Finally, in 1750,[1] after some eighty years of squabbling, the regulated Company of Merchants trading to Africa replaced the old joint stock Royal African Company. All African traders of the realm were now required to become members of the new body and thus, while London lost her old predominance, the outports were compelled to forego their dream of a completely free and unregulated traffic.

The new Company, which was expressly forbidden to trade in a corporate capacity, was to be governed by a committee of nine, annually elected by its freemen in the three principal slave ports of London, Bristol and Liverpool. Admission was to be obtained on the payment of 40 shillings, the amount previously recommended by the merchants of Bristol, and the new Company inherited the function of maintaining the forts. In 1753, 157 of its freemen belonged to Bristol, and two years later their number had increased to 237 as against London's 147 and Liverpool's 89. Here it might be pointed out that this predominance of Bristol was more apparent than real since in both Liverpool and London firms were larger. Bristol, however, still continued to complain. The old Company was only dead in name, its traders declared; wicked London rigged elections to the committee in order to maintain its control. As the nine committee men were chosen from twelve principal merchants, the committee was virtually a permanent body, but this argument is far from convincing. Again, the Bristolians protested, the Company's officials on the coast assisted London only and hindered the traders of the outports, and so on and so on, for the Bristolians of the eighteenth century were redoubtable expostulators.

Edmund Burke, when a Member for the city, often heard of the alleged iniquities of the metropolitan traders from his constituents and of the advantages of a free and unregulated commerce—but he was not convinced. The Act upon which the African trade stood, he declared, was made by the most experienced men, upon the most mature deliberation:

" It is not every man who is loud in complaint of grievance, that is equally zealous for redressing it; and nothing is more usual than

1. 23 Geo. II, c 31.

*for men to decry an establishment on account of some lesser Evils,
in order to introduce Systems productive of much greater."*[1]

Loud in her wailing, Bristol nevertheless grew rich on the slave
trade which she relinquished when other more profitable and safer
fields of investment appeared. Well into the eighteenth century
Bristol was the only outport that was largely concerned in the
African trade. Thus, in 1707-8 52 of her ships cleared for Guinea,
only two of which belonged to the Company. According to the
Liverpool historian, Gomer Williams, Bristol between 1701 and
1709 sent out an average of 57 ships to the African coast each year.
But as he was trying to demonstrate the dramatic rise of Liverpool
this figure is probably unduly high. In 1725, Bristol ships carried
16,950 slaves, and London 26,400, to the New World. In 1753 the
clearings from the African coast were London 13, Bristol 27, Liverpool 64, Lancaster 7, Chester 1, Plymouth 1, Glasgow 4. Eighteen
years later, of the 192 ships that cleared from Guinea and carried
47,146 slaves to the plantations, 107 ships with 29,250 negroes
aboard were from Liverpool, 58 from London with 8,136, 23 from
Bristol with 8,810, 4 from Lancaster with 950. Between 1756 and
1786 Bristol sent 588 ships to Africa, Liverpool 1,858. It is therefore probable that Bristol was never the principal slave port of
the kingdom. In 1787 London had 26 ships, Bristol 22 and Liverpool 73 engaged in this trade. They carried a total of 36,000
slaves from Africa, averaging 494 a ship. In the ten years 1795-1804
London sent out 155 ships to Africa and carried 46,405 slaves.
Bristol's 29 ships sailed from the coast with 10,718 negroes, while
Liverpool's 1,099 vessels carried 332,800.

By the nineties, in fact, Bristol was already preening herself
on her abhorrence of this trade, though she still made full use of
the negroes with which the wicked merchants of Liverpool supplied
her plantation owners. The author of *The New History* for 1793-4
wrote :

*" The Ardor for the Trade to Africa for men and women, our
fellow creatures and equals, is much abated among the humane
and benevolent Merchants of Bristol. In 1787 there were but 30
ships employed in this melancholy traffic; while the people of
Liverpool in their indiscriminate rage for Commerce and for getting
money at all events have nearly engrossed this Trade, incredibly
exceeded London and Bristol in it, employ many thousands of tons
of shipping for the purposes of buying and enslaving God's rational
creatures, and are the venders* (horresco referens) *of the souls and*

1. Donnan, E., *Documents Illustrative of the Slave Trade to America*, Vol. II.
p. 552.

bodies of men and women! to almost all the West Indian Islands ! ! !"[1]

According to Gomer Williams, the triumph of Liverpool was due to the greater energy and the superior business methods of the northern merchants who specialised in this trade. They trained their men better, paid lower wages, allowed more generous expenses and costs to their captains and factors than Bristol.

Before a man was trusted by a Liverpool firm with its business, either in Africa or in the colonies, he had to go through a long and rigorous training. As, however, in the nineties, the officers and sailors of Bristol were demanding higher wages, larger primage and other allowances in order to put them on a footing of equality with their fellows in London and Liverpool, Gomer Williams's explanation appears to do greater credit to his local patriotism than to his reputation as an impartial historian. It was probably true, however, that in the second half of the eighteenth century Liverpool did derive some advantage from specialisation in the slave business. Moreover, she had at her door a rapidly growing textile industry that provided her with abundant supplies of the cheap cloth she needed for the African market. Meanwhile, Bristol, during this same period, was tending more and more to specialise in the sugar industry. Numbers of her merchants had plantations in the colonies, and although this business did not offer the same glittering prizes as the slave trade it paid well, as the career of John Pinney showed, and it was free from the perils which beset the African trade.

It is still said in Bristol that slaves were bought and sold on a large scale in this port, but there is no historical justification for this opinion. Some enthusiasts will go so far as to refer to a bill of sale which at one time was hung on the wall of a famous Bristol hostelry. An examination, however, proved that this document was a bill of sale of slaves in Kingston, Jamaica, not Bristol. The champions of this legend will point out certain caves near the city which they declare were used for the reception of slaves, but again there is no evidence to support this view. In Henbury churchyard there is to be found the grave of an African slave, whose epitaph is as follows:

Here

Lieth the Body of

SCIPIO AFRICANUS

Negro Servant to ye Right

---

1. Mathews, W., *The New History, survey and description of the city and suburbs of Bristol, or Complete Guide and Bristol Directory for the Year* 1793-4, pp. 38-9.

Honourable Charles William
Earl of Suffolk and Bradon
Who died Ye 21 December
1720   Aged   18   years.

I who was Born a PAGAN and a SLAVE
Now sweetly sleep a CHRISTIAN in my Grave.
What tho' my hue was dark my SAVIOUR'S Sight
Shall change this darkness into radiant Light.
Such grace to me my Lord on earth has given
To recommend me to my Lord in heaven,
Whose glorious second coming here I wait
With Saints and Angels Him to celebrate.

Therefore, it is argued, slaves must have been sold in Bristol. The fact is that in the eighteenth century it was quite common for people of fashion to have African page boys dressed in pseudo-Roman costume and given such high-sounding names as the one in Henbury, or Numa Pompilius, Augustus Caesar, Marcus Aurelius, and so on. These servants, however, were never very numerous and after Lord Mansfield's famous judgment, in the case of the negro Sommersett (1772), slave-holding in England was definitely against the law.

The contention that slaves were brought to Bristol on a large scale, moreover; does less than justice to the business sense of her merchants in the eighteenth century. They were engaged in supplying the plantations with slaves and therefore the quicker they transported them from Africa to the colonial market the better. They would certainly never have been so stupid as to bring these poor dejected creatures up to Bristol, where they would probably have died of pneumonia, or influenza or some other disease, when they wanted to sell them in Jamaica, the Carolinas or Virginia.

Now, how was the slave trade organised? In spite of the prohibitions of the later Stuarts and the fact that such men as Edward Colston became members of the Royal African Company, it appears that a number of Bristol firms were illegally concerned with the African trade before the close of the seventeenth century, but for obvious reasons the number of these is unknown. Here it must be acknowledged that no irrefutable proof of this can be adduced, but, in view of the frequently declared interest of Bristol merchants in this traffic during the second half of the seventeenth century, this would appear to be a fairly reasonable conjecture.

Within a few years after it was thrown open Bristol's share of
the slave trade was considerable and it is hard to believe that this
started from zero in 1698.[1]

In the course of the eighteenth century mayors of Bristol, sheriffs,
aldermen, town councillors, Members of Parliament, the Society of
Merchant Venturers and, indeed, men of the highest repute in the
place were engaged in this traffic. These were not wicked men
but pillars of society in their own time and there seems to be little
justification for that macabre self-satisfaction which some
Bristolians appear to derive from the recollection of the presumed
moral depravity of their forbears. If these men are to be judged
then it should be by the moral standards of the time in which they
lived. Since the nation as a whole at that time condoned their
activities and applauded them for their enterprise, there would
appear to be no special reason why they should be selected for particular condemnation. Many of them honestly believed that though
negroes looked like men they were not really human. Furthermore,
condemnation of these merchants of a bygone age comes strangely
from a generation that is more familiar with violence, cruelty and
massacre on the grand scale than any since the Dark Ages. Wrong
they undoubtedly were and their trade was one of the most
barbarous and cruel that has disgraced the human story, but " man's
inhumanity to man " still " makes countless thousands mourn !"
Who are the inventors of poison gas, the hydrogen bomb and other
devilries to judge?

Some of the slave firms of Bristol were small one-man concerns,
but more often they were partnerships of two to six or more. A
small firm might have one ship only which it occasionally dispatched to the African coast, but by the middle of the eighteenth
century the larger ones often had several vessels and carried on a
well organised trade with Africa and the plantations. As the
century advanced this business in Liverpool tended to pass into
the hands of a diminishing number of concerns whose size increased
as smaller competitors were absorbed or eliminated. In Bristol the
moderate-sized firm continued to hold its own to the end. Indeed,
the concentration of the trade in the hands of a few large under-
takings which took place in Liverpool, with consequent economies
in overheads, may be an additional reason for her victory.

The larger firms had their agents on the coast and in the colonies,
and their correspondence with their principals in England is one
of our main sources of information on this subject. Frequently the

1. The Royal African Company from time to time licensed non-members to trade.
In 1690, it approved of proposals for a ship fitting out in Bristol. See K. G.
Davies, *The Royal African Company*, 1957, p. 126.

captain was required not only to sail his ship but to discharge the
function of factor as well.

The vessels employed were of various rigs. Ships, brigs,
brigantines, snows, galleys and schooners all appear in the records.
Perhaps it should be explained that these eighteenth century galleys
were not vessels rowed by slaves. The English galley of that period
was built for speed, its spread of canvas was twice that of other
sailing ships and it had a flush deck fore and aft.

One of the most surprising things about the vessels used in the
African trade was their diminutive size. The *Laughing Sally*, for
example, was so small that when she ran into a whale she sank,
but what happened to the whale we do not know. Of the 70 vessels
registered in Bristol between 1727 and 1769, engaged in carrying
slaves from Africa to Virginia, one was of 50 tons burden and its
usual cargo of slaves was 190. Thirteen ranged from 51 to 71 tons.
with an average carrying capacity of 166. The *Bridget*, however,
of 70 tons, carried 225 on at least one voyage. Thirty-eight were
in the group 76 to 100 tons and their average cargo capacity was
233, but the *Williamsburg*, of 100 tons, contrived to take 335
aboard. The *Tryal*, of 90 tons, took 356 on one voyage and 390 on
another. The *Ann*, of 90 tons, carried 310, and the *Bryce*, of 100
tons, took 249 on one voyage and 414 on another. In the group 101
to 150 tons there were 20 vessels with an average carrying capacity
of 250, but the *Greyhound* of 120 tons burden carried 410 on at least
one occasion. In the group 151 to 200 tons there were six vessels
whose average slave cargo was 299, but the *Hector* of 200 tons
carried 512 on a single voyage. There was one ship of 230 tons
which, however, carried only a few slaves and was not really a slave
ship. Of these 70 vessels 28 were built in Bristol, seven in other
parts of England, 25 in the colonies and 10 were prizes. At the
time of their departure from Bristol on the voyages to which these
figures apply, their average age was 10 years, but the *Marlborough*
was 29 and several others were 20 years old. From this it would
seem that it was the practice to divert ships to the slave trade
when their best days were over.

So much for the ships, and now what of the men who sailed in
them? The slave trade was never popular among sailors, but this
repugnance was due not so much to humanitarian scruples as to the
evil reputation of the Coast, for as sailors sang :

> Beware and take care of the Bight of Benin,
> There's one comes out for forty go in,

In peace time the wages paid in the West Indian and Guinea trades
were about the same, but in time of war the level in the latter was
somewhat higher. Recruitment was often far from easy, and after

the anti-slave trade campaign began it became increasingly difficult. So various forcible methods were employed to collect a crew. Men were carried aboard dead drunk or with the connivance of the taverner they were confronted with the unpleasant choice between imprisonment for debt or a voyage on a slaver. Death and desertion were all too common. Thus, out of 940 men who made up the crews of 24 Bristol ships in 1787, 216 died during the voyage and 239 deserted or were discharged in the colonies. Only 10 out of 56 who sailed in the *Brothers* from Bristol returned home; 19 out of 51 in the *Alexander* and 14 out of 44 in the *Royal Charlotte*. But as these figures were used for purposes of propaganda by the anti-slave trade campaigners it is probable that the losses on an average voyage were not as high as these.

Normally a Guineaman carried a somewhat larger crew than was customary in other trades. In Bristol ships it was the usual practice to carry 12 men for every 100 tons in vessels of 300 tons and over. In the direct trade with the West Indies, however, the number was seven. Generally speaking, it was usual in smaller vessels to carry a larger proportion of men to tons. Again, in slavers only two-fifths of the crew were able-seamen, as against four-fifths in the direct West Indian trade. Slave ships were often barricaded on poop and forecastle. The guns that peeped through in convenient places to cover the waist of the vessel where the negroes came up for exercise and air were grim reminders of the perils of this trade.

What, then, did these vessels carry with them to Africa? Usually a variety of chintzes and other sorts of cloth, muskets, pistols, powder, shot, beads, metal bars, trinkets of different kinds, spirits, a medicine chest, slave provisions, cooking utensils and a grim assortment of handcuffs, chains, shackles, irons and whips. They usually sailed for Gambia, Sierra Leone, the Windward Coast, Anamabo, Whydah, New Calabar, Bonny and Old Calabar, but the term " the Guinea coast " was commonly understood to include the whole of the African littoral between Cape Verde and the Congo. Indeed, ships sometimes traded along the coast as far down as Angola and occasionally a few sailed round the Cape to Madagascar.

With luck a firm might make three profits on a single voyage. Thus, the cargoes taken out from Bristol were exchanged on the coast for negroes at a profit. One captain sold cloth at a crown a piece which had cost him eighteen pence in Bristol. The slaves were disposed of in the colonies at a profit, and the colonial products for which they were exchanged were sold in England at a profit. But it was always a dangerous trade and a voyage might prove to be a dead loss. England was frequently at war in the eighteenth century, so enemy ships were to be looked for, and Bristol suffered grievously at the hands of French privateers. Then, in times of peace and war, as Bristol captains knew to their cost, both in the Old World and the New, there were corsairs and pirates with which to reckon. The *Callabar Merchant* of Bristol, for example, in 1719 was attacked and captured by three ships, one of which sailed under the black flag.

Life on the African coast was wont to be dangerous. Portuguese, French, Dutch, Danes, Germans, Swedes, Britons and New Englanders competed for slaves. They traded and caroused; they cheated, fought and died; they broke every law of God and Man, but some of them managed somehow to survive. Even the officers of his Majesty's ships sent out to protect the honest trader (assuming that any existed) took a hand in illicit trade and neglected their duty.

A ship might be supplied with negroes in various ways. Company vessels, or those that acknowledged its authority, resorted to its forts where they found negroes already collected and ready to be put aboard. Again, the victims might be purchased in a slave market controlled by a local chief or white trader. When the negroes were bought and branded they were driven aboard, and the sooner the ship was fully " slaved " the better. Sometimes a firm would send its agent on in advance to procure negroes in order that the delay on the coast should be as short as possible.

" *We hope that this will find you safe arrived on the Coast of Angola & with a fine parcell of Negroes ready to putt on board our ship* Union *by whom (God willing) you'll receive this.*"[1]
This agent was then ordered to proceed with the greatest expedition and care and so to justify the good opinion that his employers had of him. He was to buy about 100 slaves, " aiming chiefly at the females from 10 to 14 years of age ".

When the supply on the coast fell short, boats were dispatched up river to trade. Villages were attacked at the dead of night and all the young and fit that could be captured were carried off. Sometimes, like birds of prey, the slavers waited for the conclusion of a war, which in some instances they themselves had fomented, in order that they might enslave the conquered and, if there were not enough of these, the conquerors as well.

A ship might be on the coast for a few weeks only or, like the *Black Prince* of Bristol in the early sixties of the eighteenth century, many months might elapse before she sailed from the coast.

" *When we purchase Negroes,*" writes Snelgrave in the early eighteenth century,

---

1. *African Slave Trade of Bristol* (Bristol City Library: Jefferies MSS. XIII).

" we couple the sturdy Men together with Irons; but we suffer the Women and Children to go freely about: And soon after we have sail'd from the Coast, we undo all the Mens Irons ".[1]

According to another author, it was the practice

". . . to keep the Males apart from the Women and Children, to handcuff the former; Bristol Ships triple such as are sturdy, with Chains round their Necks;"

They kept *" their own Men sober, and on a barricado'd Quarter-deck:"*[2]

Though some captains tried to mitigate the lot of their victims as much as they were able, brutality was the rule, for captains and crews alike were never wholly free from fear. Some commanders, like the famous Captain Crow of Liverpool, were naturally kindly men, but many were brutes. There was one, for example, who was brought to trial in England because he had ordered a sick child to be thrown overboard after its mother died and no one would take care of it. He was acquitted. When an opportunity offered, grief-maddened wretches leapt overboard to escape their misery. Sometimes, as in the *King David* of Bristol, the Africans mutinied and murdered their tormentors, though in this instance the rising was made possible by the indulgence with which the captain had treated the slaves. Again, a ship arrived in New England on one occasion with a passenger aboard who was the sole survivor of the ship's company of a Bristol schooner. In addition to mutiny there was always the possibility of epidemic. Thus, in the records are to be found statements of losses which ranged from 60 to 100 and more in a single voyage.

Even when a ship arrived in a colonial port the troubles of the captain were not over. Colonial governments had the unpleasant habit of imposing special duties on the importation of negroes. As repeated petitions to Parliament prove, Virginia was a frequent offender, but South Carolina, New York, Jamaica, Barbados and other colonies were also guilty. These special impositions led not only to legal wrangling but also to the smuggling of cargoes of slaves ashore in out of the way places. Then, when there was no difficulty of this sort to worry the captain, he might find on his arrival that the local market was over-stocked or that the price of slaves had slumped because of the threat of war. For these and many other reasons the planters might be disinclined to buy, for to them slaves were just one commodity like any other.

" The John and Betty *arrived here the 4th Instant, with one hundred and fifty bight negroes, she purchas'd two hundred and fifty and*

1. Donnan, *op. cit.,* Vol. II, p. 353.

2. *Ibid,* p. 281.

*have buried eleven or more since her arrivall. They are the worst
Cargoe of Negroes have been imported for severall Years past . . . .
They were so badd Could not sell Tenn to the planters. We yester-
day sold one hundred and five . . . . at eighteen pounds Ten shillings
per head, Which Considering the Condition the Negroes were in, is
the greatest price have been given. The remainder are so very bad,
cannot gett £8 pr head for them. Wee shall be oblig'd to sell them
at Outcry for the most they will Yield."*[1]

Speaking of another cargo a writer informed his principals in
England:

*" A Brigantine arrived last Friday called the Post Boy of Bristol
with 350 Negroes. These are proper for the Havanas and Cuba.
As we want Girls we shall take those who are not too much on the
Yellow cast."*[2]

An agent in Antigua wrote:

*" We would you could be perswaded to Direct your Vessells to the
Gold Coast or Widdaw, as negroes from those places Especially
the Latter, are in most Esteem here . . . when Bonny Negroes (the
men particularly) are held in much Contempt Comparatively . . .
many of them hanging and Drowning themselves."*[3]

Writing from Kingston, Jamaica, in 1729 another agent states:

*" The people of Bristoll seem doubtfull of the Jamaica Markett for
Slaves, I think the worst Cargo since Ive been here is the Aurora,
& they turn out at abt. £19-10/- round, & is the best Sale I've been
concerned in they were in generall either Children or Greyheaded
. . ."*[4]

Again:

*" a third poor pining creature hanged herself with a piece of
small Vine which shews that her carcass was not very weighty."*[5]

There is much said in the factors' letters about the advantages
and disadvantages of cash payments, short and long credits,
brokerage charges, market conditions, but nothing about the feelings
of the unfortunate negroes who were thought of merely as horses,
cattle and sheep.

" Since my Arr[l]*,"* John Pinney wrote from Nevis in 1765, *" I've
purch*[d] *9 Negroe Slaves at St Kitts and can assure you I was shock'd
at the first appea*[ce] *of hum*[n] *flesh expos'd for Sale. But surely God
ordain'd 'em for y*[e] *use and benefit of us: other*[se] *his Divine Will,
would have been made manifest by some parti*[r] *sign or token."*[6]

1. *African Slave Trade of Bristol* (Bristol City Library: Jefferies MSS. XIII).
2. Donnan, *op. cit.* Vol. II, p. 459.
3. *African Slave Trade of Bristol* (Bristol City Library: Jefferies MSS. XIII).
4. *Ibid.*
5. Donnan, *op. cit.,* Vol. IV, p. 432, n.2.
6. *Pinney Papers, Business Letter-book,* 1761-75, fol. 67.

Sometimes all the slaves were sold quickly at the first port of call, singly or in parcels. Sometimes they were peddled round the colonies for months from Barbados to Virginia. Or, again, " soul drivers ", as middle men were often called, in some colonies herded them from plantation to plantation like cattle, selling a few here and a few there and paying no attention whatever to family ties.

The scramble was another form of sale adopted by captains in a hurry to get rid of indifferent cargo:

". . . *the ship was darkened with sails, and covered round. The men slaves were placed on the main deck, and the women on the quarter deck. The purchasers on shore were informed a gun would be fired when they were ready to open the sale. A great number of people came on board with tallies or cards in their hands, with their own names upon them, and rushed through the barricado door with the ferocity of brutes. Some had three or four handkerchiefs tied together, to encircle as many as they thought fit for their purpose.*"[1]

Again, the factors might dispose of their wares at the slave market. Pinkard describes a typical one:

". . . *the slaves were brought in, one at a time, and mounted upon the chair before the bidders, who handled and inspected them with as little concern as if they had been examining cattle at Smithfield market. They turned them about, felt them, viewed their shape and their limbs, looked into their mouths, made them jump and throw out their arms, and subjected them to all the means of trial as if dealing with a horse or any other brute animal.*"[2]

As to the question what did the slaves cost, no one answer can be given. It has been seen that the goods brought out from England were sold at high rates. The price of a slave in Africa depended upon a lot of imponderables—scarcity, abundance, place of origin, age, sex, physical condition, the bargaining power of the captain and many other things. The most common unit of exchange on the coast was a bar of iron, but the value of this was far from uniform :

" *A Barr is a denomination given to a certain Quantity of Goods of any Kind, which Quantity was of equal Value among the Natives to a Barr of Iron, when this River was first traded to. Thus, a Pound of Fringe is a Barr, two Pounds of Gunpowder is a Barr, an ounce of Silver is but a Barr, and 100 Gun-Flints is a Barr. . . .*"[3]

and, in fact, each commodity could be valued in terms of bars. All

---

1. *An Abstract of the Evidence delivered before a Select Committee of the House of Commons in the years* 1790 *and* 1791 ; *on the part of the petitioners for the Abolition of the Slave Trade.* p. 46.

2. Pinkard, G., *Notes on the West Indies,* vol. 1, p. 430.

3. Donnan, *op. cit.,* Vol. II, p. 396.

that is attempted here is to give a rough idea of the cost of raw negroes in the eighteenth century. At Anamabo in the early 1700s they fetched the equivalent of £11 to £14 and, at the same place, in 1714-15 prices ranged between £20 and £26, but from £16 to £22 on the Leeward coast. By 1719 prices fluctuated between £28 and £32, while in 1757 (that is, during the Seven Years War), at Bonny, negroes could be purchased at from £9 to £10 a piece. Between 1783 and 1787 prices ranged between £10 and £20. There therefore does not appear to have been any marked rise in the price of slaves, though violent fluctuations undoubtedly occurred.

It is equally difficult to say what they sold for in the colonies. Taking the whole period 1660-1807, however, there appears to have been an upward trend. Here again, place of origin, condition, state of the market, the political situation and so on directly affected the movement of prices, but, bearing all these things in mind, the Royal African Company in 1663 sold slaves in Barbados at £18 a piece. In 1700 the price in the same colony was £19. 15. 4d. They fetched £18 to £24 in Jamaica nine years later and from £28 to £30 in Barbados. Writing from the latter colony on January 3rd, 1723 an agent states:

" *The 10th ulto we sold the ship* Normans *cargoe of Bite Negroes (tho' they were in bad order by a teadious Passage) at 22.6.11 round, the same day was a Sla of Gold Coast wch came out at £29. 19/6 and not extraordinary. Most Plantations want a supply wch hope will keep up the Price for a considerable time.*"[1]

In a letter from Jamaica in 1728 the writer says:

"*. . . . am to acquaint you of ye arrival of ye* Virgin *from ye Gold Coast with 262 Slaves to our address the Sale of which wee've finished & they comes at £30: 17: 6 pr head round, wch is good price Considering there was so many small among them it has been our Ill luck to have too many of them in this Ship so well as ye* Tunbridge *for I begg leave to assure you that its impossible for us to bring out boys & Girls at soe great price as men & women . . .*"[2]

In 1739 a freshly-landed man slave cost £24 sterling and £37 during the forties. Anamabo negroes, which cost £9 or £10 on the Coast, sold for £29 or £30 in the colonies. In 1776 male slaves in Jamaica cost £50 and in 1791 about the same. Between 1795 and 1797 a male slave cost from £50 to £80 and women and children proportionately less. Creoles, that is, slaves born in the islands, if trained as cooks or mechanics were valued at £20, £30 or even £60 more than untrained new arrivals.

---

1. *African Slave Trade of Bristol* (Bristol City Library: Jefferies MSS. XIII).
2. *Ibid.*

Shackles used on a slave ship.

Photograph by courtesy of the Director of Bristol City Museum.

Page from " A Journal of an Intended Voyage in the Ship Black Prince From Bristol to the Gold Coast of Africa Being her 7th to the Coast commencing April 24th, 1762 ".

Photographed by A. R. Griffin.

Bristol City Library.

182   The Slave Trade

This, then was the brutal trade against which the conscience of
England revolted in the closing years of the eighteenth century and
which Wilberforce made it his life's work to destroy.   Contrary
to the views of the Marxists, the slave trade in its last years was
thriving.   The West Indian colonies were still of enormous value to
this country and it is false to maintain that Great Britain gave up
this commerce only when it ceased to be of any economic significance.   It has been computed that at the end of the eighteenth
century four-fifths of all Britain's investments overseas were in the
West Indies.

"The first place I resolved to visit," writes Clarkson, *" was
Bristol . . . . On turning a corner within about a mile of that city,
at about eight in the evening, I came within sight of it.   The weather
was rather hazy, which occasioned it to look of unusual dimensions.
The bells of some of the churches were then ringing; the sound of
them did not strike me, till I had turned the corner before mentioned, when it came upon me at once.   It filled me, almost directly,
with a melancholy for which I could not account.   I began now to
tremble, for the first time, at the arduous task I had undertaken, of
attempting to subvert one of the branches of the commerce of the
great place which was then before me."*[1]

Clarkson expected much trouble and persecution in Bristol and he
mournfully speculated on the possibility of his ever leaving it alive.
But it is hard not to feel that this worthy clergyman was given
somewhat unnecessarily to self-dramatization.   He thought of himself, on his entry into Bristol, as a gallant knight errant waging
battle for a noble ideal, as in fact he was.   He was not St George,
however, and Bristol was not a dragon, but a great, solid English
trading town.   His apprehensions of bad treatment in that city
did less than justice to its citizens.   It was, of course, natural that
slave merchants and plantation owners should not receive him with
open arms and he was bitterly attacked in the local press and on
the platform.   Still, it should not be forgotten that the Society of
Merchant Venturers allowed him full liberty to visit its Hall and to
abstract such information as he required from its records, and this
although his purpose was well known.   In fact, he found many
people in Bristol ready and anxious to aid him in his task.   By that
time of course only a few people were actively engaged in the slave
trade; yet, though some Bristolians denounced it, there were few at
first who believed that it could be abolished.

The lurid descriptions of drunkenness and vice which Clarkson
gives of the taverns in which slave crews were picked up are not

1. Clarkson, T., *The History of the Rise, Progress, and Accomplishment of the
Abolition of the African Slave-Trade by the British Parliament*, Vol. I, p. 293-4.

the concern of the present writer. Doubtless Clarkson did encounter
dreadful conditions in the taverns which he visited, but this sensi-
tive and imaginative young clergyman, who must have had little
previous experience of a pub crawl in a sea port town, can scarcely
be accepted as an unbiased witness.

After over twenty years of gallant and unremitting toil the slave
trade was at last abolished. Thereafter, Great Britain took upon
herself the task of seeing that it was abolished throughout the world.
This desirable goal, however, was not reached for many years, but
the story of this prolonged crusade lies outside the scope of the
above account.

SELECT BIBLIOGRAPHY

(a) Unpublished MSS

A Journal of an Intended Voyage in the Ship Black Prince From
Bristol to the Gold Coast of Africa Being Her 7th to the Coast
Commencing April 24th, 1762.

Jefferies MSS XIII. *African Slave Trade of Bristol.* (Bristol City
Library).

" Letter of Instruction " from the owner of the snow or ship
" Africa " to the Captain, 1774.

Pinney Papers.

Society of Merchant Venturers: *Book of Petitions.*

(b) Published

*An Abstract of the Evidence delivered before a Select Committee
of the House of Commons in the years 1790 and 1791; on the
part of the petitioners for the Abolition of the Slave Trade*
(London, 1791).

Cary, J., *An Essay on the State of England, in relation to its Trade,
its Poor and its Taxes, for carrying on the present war against
France* (Bristol, 1695).

Clarkson, T., *The History of the Rise, Progress and Accomplishment of the Abolition of the African Slave-Trade by the British
Parliament.* 2 vols. (London, 1808).

K. G. Davies, *The Royal African Company,* 1957.

Donnan, E., *Documents Illustrative of the History of the Slave Trade to America.* 4 vols. (Washington, 1930-35).

MacInnes, C. M., *England and Slavery* (Bristol, 1934).
A Gateway of Empire (Bristol, 1939).
" The Slave Trade " in *The Trade Winds,* ed. C. Northcote Parkinson (London, 1948).

Mathews, W., *The New History, survey and description of the city and suburbs of Bristol, or Complete Guide and Bristol Directory for the year 1793-4* (Bristol, 1794).

Pinkard, G., *Notes on the West Indies.* 2 vols. (London, 1816).

Royal African Company. *A Collection of 24 Broadsheets relating to the Affairs of the Royal African Company.* Early eighteenth century.

Snelgrave, Capt. W., *A New Account of Some Parts of Guinea and the Slave Trade* (London, 1754).

Stock, L. F., ed., *Proceedings and Debates of the British Parliaments respecting North America.* 5 vols. (Washington, 1924-41).

THE ANTI-SLAVE TRADE
MOVEMENT IN BRISTOL

PETER MARSHALL

The American War of Independence sharply reduced the overseas trade of Bristol and almost entirely halted the traffic in African slaves conducted from the port.[1] After the restoration of peace in 1783, however, Bristol ships resumed voyages to West Africa in search of tropical woods for the English market and negroes to supply the needs of the New World slave plantations. The dominant position of Liverpool in the slave trade, secured before the war, was not remotely threatened, but clearances from Bristol for Africa became a regular occurrence, 16 being recorded in 1785, 20 in 1786, 31 in 1787 and 17 in 1788, of which between one-third and a half represented slaving voyages.[2] This present interest was but a pale reflection of past pre-eminence, but the reputation of Bristol as a slaving port, and its continued concern in West Indian trade and property, ensured that the city would not escape controversy if demands should arise for the suppression of the trade in negroes.

Agitation against the trade did not, in fact, await its resumption. Articles demonstrating its inhumanity, reprinted from American newspapers, had appeared in *Felix Farley's Bristol Journal* during the summer and autumn of 1783 in consequence of the determination of the Society of Friends to testify against slavery.[3] This attitude was steadfastly maintained: in July 1785, the Bristol Men's Monthly Meeting directed six of its number to distribute 300 copies of Anthony Benezet's *Caution against the Slave Trade to Great Britain* "to every Person concerned in any respect in the Slave Trade", and ordered an inquiry whether any Friends were in any way involved.[4] In November the committee reported to the Monthly Meeting that:

> we find Friends are generally clear; not one person being engaged therein, or holding any one in slavery. Some few in the course of business furnish goods to merchants in that trade and only one family, who from principle have retired from the West Indies to this city and have not yet been able to withdraw their property, hold a mortgage on an estate whereon slaves are employed.[5]

1   John Latimer, *The Annals of Bristol in the Eighteenth Century* (Bristol, 1893), p. 416.
2   *House of Commons Accounts and Papers* XXIV (1789), No. 631, XXXIV (1790-91), p. 278.
3   *FFBJ* 7 June, 4 Oct., 1 Nov., 8 Nov., 1783.
4   Men's Meeting Minutes 1779-1785. 1 July 1785. Bristol Record Office.
5   *Ibid.*, 28 Nov. 1785.

The Bristol Men's Meeting numbered only about fifty, but its members were to play a substantial part in the local protest against the slave trade.

In the summer of 1787 Thomas Clarkson was despatched by the committee, which had been established in London to secure the abolition of the slave trade, to investigate conditions in provincial seaports. He made first for Bristol, where he arrived on 27 June with a letter of introduction to Harry Gandy, a conveyancer in Castle-Green, who as a young man had sailed on two slave voyages, an experience which had later led him, afflicted by conscience, to join the Society of Friends. Gandy introduced Clarkson to seven other Quaker families: these, he later recalled, "were my first and only acquaintance at Bristol for some time. I derived assistance in the promotion of my objects from all of them . . ."[6] Clarkson was seeking information on a number of questions; the state of the legitimate and slave trades of the city with Africa, conditions on the voyage to the West Indies, the danger to seamen of serving on slavers as compared with other vessels, and the general extent of the slave trade of Bristol.[7]

Clarkson did not find Bristolians to be proud of the trade: "every body seemed to execrate it, though no one thought of its abolition".[8] A report that a Bristol slave ship, the *Brothers,* had been deserted by its crew on account of cruel treatment by the captain on the previous voyage and a high death rate, directed Clarkson to an aspect of the trade with which he had previously been unfamiliar: the unwillingness of seamen to engage and their bad treatment on slave ships.[9] Through Truman Harford, a member of the Society of Merchant Venturers, he secured access to the muster rolls, which confirmed the death of 32 seamen on the *Brothers'* last voyage; evidence was obtained that John Dean, a free negro of the crew, had for a trifling offence been fastened to the deck, burned with hot pitch, and scarred with tongs. Appalled at these discoveries, Clarkson determined to continue his investigations, which were now becoming common knowledge and arousing both support and resentment. Clergymen came forward to assist him. From the Anglicans, Dr. Camplin and Dean Tucker provided help, and Clarkson secured access to the Customs House records with the Dean's aid. Henry Sulgar, the Moravian minister, produced documents relating to the killing of Africans at Calabar in

6 Thomas Clarkson, *The History of the Rise, Progress, and Accomplishment of the Abolition of the African Slave Trade by the British Parliament* (London, 1808), I. 294-295.
7 Clarkson, I. 295-296.
8 Clarkson, I. 297.
9 Clarkson, I. 297-298.

1767, of which Clarkson had previously received only vague reports.[10] Nevertheless, the search for witnesses and victims of brutality proved difficult. The surgeon's mate of the *Alfred* was reported to have been driven to attempted suicide by the attacks of his captain. He was found by Clarkson, seemed delirious, and was shortly afterwards reported dead. Continuing his quest, Clarkson was again aided by the Quakers, one of whom now brought to him another member of the crew, who confirmed that the captain had been responsible for the death of the surgeon's mate and also of a seaman, whom he had brutally beaten with a rope. Clarkson wished to see the captain tried for murder, but on approaching Burges, the deputy town clerk, whom he knew to be privately sympathetic to his cause, was advised that the cost of maintaining the crew as witnesses and the likelihood that they would be bribed away before the case was heard, made failure and high expense the most probable outcome. Reluctantly, he abandoned the idea and returned to his investigations.[11] He had heard that seamen were lured into the trade. The landlord of a local tavern, the "Seven Stars", who boarded seamen but refused any association with the slavers, escorted the young Cambridge graduate round the Public Houses in Marsh Street where crews were recruited. On nineteen occasions, in the early morning hours, Clarkson observed how landlords and ships' mates plied and stupefied seamen with drink, or encouraged them to spend beyond their means until signing on for a slave voyage remained the only alternative to imprisonment for debt. Nominally, pay was higher on the slave ships, but Clarkson concluded that the practice of paying half their wages in the local currency on arrival in the West Indies cheated seamen of any financial advantage.[12]

Despite these observations and the evidence of the muster rolls, Clarkson was unable to find witnesses prepared to testfy in public. His hopes of persuading former slave captains to do so proved quite futile: fearful of incriminating themselves or else still part owners of slavers, they refused to speak and shunned Clarkson as if he "had been a mad dog". Harry Gandy, his original friend in Bristol, offered to give evidence, but no one else came forward. The Quakers once more provided assistance, arranging a secret meeting at the house of one of their number between Clarkson and the surgeon of the slave ship *Pilgrim*, which was about to sail.

10 Clarkson, I. 298-310.
11 Clarkson, 1. 310-319.
12 Clarkson, I. 322-325. Articles of Agreement for the Bristol slaver *Sally*, 22 July 1785, are printed by Elizabeth Donnan ed., *Documents Illustrative of the Slave Trade to America* (Washington, 1931), II. 560-562.

Although he had been warned by the owner not to speak to Clarkson, the surgeon described the barbarities of the trade, claiming that he was only returning to it through inability to establish himself in his profession. Clarkson could not detain him as evidence: payment might be construed as bribery, and the committee had not yet determined when it would seek a hearing before Parliament. It was therefore agreed at a second meeting that surgeon Gardiner would testify when he returned from the voyage and would keep a journal for that purpose.[13].

The next opportunity was provided by a fragment of conversation overheard as Clarkson passed by the Exchange: a young man was speaking of his experiences on the Coast. Clarkson followed him and waited outside a house for three hours, to no purpose. He was subsequently identified as James Arnold and interviewed by Clarkson. Arnold had been on two voyages as surgeon's mate of the *Alexander* in 1785 and had recently returned from a further voyage as surgeon of the *Little Pearl*. He also had been warned to avoid Clarkson, but claimed that he opposed the trade and had therefore made no attempt at concealment. His description of the treatment of seamen on the *Alexander* was the most horrifying Clarkson had heard. Arnold was about to sail on the *Ruby*, but prior to this made depositions before the chief magistrate, George Daubeny. He also promised to keep a journal of the voyage.[14]

Clarkson had begun to suffer from physical exhaustion and emotional reaction to the evidence he had secured. Returning from a brief holiday in Monmouth he was introduced to another sympathetic surgeon, Alexander Falconbridge, who after four voyages had now abandoned the trade. He spoke with particular bitterness of the captain of the *Alexander,* and Clarkson then realized that Arnold had served on this vessel as mate to Falconbridge. A new point, to which Clarkson henceforth attached great importance, then emerged: although the muster rolls indicated a heavy mortality rate, the situation was in fact worse, since the trade was responsible for the subsequent death or permanent disablement of many seamen. Falconbridge declared himself willing to tell all he knew, either privately or in public. The dedicated investigator was quite overwhelmed by this belated success. "The joy I felt," he recalled, "rendered me quite useless, as to business, for the remainder of the day."[15]

Information was now becoming more plentiful. Thompson, the landlord of the "Seven Stars", kept him informed of the condition

13 Clarkson, I. 330-337.
14 Clarkson, I. 337-343.
15 Clarkson, I. 345-353.

THOMAS CLARKSON, 1760-1846

In the face of great difficulties Clarkson collected in Bristol a great deal of evidence in support of the case for the abolition of the slave trade. In 1808 he published in two volumes *A History of the Rise, Progress, and Accomplishment of the Abolition of the Slave Trade by the British Parliament.*

Coloured engraving by Cruikshank, published 10 April, 1792, showing Captain Kimber on the deck of a slave ship with a negro girl suspended by an ankle from a rope. See *catalogue of Political and Personal Satires in the British Museum*, vol. VI, 1784-1792, No. 8079, edit. Mary Dorothy George, 1938

of the seamen. Some, Clarkson learnt, had escaped ashore from
the *Prince* before sailing; others on the *Africa,* including one of the
mates, were alarmed at the demand that they should sign their
articles of agreement unread. Sheriff, the mate, was terrified of
his captain and appealed to Clarkson for help. Truman Harford
agreed that the only possibility was to board the *Africa* in Kingroad and attempt to remove Sheriff on the grounds that the articles,
being unseen, were invalid. Fortunately, the captain was not on
board and Sheriff was brought ashore without incident. Clarkson
made no secret of his responsibility, leaving his name as remover
of the mate at the captain's house. He heard no more of the
matter.[16]

Pursuing the line of inquiry suggested by Falconbridge, Clarkson
visited three sick seamen who had never recovered from a trip, the
previous year, on the *Thomas.* They expressed the hope that he
would not leave Bristol before inquiring into the murder of their
shipmate, William Lines. All believed that he had been killed by
the chief mate, though they had not witnessed the crime. The next
day he was visited by the mother of the dead man, in company
with four other members of the crew. Clarkson was now convinced
that murder had been committed, thought of consulting Burges,
but remembering his advice on the previous occasion, determined
to proceed directly with the laying of charges against the captain
of the *Thomas.* When Clarkson appeared before the magistrates,
he found the bench occupied by slave traders and West India
merchants, to whom the mayor had passed on the warning given
him by Clarkson the previous day of his intention to bring
accusations. The abolitionist now encountered open hostility: "I
shall never forget the savage looks which these people gave me,"
he wrote later, "which indeed were so remarkable as to occasion
the eyes of the whole court to be turned upon me".[17] The case
was referred to the Admiralty court in London. Clarkson was now
given an even wider berth by the slavers' officers but seamen from
seven other ships applied to him for redress of wrongs. The quest
for evidence had proved successful, but the accumulation of
sickening details so preyed upon Clarkson's mind that he had
come to feel that "to stay in Bristol a day longer than was necessary
would be only an interruption for so much time both of my
happiness and of my health . . ."[18] Fortunately, he could now leave
the campaign in local hands: the Quakers, Anglican and Dissenting
clergy, and Joseph Harford, twice High Sheriff and a member of

16 Clarkson, I. 354-358.
17 Clarkson, I. 359-361.
18 Clarkson, I. 363-365.

the Common Council, were committed to the cause. Having secured their promise to establish a committee to prepare a parliamentary petition against the trade, Clarkson departed for Liverpool.[19]

Although Clarkson's experiences in the major slave port of the country were far from uneventful, Bristol had provided his first and most disturbing impressions of the trade. His *History* devoted more space to his stay in Bristol than to his visit to Liverpool, which he was forced to break off on the receipt of alarming news that the case against the *Thomas* was about to collapse for the want of evidence. Two of the four witnesses had been bribed away to sea and the others were known only to be working in a mine between Neath and Swansea. Clarkson returned to Bristol to lead the search. The men were found and sent to London, but arrived just after the case had been dismissed by default.[20]

The local committee had failed in this respect, but continued during the summer of 1787 to bring the abolitionist case to the notice of Bristolians. On 21 July both *Felix Farley's Bristol Journal* and *Bonner and Middleton's Bristol Journal* printed "A summary View of the Slave Trade . . .", a concise statement of the case for abolition issued by the London committee, which had instructed its secretary on 17 July to send copies to James Harford, Richard Reynolds and Matthew Wright.[21] In August letters supporting the cause appeared in *Bonner and Middleton* and in October Clarkson informed the London committee that, due to his efforts, places in the West of England, including Bristol, were ready to petition against the trade when the committee would give the signal to do so.[22]

By the beginning of 1788 the abolitionists were ready to proceed with the preparation of petitions. The Bristol group held its first public meeting on 28 January at the Guildhall, and formed a committee to prepare a petition against the trade. Substantial support had been obtained: the meeting was called by the mayor, who was prevented by illness from taking the chair, and presided over by Joseph Harford. The list of prominent supporters included the Deans of Bristol and Gloucester, Caleb Evans and J. P. Estlin, prominent dissenting ministers, Aldermen George Daubeny and John Harris, together with doctors and merchants. It was resolved to establish a committee of correspondence, open a subscription, and place the petition in the Guildhall for signature during the

19 Clarkson, I. 366-367.
20 Clarkson, I. 427-435.
21 Proceedings of the Committee for Abolition of the Slave Trade, British Museum, Add. Mss. 21,254.
22 *Ibid.*, 16 October 1787.

following week.[23] This show of strength was sufficient to disturb
John Pinney, who wrote to his agent in Nevis that

> The present alarming crisis, respecting the abolition of
> the African Trade, operates so strongly on my mind,
> that I am resolved to contract, with the utmost expedition
> all my concerns in the West Indies. Never again, upon
> my own private account, will I enter into a new engage-
> ment in that part of the world: therefore permit me, most
> earnestly to entreat you to act with great circumspection
> and to make me as large a remittance, in bills of exchange,
> as possible. Without which, I shall be in a situation truly
> unpleasant, and most mortifying . . .[24]

Two days later the lords of the committee of the privy council
were ordered to investigate the state of the slave trade and the
conditions of the slaves in the West Indies.

Both sides were now anxious to present their cases. The Bristol
newspapers printed correspondence attacking and defending the
trade; during April and May 1788 *Bonner and Middleton* published
Falconbridge's *Account of the Slave Trade* in serial form. By the
end of March the Bristol committee was able to send a donation
of one hundred guineas to London.[25] Meanwhile, the supporters
of the trade were beginning to rally. A general meeting at
Merchants' Hall on 6 March resolved that the privy council
committee should be petitioned in support of the trade and
requested to hear the evidence of the Society of Merchant
Venturers. The support of Matthew Brickdale, one of the Members
of Parliament for Bristol, was to be sought, and information and
witnesses held ready.[26] The spirits of the West India interest began
to revive at this sign of resistance. The house of Pinney and Tobin
thought that the onslaught was declining: James Tobin, who had
returned from Nevis in 1784, had plunged into an extended
pamphlet controversy with James Ramsay, an Anglican clergyman
who had lived in St. Kitts, debating the evils and comforts of
slavery with his "reverent and virulent antagonist". The partnership
was therefore in a situation from which it viewed the controversy
with the keenest of both personal and commercial interests. For the
moment, it was felt that "much of the spirit of enthusiasm seems
to have evaporated and the minds of the generality of the nation

23 *BMBJ* 2 Feb., 1788.
24 John Pinney to William Coker, 9 Feb. 1788. Pinney Letter Book
    1788-1792, University of Bristol.
25 Abolition Committee Proceedings, 1 Apr. 1788. BM add. Mss. 21,255.
26 Society of Merchant Venturers, Book of Proceedings II (1782-1789)
    ff. 407-410. W. E. Minchinton ed., *Politics and the Port of Bristol in
    the Eighteenth Century* (Bristol, 1963), pp. 161-162.

are much opened by the ample discussion this question has undergone . . .[27] A decline in interest offered the greatest hope to the opponents of abolition, since they shrank from supporting the slave trade as desirable in principle. Tobin had refused to argue the justice of slavery, declaring himself a "general enemy" of the institution and describing the trade as an "unnatural traffic". He freely admitted that

> It has indeed ever been my opinion that neither the slavery of the West India colonies, or the commerce of the human species, are to be defended, except on political grounds, and the general practice of all the most enlightened nations.[28]

The returning complacency of those who were hoping that the agitation would dwindle into insignificance was shattered by the unexpected introduction, late in the parliamentary year, of Sir William Dolben's bill to regulate conditions on the slave ships. Pinney relapsed into prophecies of financial disaster and gloom at the ineffectual opposition being offered to the measure. "We are sorry to say," a West Indian correspondent was informed, "the slave trade seems to have but weak advocates in the House of Commons or that the question is so unpopular that gentlemen do not choose to give their real sentiments in public."[29]

Bristol interests were apparent in the opposition to the Dolben bill. In the motion for its second reading in the Commons, Gascoyne of Liverpool proposed a delay of three months, so that evidence could be heard and representations received from his constituents. Matthew Brickdale seconded the motion, but without much fervour. It was, he said, his duty to do so, though his private sentiments led him to wish for some regulation of the trade. This could not be achieved hastily and required "cool investigation".[30] The bill, which established maximum numbers of slaves to be carried in proportion to the tonnage of the ships, threatened the profitability of the trade: calculations demonstrated that the nine ships owned by James Jones, the largest Bristol trader, would be compelled to reduce their cargoes by almost a quarter.[31] It was therefore not surprising that a Merchants' petition against regulation was sent to Stephen Fuller and transmitted to the Duke of Chandos for

27 Pinney & Tobin to Ulysses Lynch, 25 Apr. 1788. Pinney & Tobin Letter Book 1784-1789, University of Bristol.
28 James Tobin, A Short Rejoinder . . . (London, 1787), pp. 23-24.
29 Pinney & Tobin to Edward Brazier, 24 May 1788. Pinney & Tobin Letter Book 1784-1789.
30 The Parliamentary History of England . . . (London, 1816), 26 May 1788, XXVII. 576-579.
31 W. E. Minchinton ed., The Trade of Bristol in the Eighteenth Century (Bristol, 1957), p. 173.

presentation to the House of Lords.[32] It did not prevent enactment of the bill.

Meanwhile, the privy council committee had been hearing evidence on the trade which, after arrangement under six subject headings, was published in 1789 as an extensive report. Bristol's concern in the trade was reflected in the number of both hostile and friendly witnesses provided by the city. The report first examined the present condition of the slave exporting regions of Africa. Evidence had been heard from Captain Thomas Deane, commander of a vessel owned by Mr. Biggs of Bristol. Deane had been engaged for the previous three years in the wood and ivory trade; he testified on the means by which slaves were obtained. John Anderson, representing the standing committee of the Merchant Venturers, emphasized the comparative humanity and order of the trade. Testimony from Bristol on the fraud and violence stemming from the trade demonstrated the value of Clarkson's visit: much of this evidence was delivered in writing by the abolitionist. Such was the case with the evidence of William James, now of the Royal Navy, who had undertaken three voyages from Bristol between 1764 and 1768; the more recent and impressive evidence of James Arnold was also submitted in this fashion. Arnold had honoured his pledge to keep an account of his third voyage, undertaken in the brig *Ruby,* which had sailed from Kingroad on 9 August 1787: his evidence related entirely to this trip. Captain Joseph Williams, he alleged, was notorious for his brutal treatment of the natives and unfair trading. Moreover, Arnold reached Bristol in time to learn that the hearings had not concluded, made his way to London, and supplemented the account in his journal by a graphic, damning, and fresh description to the committee of the evils of the trade. Gardiner, the surgeon who had also promised Clarkson to keep a journal, had died on his voyage: his notes had been found and buried with him.[33]

Sydenham Teast gave evidence as a Bristol merchant engaged in the African, but not in the slave, trade. He was not prepared to admit that the legitimate trade was especially profitable or likely to become so. Captain Deane, however, thought that opportunities existed and declared that he had made a considerable profit.

The second heading under which the evidence was reported

32 Stephen Fuller to SMV 7 July 1788, Letters 1754 — Bundle 28, Merchants' House. Minchinton, *Politics,* p. 162.
33 Clarkson, II. 19. *Report of the Lords of the Committee of Council* (1789). Unpaginated copy, Bristol Central Reference Library.

concerned the manner in which slaves were carried to the West Indies. Falconbridge gave evidence on his four voyages, but his account seems far less damaging than that of Arnold, whose statement, sworn on 5 September, 1788, of conditions on the *Ruby*, described the distress of the seamen and the cruelties of the captain during the crossing. The crew was never addressed by name, being called "Red or Blue Villain", according to the colour of their jacket. Poor food, bad quarters, floggings for the least offence, explained why four out of a crew of nineteen had died on the voyage. When Arnold appeared personally before the committee, he testified on an earlier voyage with Williams in 1786 on the *Ruby*, then called the *Little Pearl;* he declared that the seamen were treated with almost as much cruelty as the slaves.

Clarkson's own evidence presented the results of his examination of the Bristol muster rolls; from them, he demonstrated that the city's crews had suffered even higher losses than those sailing from Liverpool. He dwelt particularly on the fate of the crew of the *Thomas* as an example of the dangers run by seamen in the slave trade, though he was compelled to admit that no particular resentment had been created, since they were "in general a thoughtless set of men".

The fourth section of the report, which sought to assess the extent of the slave trade, included figures provided by the representatives of Bristol. African commerce employed 30 ships totalling 4,195 tons, compared with 72 ships of 17,391 tons engaged in the West Indian trade and 7 ships of 1,571 tons carrying timber from Honduras. The relative unimportance of the slave trade was demonstrated by the employment of 119 ships of 15,454 tons in the remaining overseas commerce of Bristol. Calculated by value, the slave trade possessed somewhat greater significance. Legitimate trade from Africa provided imports worth only £15,000, equal with those from Honduras, but dwarfed by the West Indian figure of £774,000. On the other hand, the commercial value of all ships and exports to Africa amounted to £240,000, while the West Indian trade was estimated to be worth £459,000, representing a much less decisive degree of superiority. The gross commercial value of ships and cargoes assigned to other trade overseas was assessed at £900,000, so that the legitimate and slave trades of Bristol with Africa did not, even as calculated by representatives anxious to combat a threat to their interests, represent more than twelve per cent of the city's total overseas trade.[34] This would seem a stake

34 Values and tonnage from Lords *Report.* See also Minchinton, *Trade,*
    p. 181 for numbers of ships A 1790 cargo for the Africa trade is
    printed p. 60.

sufficiently substantial to be worth defending but not large enough
to dictate local mercantile opinion, provided that the slave trade
could be isolated from West Indian interests. The abolitionists,
anxious to prevent a conjuction, denied that their ultimate aim
was emancipation in the islands: their inability to gain acceptance
of this assurance, coupled with the belief that West Indian
prosperity depended upon the constant replenishment of the slave
labour force from Africa, led to the strengthening of the limited
slave trading interest of the city by the much larger and influential
group which was now alarmed at the general threat to Bristol's
commerce. The combined value of the Caribbean and African
trades far exceeded that of the remaining overseas trade and the
feeling grew that a limited evil must be tolerated in order to sustain
a general prosperity.

Seen in this light, the privy council report appeared merely a
preliminary to attempts to legislate for the suppression of the trade.
In February 1789, the secretary of the African committee of Liverpool alerted the Bristol mercantile interest to this possibility,
urging action to "prevent a blow, so fatal to the naval strength of
Britain, and so destructive of the liberty and welfare of the human
species, as the abolition of this branch of commerce would certainly
prove . . ."[35] The London West India committee of planters and
merchants had established in February 1788 a standing committee
to oppose abolition.[36] Now, in the face of imminent danger, the
support of Bristol merchants was requested: on 3 April, 1789, the
standing committee of the Merchant Venturers was informed that
the House of Commons would in three weeks' time go into
committee to consider petitions proposing total abolition of the
slave trade. It was resolved that advertisements should be placed
in the Bristol and Bath newspapers, requesting all parties
"interested in the trade and manufactures and welfare of the West
Indian islands" to attend a meeting at Merchants' Hall on 13
April.[37] The London West India interest met to express its opposition on 9 April and the proceedings were received in Bristol in
time for their unanimous approval by "a very numerous and
respectable body".[38] A committee was appointed, with no less than
47 members, and charged with the preparation of petitions opposing
abolition, which would be subscribed by the city's West India

35 Samuel Green to James Jones, 18 Feb. 1789. Letters 1754 — Bundle
    29, Merchants' House.
36 Elsa V. Goveia, *Slave Society in the British Leeward Islands at the
    End of the Eighteenth Century* (New Haven and London, 1965), p. 23.
37 SMV Book of Proceedings, 11. f. 498.
38 *Ibid.*, f. 499.

merchants and planters, African merchants, manufacturers connected with these trades, and shipowners. The support and services of the Merchant Venturers and Members of Parliament were requested.[39]   The shift of opinion in Bristol was clearly indicated by the presence on the committee of Aldermen Daubeney and Harris who had, in January 1788, supported the initial protest against the trade.

The committee wasted no time: it met on 15 April, arranging for news of the first meeting to be printed in Bristol, Bath and London newspapers, and naming supporters who would secure signatures to three petitions against abolition. The relative importance of the interests now roused to resistance may be indicated by the numbers charged with this task: the African committee was ten strong, the West India merchants totalled 23, while the manufacturers required 34 representatives. The framing of the petitions began on 20 April; they were despatched by mail coach to London six days later. The work was completed so speedily that copies of the London petitions were received too late to be used in Bristol.[40]

Matthew Brickdale had been approached to take charge of the petitions, but declined because of illness; he reiterated his belief that the trade should be maintained under regulation.[41] Bristol's other Member of Parliament, Henry Cruger, was happy to undertake the task and reported the safe receipt of the petitions on 28 April. Their presentation was then deferred, since the slave trade interest had agreed to arrange for a joint delivery of the seaports' protests, which would take place when William Wilberforce introduced his motion for abolition. This would create the strongest possible impression and also prevent Wilberforce from using the petitions to further his attacks.[42]

Wilberforce opened his parliamentary campaign on 12 May. In the course of his speech he referred to the trade in Irish children, which he alleged had been carried on through Bristol in the reign of Henry VII until its abolition by the conscience-stricken Irish. "All I ask, therefore, of the people of Bristol," was his appeal, "is, that they would become as civilized now, as Irishmen were

39 These and subsequent proceedings were entered in the later pages of the West India New Society minute book, preserved in Merchants' House. The committee, though provided with accommodation and clerical assistance by SMV, enjoyed a separate if temporary existence from the Society and the much smaller Bristol West India club.
40 Committee minutes, 15, 20, 22, 25 Apr. 1789.
41 Brickdale to Jeremiah Osborne, 26 Apr. 1789. African Trade Box 'G', Merchants' House.
42 Cruger to Osborne, 28 April 1789, ibid.

four hundred years ago . . ."[43] On this same day, as had been
planned, the Bristol petitions were presented. They now numbered
six: besides the three prepared by the committee, protests against
the abolition of the trade were submitted by the Corporation, the
Merchant Venturers, and the Newfoundland merchants.[44] Their
objections were similar and stressed the general consequences of
abolition. The petition of the West India interest declared that
recent inquiries had shown that the African and Caribbean trade
accounted for at least three-fifths of Bristol's commerce; passage
of the bill would therefore bring inevitable decline and ruin to
thousands. Abolition would reduce British West Indian planters
to an impossible position of inferiority when compared with other
European colonists, halt any expansion, and destroy the carrying
trade, the nursery of British seamen and seapower. Investments
and investors would receive a fatal blow. The closing of Bristol
sugar refineries would throw many hundreds of labourers out of
work. It was admitted that the Dolben Act contained desirable
regulations, which could perhaps be extended, but in any event
the colonial assemblies were now considering ameliorative
measures. If, however, the demand for abolition prevailed, those
who suffered losses should receive compensation. All the petitions
stressed that the consequences of abolition would combine grave
dangers to British prosperity and no improvement of the negro's
lot; cautious regulation of the trade was the only practical step.
The organizers of the petitions were pleased with the support they
had obtained: despite the need for rapid circulation and limitation
to those materially concerned, nearly fifty signatures had been
obtained from the African trade, about one hundred from the
manufacturers, and 127 from those connected with the West Indies
and sugar refining. It was felt that this show of strength, together
with the backing of the Corporation, the Merchant Venturers, and
the Newfoundland interest, demonstrated conclusively "how large
a part of the people of property in the city are enemies to the
proposed abolition . . ."[45]

Throughout the parliamentary debate, Cruger kept in touch
with the Bristol opponents of Wilberforce. He also played an active
part in resisting the abolitionist case: on 21 May, when Wilberforce proposed that the house go into committee, Cruger spoke
in support, but as a means of proceeding to a refutation of the

43 *Parliamentary History* XXVIII. 60-61.
44 Donnan, II. 602-612. Minchinton. *Politics*, pp. 165-166 Common Council
Proceedings, 1783-1790, ff. 285, 289-290. Bristol Record Office.
45 Osborne to Cruger, 26 Apr. 1789. Letters Outward 1781-1810,
Merchants' House.

arguments for abolition. Declaring himself to be a supporter of humanitarian causes and an opponent of oppression, he proceeded to demand that the cost of ending the trade should fall not on individuals but on the nation. This required the raising of a fund amounting to at least £60 or £70 millions. He asked if emancipation formed part of the project. Nothing but evil was believed of the condition of the slave trade, but he "could venture to pronounce the picture over-charged". He therefore argued for gradual regulation leading to abolition, rather than for a "precipitate amputation". The bringing to Africa of internal peace and industry would do more than international agreement to abolish the trade. Other nations were most unlikely to join in a decision which would therefore only serve to benefit foreign slave traders. For these reasons Cruger proclaimed his support of the petitions he had presented and his intention to vote against Wilberforce's propositions.[46]

This oblique and apologetic rejection of abolition represented Cruger's public pronouncement of an already determined private agreement to work with the main body of the West India parliamentary interest for the defeat of the bill. He had reported on 18 May to the Bristol committee, in a letter to Merchants Hall:

> I am just returned from a meeting of W.I. planters—Lord Penrhyn in the chair. The business was to consult on the *mode* of proceedings in the House next Thursday. Some were for adducing *evidence* to refute all the *12 Propositions,* others for moving them to be "false, insidious, and replete with misrepresentation." A third opinion was for trying our strength by a *short* question. This was thought dangerous, 'till something was said to remove the *impressions* of Wilberforce's speech. After two hours' discussion, Lord Maitland hit upon the middle line, which met the approbation of all parties, which was, when Wilberforce moved the *first* Proposition, to oppose it upon its being ill founded and not supported by evidence. He will naturally say the evidence was given before the privy council. The answer will be, "that is no evidence for the House of Commons to proceed upon." Pitt will refuse to bring his evidence again, upon which Lord Penrhyn will move that "Sir William Dolben leave the Chair". Here a division will *try our numbers,* which we are impatient to do as soon as possible, as so many of our friends *are going out of Town*. If we are beat, as I

fear we shall be, then we shall think of bringing evidence
to the Bar to *disprove* many of the allegations contained
in the 12 Propositions, also to correct the misrepresenta-
tions with which they are said to abound. This will be a
tedious piece of work, tho' highly proper, and will of
course *oblige* the ministers to postpone the business until
next year. It was said that our Court have made overtures
to every court in Europe to unite with us in abolishing
the slave trade.

You will do me the favor to show *these hasty lines* to
Mr. Miles the chairman and as many other gentlemen as
are interested in this very important business, but do not
let my letter be published, it is not fit, nor intended for
that . . .[47]

Once roused, the Bristol opposition to abolition remained firm
in its determination to resist: on 3 June the West India merchants
resolved that the treasurer of the Bristol West India Society should
be paid "sixpence per hogshead and puncheon and so in proportion
for all other articles on our imports into this port from the sugar
colonies from the 24 April 1789 to the 24 April 1790".[48] The levy
was intended to finance the costs of opposing abolition. The
Merchant Venturers, learning that a further reduction was proposed
in the number of slaves permitted to be carried in each ship,
ordered the preparation of a petition of protest.[49] Further
immediate action was, however, rendered unnecessary by the
success of the West Indian interest in persuading the House of
Commons to declare in favour of undertaking its own inquiry into
the slave trade. The select committee did not begin to hear
evidence until 29 January 1790.

The first witness to be called by counsel for the Liverpool
petition in support of the continuation of the trade was a Bristol
slave captain. Curiously, no Liverpool commander was called, and
the choice of James Fraser was obviously not accidental. He had
been engaged in the trade for twenty years but, as even Clarkson
was prepared to admit, was the sole captain of good reputation
in Bristol: during his stay in Bristol he had been told by Burges,
the sympathetic deputy town clerk, that he knew of "only one
captain from the port in the slave-trade, who did not deserve long
ago to be hanged"[50] — meaning Fraser — and this opinion had

47 Cruger to Osborne 18 May 1789, African Trade Box 'G', Merchants'
    House.
48 Committee minutes, 3 June, 1789, Merchants' House.
49 Book of Proceedings II, 3 July 1789, f.516.
50 Clarkson, I. 313.

been confirmed by Alexander Falconbridge, who had served with him, and by Thompson, Clarkson's guide through the taverns of Bristol.[51] It is obvious that the choice of Fraser was designed to present the trade in the best possible light. His evidence emphasized the natural existence, given the current condition of Africa, of the trade; the generally low mortality among slaves during the voyage, and the good treatment of seamen whom he admitted were often half-trained and, in the case of Bristol, "in general inferior in capacity to what they are in other ports", so that their wages were no higher than those paid in the normal West India trade. Fraser was the only witness brought forward by Liverpool to testify on the state of Africa and conditions in the Middle Passage.[52]

When the committee turned its attention to the condition of the slaves in the West Indies, James Tobin was called in evidence on 25 February. In anticipation of this step, Tobin's name had been erased from the Bristol West India petition before its presentation to the House.[53]   He asserted the necessity of maintaining the importation of slaves into the islands, defended their treatment by the planters, and deplored the damage already done by the campaign to the credit facilities on which the Caribbean economy depended.[54] In March, witnesses hostile to the trade began to be heard. Alexander Falconbridge gave evidence: he agreed that Captain Fraser treated his seamen well, but insisted that on other ships the situation was quite different. He was subjected to hostile questioning, being accused of having, after the period in which he now claimed to have abandoned the trade in disgust, sought a command from a Bristol slave trader. The charge was not beyond the bounds of possibility. Falconbridge was not a man of strong character, as his later career demonstrated. After 1791 he was employed by the Sierra Leone Company, who found him unreliable and addicted to drink. He was dismissed from his appointment as commercial agent and succumbed within a short time to alcohol and the climate of the colony.[55] Later witnesses who had sailed from Bristol could report on only the more distant past. James Morley, now a naval gunner, had undertaken six voyages from Bristol between 1760 and 1776, while John Marshall had sailed on three or more occasions — his memory was uncertain — after

51   Clarkson, I. 349-350.
52.   *House of Commons Accounts and Papers* XXIX (1790) No. 698, 1-59.
53   Osborne to Cruger, 1 May 1789. Letters Outward 1781-1810, f. 80, Merchants' House.
54   *House of Commons Accounts and Papers* XXIX (1790) No. 698, 260-287.
55   *Ibid.,* 581-632. Christopher Fyfe, *A History of Sierra Leone* (London, 1962), pp. 29-47.

1762.[56] So the parliamentary inquiry dragged on, accumulating a store of information for historians of West Indian slavery and the slave trade, but for the moment effectively checking the abolitionist attempt to secure a rapid and decisive end to the trade.

The general election of 1790 saw the retirement of Bristol's members of parliament. After a poll displaying a dramatic decline from the very high vote of 1784, Brickdale was replaced by the Marquis of Worcester, son and heir of the Duke of Beaufort, and Cruger by John Baker Holroyd, Lord Sheffield. Worcester is not reported as taking part in parliamentary debates during his six years as a member for Bristol, but Sheffield spoke frequently, particularly in defence of the slave trade. Nominally a Whig, Sheffield had achieved prominence after 1783 as a continued advocate of the maintenance of the Old Colonial System: his *Observations on the Commerce of the American States with Europe and the West Indies* was regarded by many, both at home and abroad, as a major influence on the decision to exclude American shipping from the trade of the British Empire. Sheffield entered the slave trade controversy in the spring of 1790, publishing a substantial pamphlet which was reprinted, with additions and an open admission of authorship, in the following year. *Observations on the Project for Abolishing the Slave Trade* argued that it was neither practicable nor advantageous, even to the slaves, for the trade to be abolished. Sheffield denied any financial interests in the plantations or the trade and admitted that the institution of slavery had been marked by abuses and cruelty. He was not opposed to ameliorative reforms: both slaves and seamen would benefit from parliamentary regulation of shipping conditions; the West Indian Assemblies should be encouraged to pass legislation which would improve the lot of the slave in the islands. Tariffs and bounties could be employed to reduce slave imports, and the prospect was held out that, under kind but firm supervision, the slaves might progress towards a status of perpetual apprenticeship. Emancipation was rejected since the negro could not survive without the aid of white domination, and agreement between all the powers of Europe interested in the trade would not be obtainable. Sheffield's arguments were based on fervent beliefs in the sanctity of property and the necessity of maintaining a policy of enlightened paternalism. It was a clear reflection of a changed political situation that the Bristol Whigs had offered a candidacy free of financial obligation and had arranged a triumphal entry into the city for a politician renowned for his conservatism. The

56 *House of Commons Accounts and Papers* XXX (1790) No. 699, 149-161, 380-381.

constituency which had elected Burke now chose as a representative a man famous for his part in excluding Americans from participation in the benefits of the British commercial system. Once returned, Sheffield spoke in the Commons of the impractibility of abolition and the need to improve conditions in the islands by working through the Assemblies.[57]

The first attempt of the abolitionists to secure suppression of the trade had failed to secure a parliamentary decision, but the cause was not abandoned: Wilberforce and his colleagues devoted much of 1791 to study of the evidence produced at the parliamentary hearings as preparation for a further attempt to secure legislation. During March 1792 *Felix Farley* reported that abolitionist petitions had been widely supported in Bath, with more than a thousand signatures, and in the Wiltshire cloth towns, where 700 names were secured: clergy and laity of both the Anglican and Nonconformist churches were prominent in the lists.[58] The Bristol press published letters supporting and opposing the trade, but there appears to have been no flurry of organization, comparable with that of 1789, to resist abolition. This was not indicative of apathy but rather of a situation in which both sides were now advancing their cases from well-established positions: the surprise onslaught of 1789 had by 1792 become a phase in a protracted struggle.

On 2 April 1792 Wilberforce delivered his major speech on the motion for abolition and involved Bristol ships in a description of recent brutality which, he claimed, demonstrated that the pursuit of slaves entailed the complete loss of humane feelings. He declared that only the previous August, six slave ships, infuriated at an attempt to raise prices at Calabar, had bombarded the town for three hours, and had later resumed the attack until the captains' offer was accepted. The House indignantly demanded the names of the ships: three were from Liverpool and three — the *Thomas, Recovery* and *Wasp* — from Bristol. Finally, Wilberforce horrified the House by an account of how a girl of 15 had died as the result of barbarous maltreatment in the course of a voyage, and named a Captain Kimber as responsible.[59]

In Bristol, this speech aroused the greatest possible interest. The entire front and back pages of *Felix Farley's* issue of 7 April

57 *Parliamentary History* XXIX (1791-1792), 19 Apr. 1791, 358-359.
58 *FFBJ* 24, 31 Mar. 1792.
59 *Parliamentary History,* XXIX. 1068-1071. Either the parliamentary report or Wilberforce's informant erred. The *Anatree* is reported as a Bristol ship, which was not the case. On the other hand the *Wasp,* given without port, was a Bristol slaver at this time.

were devoted to an account of the debate, even though this involved postponing the printing of advertisements. The excitement was understandable in view of the mention of Bristol ships and, in particular, the singling out of John Kimber for condemnation. Kimber was captain of the *Recovery*, a slaver of 189 tons owned by four Bristol merchants, with a shore address at 27 Redcross Street, near Old Market. It was alleged that the girl had died of injuries received on board his ship. Kimber immediately denied the charge, inserting a notice in the same issue of the paper that he was preparing a narrative which would show the charges to be false and unjust. It was not surprising that, the following week, a local bookseller announced that his supply of an account of the debate had been sold out, but that he expected a further large number of copies to arrive that day from London.

In consequence of Wilberforce's charges, action was quickly taken against Kimber. He was arrested in Bristol on 8 April, and taken to London the following day, to await trial before the High Court of Admiralty.[60]   When the parliamentary debate continued on 23 April, Lord Sheffield rose to deny that abolition was desired by a great majority, but declared that

> his chief motive for rising was, to notice a new and
> very unjustifiable style of accusation which had been
> lately adopted in that House. Some gentlemen, in the
> most concealed manner, scraped together, from any
> quarter, miserable stories, and, without the least notice
> to the parties, brought the astonished person accused
> before the public, in a manner that made it impossible
> for him to justify himself. If, however, a prosecution
> took place, the efforts of eloquence they had heard were
> like greatly to prejudice a jury, and prevent a fair trial.
> Nothing could be more inexcusable than to enrage the
> public against a man before trial. In Captain Kimber's
> case, we had a melancholy instance of malice and
> credulity. He was almost ashamed of the impression the
> story had made on him. It was his duty to inquire; he
> had gone into a complete investigation of the matter;
> and it was as clear as demonstration to him, that there
> was not the least foundation for a criminal prosecution
> against Captain Kimber; and it was also the opinion
> of men more capable of judging than himself. However,
> that cruelly injured man was in Newgate, and in irons,

60 *FFBJ* 16 June 1792. Previous accounts of the Kimber incident have not indicated its Bristol origins.

and could not have the advantage of a trial sooner than 7th of June. If any more of those unfair attacks were made in that House, that he should insist on bringing evidence to the bar, that the innocent might have an immediate opportunity of exculpation.[61].

On 21 April Kimber had announced that he had been advised by Counsel not to publish a defence until after his trial. *Felix Farley* continued to give great prominence to the parliamentary debate and on 28 April again deferred advertisements for this purpose. When Kimber's trial took place, full accounts of the proceedings were given. Two members of the crew of the *Recovery,* William Dowling, the surgeon, and Stephen Devereux, comprised the witnesses for the prosecution. They fared badly under cross-examination, in which, it was reported, "their inconsistency, prevarication, and contradictions were . . . notorious". There was no lack of testimony in support of Kimber: Walter Jacks, one of the four Bristol owners, spoke in his favour, as did Thomas Phillips, who had commanded the *Thomas* during the Calabar incident; the surgeon of the *Thomas* declared that a feud had existed between Dowling and Kimber, while the second mate of the *Wasp,* the third Bristol ship involved, spoke highly of Kimber and slightingly of Devereux as a man of mutinous disposition. The defence claimed to have called not one-tenth of those willing to testify for Kimber, while the prosecution was restricted to its two witnesses. The jury acquitted Kimber without retiring; Dowling and Devereux were committed to Newgate on charges of perjury. *Felix Farley* reported these proceedings at length and accepted the truth of Kimber's story. The girl had died of disease, not maltreatment; the bombardment of Calabar had caused no casualties; Kimber was not a vindictive man and had returned home with 22 of his original crew of 25, not only six or seven as had been alleged.[62]

It is impossible to say whether the acquittal was justified. The evidence in Kimber's favour would seem to have been given by directly interested parties, and it may be significant that it was again a surgeon who laid the charges of brutality. The abolitionists seem to have mismanaged the accusation, perhaps relying on the crown to prosecute vigorously. Wilberforce did not disclose the source of his information — Clarkson makes only a passing reference to the affair — but he seems to have been encouraged in his attack by Sir James Stonhouse, the Anglican clergyman resident at Hotwells and a prominent supporter of abolition. He

61 *Parliamentary History* XXIX 23 Apr. 1792, 1225-1226.
62 *FFBJ* 9, 16 June 1792.

Reproduced by courtesy of the British Museum

The Seven Stars public house in the lane leading from St. Thomas Street
to Redcliff Street in which Clarkson collected evidence from seamen in
support of the case for abolishing the slave trade.

Photograph by Reece Winstone

Of taking into Consideration the Report of the Committee to whom the expediency of petitioning the House of Commons and if tho.t necessary to prepare a Petition against the Abolition of the Slave Trade, and said Report being read, and the Draft of a Petition being produced and also read and some alteration being made therein by the House & was now Agreed to, and was ordered to be Engrossed, That the City Seal be affixed thereto And that it be presented to parliament by the Members for this City to whom Mr Town Clerk is requested to write unto requesting their support.

On 22 April 1789 the Mayor asked the Common Council to consider a report of a committee which had been drawing up a petition to the House of Commons against abolition of the slave trade (Bristol Archives Office: *Common Council Proceedings, 1783-90*, pp. 289-290).

Photograph by Photo Prints (Bristol) Ltd.

had assured Wilberforce that Kimber "is a very bad man, a great spendthrift; one who would swear to any falsehood, and who is linked with a set of rascals like himself."[63] Wilberforce and his friends remained convinced of Kimber's guilt. Although recognizing that their witnesses had not proved convincing, they stressed the "shameful remissness of the Crown lawyers, and the indecent behaviour of the judge. Wilberforce considered Kimber "in no degree acquitted *in foro conscientiae*, of the cruelties with which he is charged". His friend Lord Muncaster agreed; even in the version of the trial published by the captain's friends he detected "conscious guilt throughout".[64]

After his release, Kimber proceeded to harass Wilberforce, who received a letter on 11 July demanding a public apology, payment of £5,000, and a governmental post. After consulting Pitt, Wilberforce rejected the demands. Kimber then called on several occasions, becoming more menacing at each visit. Wilberforce's friends became alarmed for his safety; Lord Muncaster implored him to take care and Lord Rokeby, armed against attack, insisted on accompanying Wilberforce on a journey to Yorkshire. Lord Sheffield brought an end to the threats — Wilberforce's sons and biographers term him "an honourable opponent"[65] — but the episode was not forgotten. The subsequent trials of the witnesses for perjury involved Wilberforce in considerable expense, and in later years he noted in his diary that the Kimber incident was one of the two events in his campaign for abolition that had caused him great alarm and distress.[66]

For Bristol, the Kimber case marked the climax of the 1792 campaign. The House of Commons' acceptance of Dundas's amendment, proposing abolition of the slave trade to the British West Indies in 1796, may have been regarded with justified suspicion by committed abolitionists, since the delay in enforcement proved to be fatal to their hopes, but combined with the Kimber fiasco probably proved sufficient to quieten general opposition to the trade in Bristol. In any event, slaving from the port now entered a rapid and final decline. In the summer of 1791 Wilberforce had paid a brief visit to Bristol, where Harford had told him over breakfast that "the slave trade is growing disgraceful".[67] Matthew's *Directory* for 1793-4 observed that "the ardor for trade to Africa for men and women, our fellow creatures and

63 Robert Isaac and Samuel Wilberforce, *The Life of William Wilberforce* (London, 1838), I. 356-357.
64 *Ibid.*, 357-358.
65 *Ibid.*, 358-359.
66 Wilberforce, II. 29, 51, 166, 305.
67 Diary, 5 July 1791, Wilberforce I. 305.

equals, is much abated among the humane and benevolent merchants of Bristol".[68] Between 1795 and 1804 only 29 slaving voyages are recorded from Bristol, and these vessels carried only 10,718 of the 380,893 slaves transported in these years by ships sailing from Bristol, London and Liverpool.[69] The last decade of the slave trade was therefore marked by a dwindling to insignificance of Bristol's share of African commerce: to what was this due?

The collapse of the Bristol trade was not brought about primarily by the abolitionist agitation, since there were no signs of decline in the period of most intense local protest. In 1792 Parliament was provided with official figures of the numbers, names, owners and capacity of ships engaged in the slave trade between 1789 and May 1792. Bristol ships had carried 2,691 slaves in 15 voyages during 1789, 4,968 slaves in 27 voyages in 1790, 4,069 slaves in 22 voyages in 1791, and 2,180 slaves in 11 voyages during the first five months of 1792. Throughout this period Bristol had replaced London as the second slave port of the country, and although Liverpool easily retained its premier position, Bristol voyages and cargoes were only outnumbered by one to four, compared with a ratio of one to thirty eight in the decade from 1795.[70] The outbreak of war with France had made the trade more hazardous but Liverpool was evidently able to surmount difficulties which Bristol found insuperable.

Abolitionist agitation may have aroused moral distaste for the traffic, but the Bristol slave trade was gravely affected in material matters by the economic crisis of 1793. This followed a period of confident growth in which credit had been easily obtainable. Alarm at the prospect of a war with France brought an end to financial optimism; there followed a collapse of over-extended country banks and a disastrous contraction of mercantile credit.[71] Bristol was particularly vulnerable in this crisis, since its banking, mercantile and shipping interests were closely linked. Most of the Bristol banks contained partners with mercantile interests; unlike London, Bristol merchants owned their ships.[72] There was therefore no possibility of unaffected sections of the community assisting the afflicted: all were involved. On 7 March 1793 Henry

68 W. Matthews, *The New History . . . of Bristol* (Bristol, 1794), p. 38.
69 Gomer Williams, *History of the Liverpool Privateers . . .* (London, 1897), Appendix XI.
70 *House of Commons Accounts and Papers* XXXV (1792), Nos. 768 (1) 768 (2).
71 T. S. Ashton, *Economic Fluctuations in England* 1700-1800 (Oxford, 1959), pp. 132-134, 166-169. L. S. Pressnell, *Country Banking in the Industrial Revolution* (Oxford, 1956), pp. 49-50, 458.
72 Richard Pares, *A West India Fortune* (London, 1950), p. 209.

Thornton, the London banker, prepared an estimate of the bankruptcy brought about by the crisis. Noting that he had omitted many Bristol failures, his list of the more prominent showed bankruptcies in the city for an estimated £1,100,000 out of a possible national deficiency of some six million pounds. The names of many of the bankrupts are to be found in the parliamentary list of slave ship owners: Rogers and Fydell, Walter Jacks, J. Gordon, Patrick Fitz Henry are all noted by Thornton to have failed for large sums. Of the sixty voyages undertaken from Bristol between the beginning of 1790 and May 1792, twenty seven were supported in part or in whole by those reported bankrupt in 1793.[73] Unlike Liverpool, which rallied promptly and effectively to restore its trade and finances by civic action,[74] Bristol seems to have accepted the situation. Consequently, Liverpool prevailed not only in the slave trade but in the general West Indian commerce. The West India convoys of 1796 to 1798 contained only a small proportion of Bristol ships, and local sugar refineries were reduced to obtaining supplies from Liverpool.[75]

The reduction of the West India interest by economic crisis and war meant an abrupt curb of material support for a trade that was considered beyond defence on moral grounds. The slavers' ranks were further thinned by the death in 1795 of James Jones, who a decade earlier had owned nine ships, but had escaped bankruptcy. The last years of the slave trade were therefore largely a period which displayed the indifference of the much lessened mercantile and shipping interests of the city. Lord Sheffield continued to the last, though from the House of Lords, to maintain his opposition to abolition, and Charles Bathurst, who had succeeded the Marquis of Worcester as member in 1796, urged that abolition be gradual in order to preserve the value of West Indian property,[76] but these were isolated gestures of protest. When in 1806 the ministry and Parliament finally resolved to abolish the trade, Bristol newspapers reported favourably but cursorily on the event. Looking back on the year, *Felix Farley* hailed the abolition of a trade "so long the disgrace of a civilized

---

73 Thornton's list is printed by Pressnell, Appendix 28, pp. 546-547. See also Minchinton, *Trade*, p. 190, for additional bankrupts and a correction of Presnell.

74 Francis E. Hyde, Bradbury B. Parkinson and Sheila Marriner, "The Port of Liverpool and the Crisis of 1793", *Economica* N.S. XVIII (1951), 363-377.

75 John Latimer, *The Annals of Bristol in the Eighteenth Century* (Bristol, 1893), p. 519.

76 *Hansard's Parliamentary Debates* VII. 235-236, VIII. 972-973, 1050, IX. 62.

nation".[77] Relief was doubtless general in Bristol at the passing of a trade which had once seemed both indefensible and essential: the abolitionists had done much to stir consciences, but the economic crisis of 1793 had fatally sapped the material strength of the slave trade from Bristol.

[77] *FFBJ* 3 Jan. 1807, 14 June 1806.

BIBLIOGRAPHICAL NOTE

Materials relating to the last years of the Bristol slave trade and to the movements which sought to defend or extinguish it are substantial in bulk but scattered in distribution. One may best begin with the major secondary works bearing on this period of the city's history; John Latimer, *The Annals of Bristol in the Eighteenth Century* (Bristol, 1893), for modern accounts of Bristol trade, C. M. MacInnes, *A Gateway of Empire* (Bristol, 1939) and Richard Pares, *A West India Fortune* (London, 1950), and for conditions in the Caribbean, L. J. Ragatz, *The Fall of the Planter Class in the British Caribbean 1763-1833* (New York, 1928) and Elsa V. Goveia, *Slave Society in the British Leeward Islands at the End of the Eighteenth Century* (New Haven and London, 1965). Valuable though these accounts are, it is necessary to return to the sources on which they were based: the Bristol newspapers, all of which commented on the question and printed correspondence from both sides, the Pinney papers deposited in the University of Bristol, pamphlet controversies, and parliamentary reports and papers. Much documentary evidence is, however, more accessible. Volume II of Elizabeth Donnan's *Documents Illustrative of the Slave Trade to America* (Washington, 1931), and, in particular, Volumes XX and XXIII of the Bristol Record Society's *Publications,* edited by W. E. Minchinton, contain essential materials and commentary. It has been possible, through the courtesy of the Society of Merchant Venturers, to obtain further evidence from their archives of the growth of local resistance to abolition. The establishment of a Bristol opposition to the slave trade has been incomparably described by Thomas Clarkson in the first volume of his *History,* which remains a major source. Secondary works on abolition contain only passing reference to Bristol, though something may be gleaned from R. Coupland, *Wilberforce. A Narrative* (Oxford, 1923), and the

Wilberforces' *Life* of their father. Although the Privy Council Report of 1789 has been frequently drawn upon, insufficient use has been made of the volumes of the *House of Commons Accounts and Papers* containing official returns on the activities, slave capacity and ownership of Bristol ships. Further details on some of these ships can be found in J. W. Damer Powell, *Bristol Privateers and Ships of War* (Bristol, 1930) and Grahame E. Farr ed., *Records of Bristol Ships 1800-1838* (Bristol Record Society, 1950). The effect on Bristol commerce in general, and the slave trade in particular, of the economic crisis of 1793, requires further investigation: the circumstances attending the bankruptcy of James Rogers, one of the largest slave merchants of this period, will be illuminated by the research of Mr. A. F. Day, to whom I am obliged for many references to local materials bearing on the trade.

Index of Names, Places and Selected Subjects

Quay Warden, 141
Queen Square, 24, 83, 128, 146, 153;
  illustration, 32
Quick, the actor, 72

Races, on Durdham Downs, 120
Rackhay, 67, 85
Radicals, in Bristol, 48, 49; 83; policy, 51
Railways, 132
Ramsay, the Rev. James, 195
Randolph, Dr., 114, quoted, 115, 116
Receiver of the Customs, 146
Recovery, ship, 206-208
Red Cliff, the proposed dam, 155
Red Cliff Back, 141
Redcliffe, 108; cross, 101; hill, 90; parish,
  90, 100
Redcliff Parade, 153
Redcliff St., 97, 209
Redcross St., 207
Reddish, Samuel, actor, 71, 72
Red House, of Chatterton, 97
Redwood, 164
Reform Act, 47
Regency Theatre, 80
Reid, Richard, Sculptor, 108
Religious Toleration, Burke's attitude, 57
Rents, low in Bristol, 24
Resolution and Independence, by Words-
  worth, 105
Respirators, sold at the Hotwell, 123
Revenge, The, by Chatterton, 101, 104
Revenue Cutters, 138
Review of Mr. Burke's Conduct,
  pamphlet by Burke, 58
Reynolds, Richard, 194
Rice, imported, 130
Richard II, 80, 82
Richard III, 69; adapted by Cibber, 74, 83
Riding, 113, 118, 119, 120, 123
Riga, 130
Road Carriage, 133
Roads, 132, 133
Roadsteads, 138
Road Systems, illustration, 21
Road Traffic, volume of, 132
Rockingham, Lord, 45, 46, 47, 59; his
  party, 49, 51, 56
Roehampton, ship, 140
Rogers and Fydell, bankrupt slavers, 213
Rogers, Woodes, 132
Rokeby, Lord, 211
Romantics, 105
Romeo, William Dimond as, illustra-
  tion, 75; Montague's performance as,
  84
Rope Walk, The, 120, 153
Rope Walks, 142
Rosetti, D. G., 105
Rosin, 140
Rossini, his opera *Cinderella*, 85
Rotherhithe, 139
Rotterdam, 130
Rowe, Nicholas, 96
Rowley, Thomas, 95-100; Rowleians, 105,
  108
Rownham, 139, 155; ferry, 120;
Royal Academy, 158n
Royal African Company, 164, 168, 179
Royal Charlotte, ship, 174

Royal Exchange, 27
Royal Librarian, 146
Royal Navy, 134, 197
Royal Patents, for theatres at Bath and
  Norwich, 71
Royal York Crescent, 128
Ruby, ship, 174
Rule Britannia, 83
Rum, 129, 130, 134
Rumsey, Maria, 100
Russia, 18

Saddlery, 15
Sailcloth, 134
Sailing, on the Avon, 120
St. Augustine's Back, 36, 91, 141, 153
St. Augustine's Bridge, illustration, 44
St. Augustine the Less, illustration, 31;
  97
St. Augustine's Parade, 67
St. Austin's Wharf, 27
St. George's Channel, 135
St. Giles's Bridge, 153
St. James's Square, 128
St. John's, 95
St. Kitts, 177, 195
St. Mary Redcliff(e), 91, 97, 100, 103, 105;
  churchyard, 107, 108; illustration, 150
St. Michael's Church, 96
St. Nicholas' Church, 96
St. Paul's Cathedral, 90
St. Paul's Church, 96
St. Petersburg, 130
St. Philips, out-parish of, 17
St. Thomas Church, 128
St. Thomas Parish, 90
St. Thomas St., 27, 209
St. Vincent's Rock, 112, 139; illustration,
  137
St. Vincent's Spring, 113
Salisbury, Countess of, 72
Salmon, 27
Sandwich, 60
San Joseph y Animas, ship, 135
Saul, King, 100
Saunders, Mr., carpenter, 66, 67
Savage, Richard, poet, 30; death of, 37;
  quoted, 30; 104
School for Scandal, 72
Schooners, 173, 176
Scotland, 37, 38, 132
Scott, Sir Walter, dramatisations, 82
Scurvy, 114
Sea Mills, 139
Sea Mill Docks, 140
Septennial Act, 48, 58
Seven Stars, tavern, 189, 190; illustration,
  209
Seven Years' War, 46, 132, 139, 153, 179
Severn, River, 15, 19, 24, 132, 138
Sewers, 25, 26
Shackles, 174; illustration, 180
Shakespeare, William, 82, 98, 105
Shawl Pins, 123
Sheep, 27
Sheffield, 205, 207, 211, 213
Shelley, Percy Bysshe, 91, 105
Sheridan, Richard Brinsley, 112
Sheriff, Sailor, 193
Sheriffs, 50

224

Worcester, 27, 132; marquis of, 205, 213
Worcester, William, earliest reference to
    the Hotwell, 114
Worcestershire, 81
Wordsworth, William, on Chatterton, 105
Workhouse, 105
Wrens, 28
Wright, J. T., and J. A., 156
Wright, Matthew, 194
Wye, River, 14
Wyndham, Capt. Thomas, 162

Yarn, 129
Yates, Mrs., actress, 81
Yearsley, Ann, 105
York, 74, 108; circuit of theatres, 74;
    Duke of, 79
Yorkshire, 211; association, 56
Youghall, 129
Young, Arthur, 16